To Jane from Virginia 2015

See page 128 for Georgiana M.

JOSEPH MAFFRE
Master of the Band

Mark Griep

Marjorie Mikasen

Keeper's
Cottage
Press

Keeper's Cottage Press

ISBN-13: 978-1508491750

ISBN-10: 1508491755

For Jim

CONTENTS

FOREWORD

The early years of military bands in Britain are very poorly documented. Major battles and campaigns attracted historians from the outset, while individual regiments have always jealously guarded the memory of any encounter, however minor, in which they were involved. But the culture of the army, the everyday reality of soldiering, was considered of little interest. This was particularly the case with bands, partly because of what was, for many decades, their informal, unofficial status.

The story of military bands starts with the Seven Years' War in the mid-18th century, when, inspired by the example of the bands they encountered in Germany, the Royal Artillery recruited eight local musicians and brought them home to serve in a dual capacity: providing music for men on the march and entertainment for officers in the evening. Other regiments followed their lead and, by the time of the Napoleonic Wars, music had become an integral part of military life. It was not, however, recognised as such by the central authorities. Only two bandmasters – those of the Royal Military College and of the Royal Artillery – were paid directly by the War Office; for the rest, it fell to the officers of each regiment to recruit, and to meet the costs of, their own bandsmen and bandmasters.

Consequently many military bands were British in name only. There was a widespread prejudice in the army that British musicians were inherently inferior to their European counterparts: 'Germans alone can play the trumpet as it ought to be played,' as the Duke of Cumberland wrote in 1820. The Prussians had shown the way forward, and the foundation of a central college of military music in France in 1836 reinforced the belief that that country too was far ahead of Britain. As a result, German and French musicians were at a premium, and this bias was even more pronounced in the case of bandmasters, where foreign civilians were much preferred, becoming something of a status symbol.

All of this was gradually to change, the key moment coming with the foundation of the Military School of Music at Kneller Hall in 1857. Even so the old practices were slow to disappear. As late as 1876, when there were around 120 enlisted military bandmasters in the army, there still remained thirty-five civilians leading bands, most of them foreign born. Indeed, it was not until 1938 that the last civilian bandmaster, Randolph Ricketts of the Royal Corps of Signals, finally retired.

It is this piecemeal, decentralised history that perhaps accounts for the lack of documentation about the first century or so of British military bands. And the absence of official records is what makes this book by Griep and Mikasen so invaluable.

Joseph Maffre was one of those foreign-born civilian bandmasters who proliferated in the first half of the 19th century. His story, told here for the first time, should not be considered typical, for each of these men would have had their own extraordinary experiences, but it does bring to life an era when joining the army could offer a path into the world of music for many who would otherwise have struggled to find their way forward. It demonstrates too the contribution that was made by such men; Joseph Maffre's subsequent career as a leading light in the cultural life of Montreal is as fascinating as his early years in military service.

When I was first contacted by the authors, more than a decade ago, at the start of this formidable project, I had to apologise for the lack of help I could offer. 'This is such an obscure area of historical research,' I observed, 'that virtually every fact you uncover will be new.' I little realised then just how extensive the research would be and quite how much new material would be revealed. The resulting book is one of the most important contributions ever made to the history of military music.

Alwyn W. Turner
London
February 2015

PREFACE

This book began life as a family history project. The more we learned about ancestor Joseph Maffre, however, the more we realized he was an important historical figure whose story needed to be told. This chronological outline is the result.

Marjorie first became aware of her family's musical background in junior high school when she was learning how to play the bass clarinet. Her grandmother told her that Marjorie's great grandfather, Fred Maffre, played the cornet in a military band and that her great, great grandfather, Joseph Maffre Jr. (son of the biographee but known as simply Joseph Maffre at the time), was a Professor of Music. These facts were inspiring to a budding musician. One reason the family may have forgotten that Junior's father was the leading musician in Montreal in the 1840's is that father and son had the same name and same profession. Such situations are not always easy to remember or to disentangle.

We began to explore Marjorie's family history after we married. Our first good leads on Marjorie's Maffre line came in 1989, when Jim Maffre, great, great grandson of Joseph Maffre, sent us a copy of his Maffre Family History. Later, he sent us Will Fairbairn's 1940's outline of the Maffre succession. Fairbairn's history said that Joseph Maffre was son of the Harbormaster of Toulon who fled France during the Revolution. This was great stuff for a family historian because it points you in specific directions. We collaborated with Jim for the next decade, each of us spurring the other to dig deeper. One of our earliest finds was the entry in Elinor Kyte Senior's *British Regulars in Montreal* where she mentions that Joseph Maffre had been a military bandmaster who had set himself up as a music instructor and performer in Montreal in 1841. In 1993, we visited Montreal to meet Jim Maffre and to see the historical and genealogical sites. We spent an entire day in the McCord Museum Archives to search rare military records and the Notman photographic archive. Although our searches came up empty-handed, one of the archivists brought us the *Encyclopedia of Music in Canada* because it contained a brief entry for Joseph Maffre. This is when we realized that he was an important historical figure. It has since become apparent to us that this entry merges the history of father and son.

We followed Joseph Maffre's trail during two visits to the United Kingdom. In 1997, we toured the city and museums of Leicester, the Leicester Local Studies Library, and His Grace the Duke of Rutland's Belvoir Castle. In 2008, we visited the Leicestershire Record Office, Lymington and its museums, the Somers Town area of London, and the British Library in London.

Beginning in 2001, online access to archival documents increased in importance and led to many great finds. The following sources proved invaluable: Google search, Google Books, Google Newspaper Archive, British Newspaper Archive, Findmypast.co.uk, Ancestry.com, Familysearch.org, National Archives UK, Worldcat.org, Gale 19th century database, Library and Archives of Canada,

BanQ, Montreal Rootsweb curated by Patty Brown, Early Canadiana online, the National Library of Ireland, and the Cambridge University Library.

The following individuals provided invaluable assistance. First, we would like to thank music and social historian Alwyn Turner who gave us the benefit of his knowledge by posing insightful questions that helped us to see the potential for exploring Joseph Maffre's story in greater depth. We are also indebted to musicologist Peter Slemon for his keen observations about music in Montreal during the period in which Maffre was active. We would also like to thank archivist Richard Reeves at the New Forest Library, postman Tony Johnson from Brockenhurst, historian Jude James from Lymington, family historian Claude Maffre (no known relation), Jim Maffre's son Gerry Maffre who provided encouragement and enthusiasm, pianist Robert Palmai who recorded the Leicester and Canadian Quadrilles for Jim Maffre, and family historians Warren Sadler and Virginia Stotz.

We hope you enjoy learning about the life of Joseph Maffre as much as we've enjoyed our decades-long search.

Mark Griep and Marjorie Mikasen
Lincoln, Nebraska
February 2015

Figure 1.1: "The Original Canadian Quadrilles" Sheet Music Cover, 1847. The authors' personal collection.

1

A LIFE LIVED IN MARCH TEMPO

Joseph Maffre's musical career can be defined by his service in the British Army. He joined the Royal French Artillery Regiment as a youth and learned how to play the most primary of military instruments — the drum. Over a very short time period, possibly while serving in the West Indies, he learned to play many other instruments. When he arrived in Leicester as a young married adult, he knew how to lead a band. After a musically fruitful ten years in Leicester as a music teacher, choral master, performer and composer, the economy sent him back to the British military. Here, he was talented enough to be selected to perform for Lord Durham (John Lambton) on his voyage to Canada following the 1837 Rebellion. Once in Canada, Maffre settled in Montreal. When he left the military for good in 1842, he became one of Montreal's most prominent music professors and promoters throughout the rest of the 1840's. Each chapter describes a different period of Maffre's life.

Chapter 2 (Born on the Run) describes Joseph Maffre's family and the journey that took them from Toulon, France, to Bastia, Corsica, where Joseph was born. Joseph's parents, Barthelemy and Cecile, fled Toulon with other Royalists on December 18, 1793 with their children. They were refugees on the island of Elba for a few months, where Barthelemy and his two sons must have joined the English forces in the fight against the French Revolutionaries. One son even lost his life in a battle over Corsica. After Corsica came under English rule, the eldest son sailed to England with many other French Royalists, where he joined the Loyal Emigrants Regiment to fight in Flanders and later in Portugal. In the meantime, the rest of the family moved to Bastia where Joseph was baptized on December 6, 1794.

Chapter 3 (Barracks and Bastardy) relates how many Toulonnais, including the Maffres, made their way to Lymington, England, because of the foreign regiments. Barthelemy and Cecile Maffre arrived in Lymington in early 1795, just in time for Barthelemy to join the ill-fated Quiberon Expedition, during which he appears to have been killed or drowned. Joseph would grow up here, impregnate a local girl, Lucy Thomas, when he was a 20-year-old drummer in the Foreign Regiment, marry her, and then leave Lymington in 1817 when he was 24 years old.

Chapter 4 (The London Connection) paints a broad picture of the two and a half years Joseph Maffre spent in the Somers Town district of London. He was there long enough to have performed in three of London's musical seasons. The experience professionalized him as a musician through his interactions with other performers at the nascent Royal Philharmonic Society and at Almack's Assembly Rooms, where the elite met to dance.

In Chapter 5 (Respectfully Dedicated), Maffre's career as a professional musician took off in Leicester. He moved there in late 1819 and was gone by late 1829. It is not known how he chose Leicester as his home base but it was a shrewd move. Leicester was small enough for someone with ambition to make a big impact and it was centrally located to the many other cities in which he would perform in three-day Grand Musical Festivals that were popular at the time. It was during his Leicester period that he and Lucy completed their family of nine children. There is no information how the children were raised so we are left to imagine how Joseph taught them the family business.

Chapter 6 (A Tropical Climate) paints another broad picture, this time of military life in the West Indies when Maffre left Leicester abruptly in 1829 to join the 19th Regiment of Foot. His stint began with a concert in Barbados and lasted about four years. There is little information about his life during this period but we take this opportunity to summarize his 25 years in the military and speculate on how he may have been recruited to the 19th.

Chapter 7 (Hitting the High C's) gives the details of how Maffre led the band of the 71st on the ship that took Lord Durham and his family to Canada following the 1837 Rebellion. Upon their arrival, the band played music for Lord Durham's receptions and helped set exactly the right tone. Maffre was a bandleader who knew how to use music to impress and unite people so it is perhaps no wonder that he performed for the first six pre-Confederate Governor-Generals of British North America.

Chapter 8 (Montreal Melodies) explains how Maffre rose to the top of Montreal's musical scene between 1840 and 1848. He did everything possible to raise the public's interest in all types of music. Montreal was an excellent fit for someone fluent in English and French and who had something to offer families. He appealed to the Anglo Canadian politicians and military because he was a royalist and military man. He appealed to the French Canadians because he had French heritage, they were already more culturally refined, and perhaps most of all because he favored the quadrille (Figure 1.1), which was derived from French country dance music. In the later years of this period, he even planned musical events that were designed to unite the diverse populations of Montreal. Maffre brought his children into the family business as they came of age and this helped him expand his influence.

Chapter 9 (Cholera in the City) describes the final year of Joseph and Lucy Maffre's lives. They died in the 1849 cholera epidemic that began among the troops occupying the city. Joseph probably contracted cholera when he visited the 19th or 71st Regiments during the month after what would turn out to be his final concert in June 1849. These two Regiments were garrisoned in the city because a mob had burned down the Parliament House after Lord Elgin assented to the Rebellion Losses Bill. The roots for that Bill date back to the reason Maffre and the 71st Regiment came to Canada in the first place – the 1837 and 1838 Rebellions.

Chapter 10 (Notes on the Firm) sketches the lives of Joseph and Lucy Maffre's children. Eldest son, Joseph Jr., was the most successful at continuing the Maffre musical legacy and even passed it on to his son Leopold Alfred Maffre. Son Henry was also a musician but he died as a young man. Joseph and Lucy's younger son Alfred became a Professor of Music but we have not been able to trace his activities past the year he earned his degree. The fate of eldest daughter Ann is unknown whereas daughter Maria married a very successful businessman who ran the largest dry dock in Montreal. Maria's descendants sold the dry dock to the City of Montreal so it could widen the Lachine Canal. One of their daughters, probably Charlotte, taught dance but gave it up after her parent's sudden deaths. Charlotte married a pawnbroker and then died suddenly herself in Toronto a few years later. Mary Anne married a man who died shortly after they moved to New Orleans. Sons Frederick and Francis became carpenters.

Chapter 11 (Music by Joseph Maffre) contains copies of the six extant works by Joseph Maffre. He composed lively pieces that could be performed at home on the piano. Chapter 12 (A Perfect Knowledge) gives scores of entries from newspapers that mention Joseph Maffre in advertisements, playbills, and reviews. There are also excerpts from city directories and magazines.

7   *TOULON. — Le Quai Cronstadt. — LL.*   Selecta

Figure 2.1: Postcard of Toulon Harbor in the 1930's. The authors' personal collection.

2
BORN ON THE RUN

This chapter is about Joseph Maffre's parents and siblings and the journey that took them from Toulon, France, to Bastia, Corsica, where Joseph was born. Joseph's parents, Barthelemy and Cecile, fled Toulon with other Royalists on December 18, 1793 with his three elder siblings, François, Pierre, and Ann Harriet. They were refugees on the island of Elba for a few months, during which time Barthelemy and his two sons must have joined the English forces in the fight against the French Revolutionaries and during which brother Pierre lost his life in one of the battles over Corsica. After Corsica came under English rule, brother François sailed to England with many other French Royalists and then joined the Loyal Emigrants Regiment to fight in Flanders and later in Portugal. Around the time that François left, Barthelemy, Cecile, and Ann Harriet moved to Bastia, Corsica, where Joseph was baptized on December 6, 1794.

1793: Evacuation of Toulon

The authors first learned of Joseph Maffre in the early 1980's when we read the tantalizingly brief entry in descendant Will Fairbairn's *Maffre Chart* (see transcription below). We speculate that Fairbairn received this information from his great aunt Maria Tate, Joseph Maffre's daughter. Frederick William "Will" Fairbairn printed his story in May 1948 and then mailed it to a few dozen relatives by which route it eventually came to us.

Opening lines from Maffre Chart by Will Fairbairn, May 1948

[1.]   ***** MAFFRE, harbormaster of Toulon, France, killed or drowned in the expedition of Napoleon's return from Elba in 1815. Had two sons who were then taken to London by their mother.

[2.]	JOSEPH	OTHER SON
	Born, Toulon France.	No record available
	Married Lucy Thomas in England about 1816.	

After decades of research, we know that Joseph Maffre's parents were Barthelemy and Cecile, we theorize that his brother, the "other son," was François, and we speculate that he had two other siblings named Pierre and Ann Harriet. Nevertheless, we confess to having spent hours re-reading and discussing Fairbairn's brief statement about Barthelemy for guidance on where to search next. One frustration is that we have never been able to connect Barthelemy's life to the very specific occupation of harbormaster. His name is not listed among the Toulon Harbormasters during the period immediately preceding the French Revolution. We also know that Barthelemy admitted he couldn't sign his name at his son Joseph's baptism (see below). Surely, a harbormaster would know how to read, write, and keep accounts. On the other hand, Fairbairn got quite a few things right. Barthelemy's life is connected to Napoleon, Toulon, Elba, and a disastrous military expedition during which he was probably killed or drowned. They just aren't connected in the way that a literal reading of Fairbairn's note would suggest. We can also place Joseph and his brother François in London in 1818. Even so, we still have to take Fairbairn's word that their mother was with them because we have not found any evidence regarding her whereabouts after she gave birth to Joseph.

Ninety-eight and a half years before Fairbairn published his family history, a short obituary for Joseph Maffre (see transcription below) painted a very different picture of the family connection to Toulon and Napoleon. The obituary was printed closer to the actual event and is undoubtedly more accurate. Taken together, the earliest documents about the family describe a compelling story about how the Maffres fled from Toulon, helped the British Navy to take Corsica, and then made their way to Lymington, England, where they made their home for about two decades.

Montreal Transcript
August 2, 1849
The late Mr. Joseph Maffre, was formerly Band Master of the 19th Regt., and subsequently of the 71st. He was son of a French loyalist, and, when a child, was, upon the evacuation of Toulon by the English in consequence of Napoleon's capture of one its principal outworks, taken by his parents to England.

Napoleon Bonaparte defined an era so it is perhaps no surprise that his name was remembered in a family story nearly 150 years later. The Bonaparte family is from Ajaccio, Corsica (Figure 2.2) but Napoleon spent most of his youth in a boarding school on mainland France. After graduation, he joined the French Army and worked his way through the ranks while serving the Revolutionaries in their efforts to overthrow the French Royalist government that had been in place for centuries. After the Revolution was won, there was counter-revolutionary chaos during which Napoleon joined in a coup and crowned himself Emperor in 1804. He then pushed his Imperial Army until the boundaries of his Empire stretched from Spain to Poland. After a decade of hard fighting and a few defeats, he was forced to abdicate and was exiled to the island of Elba in 1814. After one year and with the help of friends, he was able to escape quietly back to the mainland and regain his crown. His glory was brief, however, because his troops were defeated in June 1815 at Waterloo (now in Belgium) by British and Prussian troops. This time he was exiled to the remote island of St. Helena, located in the southern Atlantic Ocean about midway between Africa and South America. He died there in 1821 at age 52.

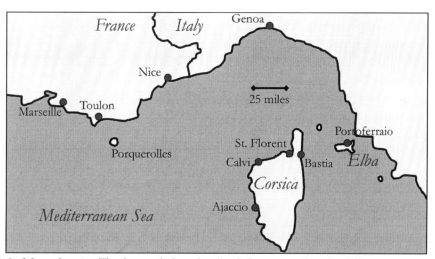

Figure 2.2: Map showing Toulon and the islands of Corsica and Elba. Illustration by Mark Griep.

The key phrase in the preceding sketch of Napoleon's life and career is that "he was able to escape quietly back to the mainland" from Elba. Fairbairn's version of the Maffre story can only be true if there was a skirmish of some sort "in the expedition of Napoleon's return from Elba in 1815." Instead, Napoleon escaped Elba because his accomplices chose a night with a new moon so there was no moonlight and they quietly rowed their ship rather than set sail so there was little sound or reflection. He escaped Elba without being noticed and without any conflict whatsoever.

Fortunately, Joseph Maffre's 1849 obituary (reproduced earlier in the text) connects his parents to Napoleon's career in a different way – they are fleeing Toulon after it finally succumbed to the Revolutionaries as a consequence of Napoleon's tactical skill. The Maffres and other refugee Royalists fled with the British Navy to Corsica except that a storm pushed them to Elba instead.

The French Revolution started on July 14, 1789 when the "Bastille" prison was stormed by a mob of peasants who were frustrated by the slow pace of political reform. At this time, French society had a large peasant class of about 85%, a middle class and clergy of about 10%, and nobility and the church hierarchy at about 5%. Needless to say, the peasant class wanted more economic mobility, fewer taxes, and fewer privileged nobles. Many nobles fled the country in 1792 and 1793 when radical political reforms were passed. These nobles are referred to as émigrés rather than emigrants because they left for political reasons and worked to overthrow the regime now in control of their home country. The émigrés sought help from all quarters and, very soon, the other European Kingdoms were at war with France, fueled by the fear that revolutionary fever would spread.

The Revolution really got rolling in January 1793 when Louis XVI was beheaded. Within a few months, the Revolutionists took control of nearly all of France. The last Royalist holdouts were the southern cities of Lyon and Toulon. Toulon had one of France's finest naval ports and a large fleet of the French Royal Navy. Its trade centered on fishing, shipping olive oil and cloth, ship repair, and ship construction. Before the Revolution, it was among the thirty largest cities in France with a population of about 20,000. The advances of the Revolutionary forces, however, had driven many French Royalists into the city just before its fall and it was now overcrowded.

The Revolutionists took Lyon in October 1793 but waited until December to try for Toulon. English Admiral Samuel Hood had situated his fleet just a few miles off the Toulon coast to prevent food and supplies from entering. Admiral Jean-Honoré de Trogoff-Kerlessy was the French Royal Navy's commander-in-chief of Toulon Harbor. While waiting for the final assault, Trogoff was concerned the city's food supplies were running low and began bargaining with Hood. At almost the last minute, Trogoff handed over all French Naval ships and forts in return for defense against the Revolutionists. Understandably, many French naval troops were not pleased with this action and 5000 of them were allowed to sail on four ships out of the port before Hood took control. The taking of Toulon was considered a great prize for the English and Hood became Lord Hood as a result. By this time, the English had joined forces with Naples and Spain to help defeat the Revolutionists.

On December 16, Napoleon Bonaparte, a young and relatively undistinguished artillery captain, led the Revolutionists in the attack of Toulon. He carried out a very simple plan. From the hills above Toulon, the cannons kept up a steady volley on the ships in the harbor. Soon, Admiral Hood decided it was best for his ships to leave rather than to return fire over the city. Napoleon was promoted to Brigadier General for his victory over the English. His accomplishment in Toulon is now treated an early indication of his greatness.

During the three days of military fighting, Toulon's citizens began killing each other over their Revolutionary or Royalist principles. Trogoff was alarmed and requested that Hood allow Royalist

Toulonnais citizens to evacuate on the Navy's ships. Admiral Hood gave the order – once the rearguard troops were aboard, fugitives should fill the remaining space. It is now estimated that 7500 people took this offer but that many more were left behind. The Spanish ships were the first to leave with 3000 people, whom they brought to Spanish ports. The Italian fleets took 400 people to Italian ports. About 1500 émigrés left with the first division of three French ships, commanded by the English Captain Elphinstone. They sailed for Portoferraio, Elba, then for Gibraltar, and finally for England. While these Royalists were glad to escape with their lives, they were sad to leave their country and many would eventually return.

On December 18, 1793, the Barthelemy Maffre family (Barthelemy 40, Cecile 40, François 20, Pierre 16, and Ann Harriet 11) was among the final 1500 emigres who left with the second division of French ships, commanded by Admiral Trogoff on the *Commerce de Marseille*. The other four ships in this second fleet were the *Topaze*, the *Perle*, the *Poulette* and the *Tarleton*. The *Commerce de Marseilles* was among the largest French ships and had three decks and 120 guns. This fleet spent one month at sea before arriving at the village of Portoferraio on the Isle of Elba (Figure 2.2).

Admiral Hood left Toulon harbor with his battle ships on December 19th but then anchored near the island of Porquerolles for a few days to ensure that no one pursued the evacuees.

French Sou (12 deniers), 1792, showing "Ludov XVI Roi Des Francois" on the obverse.
Louis XVI was guillotined in January 1793. From the Robert Mikasen Collection.

1794: Corsica

The next document of importance to the family is Pierre Maffre's death record (see below) in Bastia's Church of St. John the Baptist (Figure 2.3). Pierre died a day or two before September 6, 1794 in Bastia at age 16. The record says he is the son of Barthelemy and a native of Toulon. He was a sailor who died in a military hospital in the service of the English. The simplest interpretation is that Pierre died of wounds obtained one month earlier when he fought with the British Navy against the French who were holding the city of Calvi in Corsica. It is therefore likely that Pierre was a member of the Royal French Artillery Regiment, raised in Elba by the British from among the French Royalists who fled with them during the evacuation of Toulon.

Pierre Maffré's burial record from Saint Jean-Baptiste Church, Bastia

The original is in Italian: L'anno mille sette cente novanta auattro, li sei settembre, e stato sepolto nel cimitiero di questa città, il fancuillo Pietro Mafre figlio di Bartolomeo Mafre nativo di Tolone in Provenza, in età di anno sedici, morto all'ospedale militare, a servizio dell'inglesi, in qualità di marinaro. L'accompagnamento e l'interro e stato fatto all nostra presenza ed'alla presenza dei reverendi Guiseppe Mattei e Sebastiano Pino quail sottoscrivono con noi.

Translation: The year one thousand seven hundred ninety-four, the sixth of September, and was buried in the cemetery of this city, young Pietro Mafre son of Bartolomeo Mafre native of Toulon in Provence, at the age of sixteen years, died at the military hospital in the service of English, as a sailor. The service and burial were performed in our presence and in the presence of the Reverends Guiseppe Mattai and Sebastiano Pino and is subscribed by us. [*The transcription was not accompanied by a signature.*]

Here are the events leading up to Pierre's death in Bastia. On January 20, 1794, after one month at sea, the second French fleet arrived at the village of Portoferraio on the island of Elba, where the British had set up a base of operations in cooperation with the Italians. A contagious fever raged over the Isle and many of the disembarked passengers and crew soon became sick or died. Many émigrés made their way to Elba before Toulon was evacuated and the British Navy had formed the Royal French Marine Artillery Company, called the Royal French, on December 8. The Royal French fought for the British in Corsica and Portugal. It seems reasonable to propose that Barthelemey 40 and his sons François 20 and Pierre 16 joined this company. This is a hint they may have been sailors in the French Navy.

Figure 2.3: Two postcards of St. John the Baptist Church in Bastia's Old Port. On the left is a detail showing the Church behind riverfront buildings. On the right is the church's interior. Pierre Maffre's burial service took place in this church. The authors' personal collection.

Corsica is a French island in the Mediterranean located closer to Italy than France. It is the least populated of the large Mediterranean islands because its mountains rise so sharply. Nearly all of Corsica's cities are located in alcoves along the coast and over half the population resides in the cities of Ajaccio and Bastia. Beginning in 1347, Genoa had political control over the island. In the 1700's, the Corsicans revolted against paying taxes and, after a few decades of skirmishes, Genoa ceded Corsica to France in 1769. After Louis XVI was beheaded in January 1793, the French Royalist-appointed Corsican leader Pascal Paoli declared that Corsica had seceded from the new French Republic. Then, Paoli raised a militia that was able to confine the French forces to the three cities of Calvi, Bastia, and St. Florent. Next, he contacted Admiral Hood for help when Hood was blockading the Toulon harbor.

In February 1794, the Royal French helped the British Navy take the Corsican port of St. Florent from 550 French troops. In March, Admiral Trogoff died of the fever on Elba. After he was buried at sea, some Toulonnais émigrés were brought to St. Florent on the *Commerce de Marseille* and *Royal-Louis*. This relieved some of the overcrowding at Elba. March is also the month during which Cecile was impregnated with Joseph.

During April and May, the British fought for the city of Bastia against 5000 defending French troops, of whom 1000 were Army regulars. After the British succeeded, the Corsicans held a General Assembly during which they voted to offer the Crown of Corsica to His Majesty the King of England. On June 19, 1794, Sir Gilbert Elliot received the Corsican crown as His Majesty's Plenipotentiary. For the next two years, Corsica was under British control. When the French Revolution was finally over, the English returned ownership of Corsica to France on September 29, 1796. Since then, it has remained a French département with the same rights as any other on the mainland. Given that Joseph Maffre was born in December 1794 in Bastia, it is interesting to note that he lived his entire life on land controlled by the British.

Even though Napoleon was from Ajaccio, many Corsicans remained church-loving Royalists and chafed under his rule. As a result, there were four revolts instigated by the Corsican clergy between 1797 and 1799, each of which was severely repressed by the French. Between 1801 and 1811, General Morand was the military Governor of Corsica and he ruled with terror rather than with justice. In 1811, a new military Governor was put in place and the capital was transferred to Ajaccio, Napoleon's birthplace.

The last battle for Corsica took place in Calvi. In June 1794, only 400 out of the 1100 émigrés men were able to fight with the Royal French Regiment because so many were sick. There had also been many deaths and two of the battle ships had to be disarmed and sent out to sea with minimal crew. The Royal French were placed on the *Commerce de Marseilles* under the command of Captain Pasquier, sailed to St. Florent, and finally to the battle of Calvi. The battle raged from July 4 to August 5, during which time Admiral Nelson lost sight in his left eye (possibly a detached retina). The British had lost 90 regular and irregular troops during the battle but with many more deaths afterwards from the sickness and disease spread by war. As noted above, Pierre Maffre was one of the irregulars who died a month later. When Corsica was won, the regular British troops were down to 700 men.

On October 1, Sir Gilbert Elliot received notice that he was now the Corsican Viceroy and that his request to raise a Corsican Corps of 1500 men and a regiment of 2500 émigrés was approved. He needed the Corps to act as a police force on the island and to defend against a possible invasion from France. He immediately ran into two problems – the locals didn't want to join and many émigrés were leaving for England to join regiments so they could continue fighting the Revolutionaries. By November, Sir Gilbert managed to raise only 76 troops for his Corsican Light Dragoons. It seems that François Maffre was among those who left. We know that Barthelemy and Cecile stayed behind because Joseph was born in Bastia two months later. Cecile's pregnancy may be the reason they chose not to leave. Sir Gilbert moved the government to Bastia in an attempt to lessen Paoli's influence. It was during this time that the Royal French troops were issued full uniform and fatigue dress consisting of a round hat, flannel waistcoat and breeches, linen pantaloons, and blue stockings.

We know that François Maffre was among the men who sailed from Corsica to Portsmouth, England with the British Navy because his service is summarized on pension rolls, now in the UK National Archives under WO 69/618 (Table 2.1).

Table 2.1: Francis Maffre's Royal Foreign Artillery Pension Record, 1816

(1) Names (Non-commissioned officers)	*Maffre, Francis*
(2) Regiment or Corps	*Foreign Artillery*
(3) Battalion	
(4) Company or Troop	*Prevosts*
(5) Periods of Service, or on the Out-Pension	
(a) Date of Inlistment [*sic*]	*1 Ap^L 1805*
(b) Age at time of Discharge	*41*
(c) Period of Service in Each Rank	
Private	*3 years, 92 days [that is, 3 years & 3 months]*
Bombadier or Corporal	*7 years, 92 days [that is, 7 years & 3 months]*
Serjeant	
Staff Serjeant	
(d) Previous Service in any other Corps, and Period on the Out-Pension	
Period of Service in any other Corps	*Loyal Emigrants*
Period on Out-Pension	
(e) Service in each Corps when in more than one, or half the Period on the OUT-PENSION	*5 years*
(f) Deductions to be made from the Periods of Service	
Having Inlisted under 18 Years of Age	
ABSENT by DESERTION previous to 24th June, 1806	
DESERTION since 24th June, 1806, with	
Date to Return to Corps	
Date of being reduced to Private	
Amount of Deductions	
(g) Total Service after making the proper Deductions not including East or West India Service	*15 years, 184 days [that is, 15 years & 6 months]*
(h) Additions to be made	
Whole Period in EAST or WEST INDIA	*3 years, 273 days [that is, 3 years & 9 months]*
Total to be reckoned with the Addition for EAST or WEST INDIA Service	*19 years, 92 days [that is, 19 years & 3 months]*
(6) Period of Discharge	*31 dec 1815*
(7) Rates of Pension per Diem	
When Discharged	
British	*1 s. 3 ½ d. [15.5 pence/day or £240/year]*
Irish	
Date of Board's Orders	*11 dec 1815*
Increased to, under subsequent Orders	
British	
Irish	
Date of Board's Order	*Struck off BO 10 Janry 1825*
(8) REMARKS	

Based on his age when pensioned in 1816, Francis Maffre was born 1774. As already mentioned, at age 20, he joined the newly formed Royal French Marine Artillery Company in Elba along with his father and brother Pierre. After Corsica was safely under British protection, Francis sailed with many others to Portsmouth, where his pension says he joined the Loyal Emigrants in November 1794 and then served that company for 10 ½ years. The Loyal Emigrants were originally called La Chatre's Regiment after their commander. It was created in May 1793 in London for the growing number of émigrés in that city. Shortly after he joined, Francis and several thousand Loyal Emigrant troops were shipped to a battle in Flanders where they suffered heavy casualties. Upon their return, they numbered only 400 to 450 and were quartered in Lymington, located southwest of London on the coast. Over the next eight years, many other regiments were merged with the Loyal Emigrants and sent to fight in Quiberon and then Portugal. As we will see, Francis survived all of this and more and then got married in London in 1818.

Joseph Maffre was baptized on December 6, 1794 in Bastia, Corsica (see below). It occurred at the end of Barthelemy and Cecile's tumultuous first year on the run. Cecile's pregnancy would certainly have slowed her down but thoughts of having a baby may have given her some comfort in the face of their losses and uncertainty. Their second son Pierre 16 died in Bastia a few months earlier of battle wounds. Their eldest son François 20 had just left to fight in Flanders with the Loyal Emigrants. In Bastia, Cecile and Barthelemy had each other, their 11-year-old daughter Ann Harriet, and now a baby boy named Joseph.

> *Joseph Maffre's Birth and Baptism entry in Bastia Record book 1 E 39*
> Translation: In the year one thousand seven hundred ninety four, the sixth of December, in the Church of Santa Maria, parish of Terranuova, solemnly was baptized Guissepe, born yesterday legitimately to Bartolomeo and Cecilia Mafre, and witnessed by godparents Guiseppe Gioachino Janelle and Cecilia Bonnen [*or Ronnen*], all from Provence of France, living in this parish. The godparents have undersigned for the celebrants, on behalf of the father and mother who declared they could not write upon questioning etc. So much etc. In faith etc.
> [*Signed*] *Joseph Joachim Janelle*
>
> [*Signed*] *Mottini*, priest

Joseph Maffre's godparents were Joseph Joachim Janelle and Cecilia Bonnen [*or Ronnen*], also of Provence. It has not been possible to find further information about Bonnen but Janelle's entry in *Departmental Records of the Var* by historian Louis Honoré reads:

Janelle Joseph, A maitre de billard émigré le 28 frim. II Rentré en France le 26 vente. III.

To decode this, we need to know that the new French Republic renamed all the months and weekdays to a rational system. Frimaire means the cold season and was the third month from November 21 to December 20. Ventôse means windy season and was the sixth month from February 19 to March 20. Year I was 1793. Therefore, the entry tells us that billiards master Joseph Janelle emigrated from Toulon on December 18, 1793 and returned to France on March 16, 1795. In other words, he left Toulon on the same day as the Maffres and obviously ended up in Bastia. He returned in 1795 when French laws and attitudes were relaxing toward those who fled. Even so, many of the returning émigrés had ties or affinities to the previous Royal government and were never able to regain their previous position in society.

Another record indicates Joseph Janelle didn't fare well upon his return. In Pierre-Dominique Cheynet's *Inventory of Arrests* dating from late 1798 and early 1799, an entry says Janelle left Toulon with the British and then returned to Marseilles in 1795 by invoking the need for workers. Apparently, he used a fake certificate and was arrested.

Joseph Janelle, epart de billard à Toulon ayant quitté la ville au epart des Britanniques, rentré à Marseille en l'an III, invoquant l'exception en faveur des ouvriers, laboureurs et artisans et usant de faux certificats.

In 1923, historian Louis Honoré published a list of 2,519 Toulonnais who left in December 1793 after the town fell. It is such an important document for understanding the social upheaval in this final Royalist holdout that Colette Vitse analyzed it in some detail as part of her 1972 master's thesis in history. She was even able to add over 100 more names. Based on Vitse's analysis, Malcolm Crook cautions in his book *Toulon in War and Revolution* that Honoré's list includes more than just Toulonnais who fled. There are also fugitives from adjacent communities and even some men who remained behind and were executed in the days immediately following the fall of Toulon. Even so, an analysis of the occupations for the 1,469 Toulonnais men on Honoré's list with Vitse's amendments indicates 20% were from the upper class (nobles, military officers, leading administrators), 58% were from the middle class (artisans, shopkeepers, merchants, priests, and clerks), and 22% were workers (dockyard workers, sailors, fisherman, soldiers, and rural workers). This shows that the upper and middle classes were fleeing in much higher proportion to their population than the workers (which were probably about 60% of Toulon's citizens). Based on all of this prior work, it is confusing that the Maffres are not on this important list since several documents indicate they are from Toulon. Perhaps they have been overlooked because they left as an intact working class family unit and never returned, or because they are among the 5000 poorly document non-Toulonnais Royalists who fled from Toulon in December 1793.

Figure 3.1: Malt Hall commemorative plaque in Lymington, England. Photo by the authors.

3
BARRACKS AND BASTARDY

Many Toulonnais, including the Maffres, made their way to Lymington, England, because of the foreign regiments. For instance, the Maffre's eldest son François was in Lymington after returning from Flanders with the Loyal Emigrants Regiment. It must have been a family reunion when Barthelemy and Cecile Maffre arrived in Lymington in early 1795 with daughter Ann Harriet 12 and six-month-old baby Joseph. Barthelemy arrived just in time to join the ill-fated Quiberon Expedition, during which we think he died. Ann Harriet would marry here in 1802. Joseph would grow up here, impregnate a local girl, Lucy Thomas, when he was 20 years old, marry her, and then leave Lymington in 1817 when he was 24 years old.

1795: Lymington

Lymington is located about 100 miles southwest of London on the coast (Figure 3.2). Its waters are calmer than many coastal cities because the Isle of Wight acts as a buffer. The population of this sleepy town was about 2000 before the French émigrés arrived. It was a popular location for retired seaman and most of its commerce involved exporting salt obtained from heating seawater in long, shallow saltpans. At its peak in 1795, however, there were 3500 foreign troops in town, more than double its usual population. The foreigners made sure the taverns were full but never caused any real problems beyond a handful of murders, duels, suicides, and unmarried pregnancies.

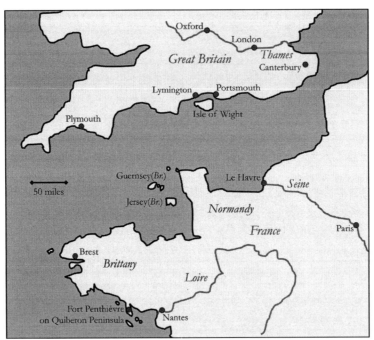

Figure 3.2: Map showing Lymington, England, and the Quiberon Peninsula of France. Illustration by Mark Griep.

During the French Revolution, Lymington hosted three émigrés Regiments — Loyal Emigrants, Hector's Regiment, and Rotalier's Regiment. All three were also known by other names, which makes it hard to decipher old records.

The Loyal Emigrants was the oldest émigrés Regiment. Its earliest troops were from the noble and middle classes who had fled France in 1792 and 1793. When it was formed in London, it was initially called La Chatre's after its commander but its official name became The Loyal Emigrants. They suffered heavy casualties in Flanders until it numbered only 400 men in 1795. We know from Francis Maffre's pension record that he joined the Loyal Emigrants in November 1794 so he was among the survivors. When they were in Lymington, this Regiment's troops were quartered in tradesmen's houses.

Hector's Regiment (often called Regiment d'Hector or Royal Marines) was formed from the sailors and officers of the French Naval Service in Southampton on October 1, 1794. In 1795, the troops numbered about 600 men. Their colonel was Jean Baptiste Hector comte d'Estaing. They were quartered in Buckland Manor, a large farmhouse located in the north of Lymington.

Rotalier's Emigrant Artillery (sometimes called the French Artillery, or French Emigrants) was formed "principally from the gunners who had defended Toulon against the Republicans" according to *A Walk Through Lymington* by Edward King. Their colonel was Pierre-Alexis Petijean de Rotalier (also spelled Rothalier). The 400 troops were quartered in the Lymington Malt-House (now the Community Centre; Figure 3.1) and a long row of stables (now destroyed) across the street.

1795: The Quiberon Expedition

We believe there is a kernel of truth in Will Fairbairn's *Maffre Chart* statement that Barthelemy Maffre was "killed or drowned in the expedition." The ill-fated Quiberon Expedition of June 1795 began in Lymington (Figure 3.2) and ended in the Quiberon Peninsula where hundreds of French royalist troops were "drowned or slaughtered on shore," according to King's *A Walk Through Lymington*. Given that Joseph was born in December 1794, the family had six months to make their way to Lymington so that Barthelemey could participate and then die at Quiberon.

When commander-in-chief Joseph de Puisaye was putting together the Quiberon Expedition, he needed all the troops he could get for his risky venture. He had just returned from a secret visit to western France where he had made contact with Royalist supporters known as the Chouans. The plan was for thousands of Royalist troops to land in the Loire Valley and unite with the Chouans to spread the counter-revolution. Instead, the British venture was defeated so decisively that the Quiberon Expedition was the last blow to the Royalist cause. By the time it was over, about 90% of the émigrés troops were "killed or drowned" in this "expedition" that doesn't involve Elba or Napoleon.

The 3500 émigrés troops were in two divisions of about equal numbers of troops. Puisaye's division included the Loyal Emigrants and Regiments led by Hector, Rotalier, Léon, and Williamson (also spelled Oilliamson). Louis Charles d'Hervilly led the other division. The émigrés troops were accompanied by about 4,500 British Regulars from the 19th, 27th, and 90th Regiments. They set sail on June 23, narrowly avoided detection by the French Navy at Brest, and then anchored off the Quiberon peninsula on the 26th. Because a mist concealed their presence, they could have made a very dramatic assault on Fort Penthiévre located on the Quiberon peninsula but that isn't what happened. Instead, Hervilly pulled out some papers claiming he was now commander-in-chief of the Expedition. This caused Puisaye and Hervilly to argue for an entire day. Even though Puisaye finally won the debate, this delay was their undoing. The Republican Army had time to start moving before the Chouans knew the English troops were waiting.

On June 28, the 8000 troops disembarked and easily took Fort Penthiévre. This was their last victory. By July 6, Republican General Lazare Hoche blocked the peninsula with 13,000 troops before the Chouans had even received their first communication. Over the next two weeks, many British assaults were rebuffed and there were many deaths. The only positive development during this time was assistance for the British from an additional 2000 émigrés troops who arrived on July 15 under the command of Charles Eugène Gabriel de Sombreuil.

It is estimated that only 1500 of the original 3500 émigrés troops were still alive when, on July 20, the Republicans began their assault on Fort Penthiévre (Figure 3.3). Unfortunately, the émigrés troops included many foreign prisoners of war who had agreed to join the expedition to get out of British military prison. As the Republicans approached the Fort, the former prisoners deserted and the Republicans were able to enter and begin their slaughter. To add to the misery, the British ships began firing on the Fort, killing friend, foe, and civilians. Puisaye ordered his men to row back to the ships but it was a blustery day and the sea was stormy and rough. On that day, thousands of émigrés and Chouan troops were either killed by bayonets or drowned. Among those who were captured, Sombreuil and 750 of his remaining men were condemned to death and shot. A monument called *Champs de Martyrs* was erected years later that gives a list of their names.

It is not certain how many troops returned to Lymington but it may have been as few as 500 out of the 8000 that participated. Puisaye was among those who returned safely and he lived under a cloud of suspicion for the rest of his life. In his 6-volume *Memoirs*, he includes detailed descriptions of the Expedition's hopelessness.

FORT PENTHIEVRE.

Figure 3.3: Fort Penthievre woodcut showing British troops in the foreground from The Pictorial History of England during the Reign of George the Third, *1841.*

After the Quiberon Expedition, the remaining émigrés troops were quartered in Lymington for one year as the Regiments built up strength. In November 1796, François Maffre was still with the Loyal Emigrants when they were sent to Portugal. Once there, they merged with the Franco-Maltese and were stationed in the Portuguese cities of Feitoria, Berqunha, Belem, and Lisbon. They disbanded in Gosport, England, on August 24, 1802.

1802: Ann Harriet Maffre

The only documentation for Ann Harriet Maffre is her marriage on December 27, 1802 in Lymington Parish Church to Jerome Rostange (see below). For our convenience, we have assumed she was twenty years old when she married giving her a birth year of 1792. Her relationship to Cecile, Joseph, and François is circumstantial in that she is "a foreigner in the parish," and she is the only other Maffre in the Lymington church records. Her husband Jerome Rostange is one of the "French Emigrants of this place," making him a colleague of her brother François.

> *Ann Harriet Maffre's marriage record from the Lymington Parish Church*
> **Jerome Rostange** of the **French Emigrants of this place** and **Ann Harriet Maffré** of this **parish (a foreigner in the parish)** were married in this **Church** by **Bannes** this **27** Day of **December** in the Year One Thousand **Eight** Hundred and **Two** by me **Ellis Jones**
> This Marriage was solemnized between Us **The Mark of Jerome Rostange + The Mark of A. Maffre X**, in the Presence of [*two indecipherable signatures*]

1805-1815: François Maffre

On April 1, 1805, Joseph's brother François Maffre enlisted in Captain George Prevost's Company of the Royal Foreign Artillery as a private after the Loyal Emigrants Regiment was disbanded. He served a total of 3 ¾ years in the West Indies. Prevost's Company was stationed in Trinidad with detachments in Grenada, St. Vincent, Barbados, and St. Lucia (Figure 3.4).

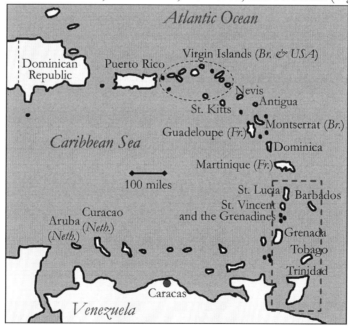

Figure 3.4: Map of the Caribbean Islands. Captain George Prevost's Company of the Royal Foreign Artillery was headquartered at Trinidad with stations at Grenada, St. Vincent, Barbados, and St. Lucia. Illustration by Mark Griep.

The Caribbean islands are the lower half of the West Indies, the collection of islands stretching from Florida to Venezuela that were named by Christopher Columbus in 1492. Europeans colonized these islands and, after finding an insufficient indigenous people to subjugate, brought slaves from Africa to raise sugar cane. Over the centuries, the Europeans fought each other over possession of many of these islands. Today, most are independent nations while a few remain affiliated with a European country. All of these, except Barbados, were French colonies before they were ceded to Britain in the 1780s.

From its creation out of various other regiments in March 1803 until its dissolution in January 1817 in Lymington, the Royal Foreign Artillery was the fourth unit of the Royal Artillery and was headed by one Major and four Captains, each with their own company. In 1804, there were 12,633 men, 785 women, and 515 children garrisoned in the Windward and Leeward Islands (St. Kitts, Nevis, Antigua, Montserrat, Dominica, St. Lucia, Barbados, St. Vincent, and Grenada). On July 1, 1808, Francis Maffre was promoted to corporal in Prevost's Company. He must have returned from West Indies in about September 1809. On October 26, 1815, Francis was godfather at his nephew Frank Maffre's baptism in Lymington, Hampshire. On December 11, 1815, Francis is discharged from Prevost's Company as Francis Maffre, age 41, and was pensioned at 15 ½ pence per day, which is £240/year.

1813-1817: Lucy Thomas Maffre

One of the most unusual documents from the Lymington years is Lucy Thomas's Bastardy Bond of November 3, 1813 from the Lymington parish records (see below). During this era, every town was charged with caring for its poor and bastardy bonds were the mechanism by which support was arranged for illegitimate children. The document says Lucy Thomas had a baby girl and she identified Joseph Maffre as the father. It is the first time Joseph appears on record since his birth in 1795. She was in the Lymington Poor House and Joseph was a drummer with the Foreign Artillery. Joseph agreed to pay two shillings [*24 pence*] per week for the child's keep, and Lucy agreed to pay six shillings [*72 pence*] per week. Lucy and Joseph were married three months later. The bastard child was not named in the document but we know from later documents that it was a girl named Ann. There were so many bastardy cases that a printed form was used and the relevant information entered by hand, as represented below with **Bold** font.

Bastardy bond for Lucy Thomas and Joseph Maffre (Lymington 42M75/P05/12)
   The Order of **Percival Louis and Charles St. Barbe Esquires County of Southampton** two of His Majesty's Justices of the Peace in and for the said **County** one whereof is of the Quorum, and both residing next unto the Limits of the Parish Church within the Parish of **Lymington** in the said **County** made the **Sixth** Day of **November** in the **fifty fourth** Year of the Reign of his said Majesty King George the **Third** concerning a **female** Bastard Child, lately born in the **Parish of Lymington** aforesaid, of the Body of **Lucy Thomas** single woman.
   Whereas it hath appeared unto us the said Justices, as well upon the Complaint of the Church-wardens and Overseers of the Poor of the said **Parish of Lymington** as upon the Oath of the said **Lucy Thomas** that she the said **Lucy Thomas** on the **Third** Day of **October** now last past, was delivered of a **Female** Bastard Child, at the **Poor House** in the said **Parish of Lymington** in the said **County** and that the said Bastard Child is actually chargeable to the said **Parish of Lymington** and further, that **Joseph Maffre** of **the Foreign Regiment of Artillery now in barracks in Lymington**

Drummer did beget the said Bastard Child on the Body of her the said **Lucy Thomas.** And whereas **the said Joseph Maffre has this day appeared before us and hath not shown any just cause why he is not the reputed father of the said Child**.

We therefore, upon Examination of the Cause and Circumstances of the Premises, as well upon the Oath of the said **Lucy Thomas** as otherwise, do hereby adjudge him the said **Joseph Maffre** to be the reputed Father of the said Bastard Child. And thereupon we do order, as well for the better Relief of the said **Lucy Thomas** as for the Sustentation and Relief of the said Bastard Child [*material crossed out relating to charges for the "Lying in" of Lucy Thomas*] that the said **Joseph Maffre** shall pay or cause to be paid, to the Churchwardens and Overseers of the Poor of the said Parish of **Lymington** for the Time being, or to some or one of them, the Sum of **Two Shillings** weekly and every Week from the present Time, for and towards the Keeping, Sustentation, and Maintenance of the said Bastard Child, for and during so long Time as the said Bastard Child shall be chargeable to the said **Parish of Lymington.** And we do further order that the said **Lucy Thomas** shall also pay or cause to be paid to the said Churchwardens and Overseers of the Poor of the said **Parish of Lymington** for the Time being, or to some one of them, the sum of **Six Pence** weekly, and every Week, so long as the said Bastard Child shall be charge- able to the said **Parish of Lymington** in Case she shall not nurse and take Care of the said Child herself. Given under our Hands and Seals the Day and Year first above-written.

On January 3, 1814, Joseph Maffre 19 and Lucy Thomas 21 are married in the Lymington Parish Church, Hampshire. The marriage witnesses are George Thomas and Elizabeth Thomas. Her brother George lived in Lymington so the witnesses are Lucy's brother and his wife. Lucy Thomas was born June 10, 1792 in East Boldre immediately to the north of Lymington, and was baptized February 13, 1793 in Beaulieu Abbey Church. Her family lived in Beaulieu Rails located six miles northeast of Lymington. Her brother George was the first in the family to move to Lymington and she must have followed him.

The marriage certificate says Joseph was in the *Foreign Depot* in Lymington. This is another name for the *French Artillery Regiment* listed on the bastardy bond. As mentioned earlier, Depot Company of the Royal Foreign Artillery Regiment was commanded by Colonel Rotalier and was formed in April 1806. It supplied replacement troops for the other Royal Foreign Artillery Regiments stationed in the West Indies, an assignment considered to be a death sentence because so many died of Yellow Fever.

On October 26, 1815, Joseph and Lucy's first legitimate child Francis was baptized in Pylewell House Roman Catholic Chapel (see below). Francis' godfather was his uncle Francois Maffre. His godmother was Rosa Carmine. On November 6, 1815 in the Pylewell House Chapel, Joseph Maffre was godfather to Maria Carmine, daughter of Joseph and Rose (Roger) Carmine.

Francis Maffré's certificate of baptism from the "Registers of Pylewell House, Lymington" *chapter of* The Catholic Register, *volume 14, p. 301.*

Transcription: Die 17ª Octobris 1815 natus, die vero 26ª ejusdem mensis & anni baptizatus est Fransciscus Mafre, filius Josephi & Lucie Mafre, olim Thomas, conjugum. Patrinus fuit Fransciscus Mafre. Matrina Roza Carmine. A me Joanne Browne Missº Aposᶜᵒ

Translation: The 17th of October 1815 born, the true 26th of the same month and year baptized was Frank Mafre, son of Joseph and Lucy Mafre, formerly Thomas, married. Godfather was Francois Maffre. Godmother Roza Carmine.

By me John Browne, Missionary Apostle

Pylewell House was Joseph Weld's home from 1801 to 1864. The Weld family was the most prominent English Catholic family at this time. Joseph Weld's father Thomas is lauded for having relieved the misfortunes of the refugees of the French Revolution and for one of the first English Catholics to entertain the king, which he did in 1789 and 1791. Joseph Weld maintained a Roman Catholic priest at his private chapel, which was used by a number of the émigrés troops since it was located only three miles east of Lymington.

Over a period of years ending in January 1818, Pastor Henry Comyn prepared a census of his two parishes (Boldre and Brockenhurst) that is rich with genealogical information for his successor Charles Shrubb. Comyn listed all members of each family, birthdates, maiden names, as well as the whereabouts of absent family members. The entry for Lucy's parent's home number 31 in Beaulieu Rails South (see below) indicates that Lucy was married to Maffre and in America when the census was taken. Her father George Thomas was a shoemaker, he was married to Hannah Burnett, and they paid £3 rent to Captain Perry for their home. George was of the few residents with a listed occupation in Beaulieu Rails. Most of the others are thought to have been smugglers.

Comyn's 1817 Census entry of for Lucy Thomas Maffre's parent's family	
[BRS 31] £3 *Captn Perry*	
George Hannah (Burnett) **THOMAS**	shoemaker
George...23 May 1790	Lym.
Lucy (*Maffrey*)............................ 10 June 1793	America
Sarah .... 3 June 1800	
Jane ....16 July 1804	<Lym'ton> [in pencil]
Robert <Sch*> ....11 May 1807	
Eliza ....27 May 1810	
[* or "in pencil" means it was in Comyn's successor Shrubb's hand]	

We have yet to discover Joseph's Company in the West Indies. Even so, it is reasonable to propose that Joseph, Lucy, and their two children were deployed to the West Indies after their son Frank's birth in November 1815. All the troops returned home in January 1817, a date consistent with the birth of their third child Joseph Jr. in London in August 1817. Therefore, they spent approximately one year in the West Indies.

When Joseph Maffre left the military in March 1841, he wrote that he had served 25 years. We have evidence he was in the military from November 1813 until about 1817 and then from about 1828 to 1841 but this adds up to only 17 total years. As such, we propose that Maffre joined the Foreign Depot in 1806 because (1) he was a member of that regiment in 1813, (2) the Depot was formed in April 1806 in Lymington under the command of Colonel Rotalier, (3) it was highly unusual for anyone to change regiments, (4) his father Barthelemey served under Colonel Rotalier in 1795, and (5) it was common for a son to join the same regiment as his father. If he joined Rotalier's Company in 1806, he would have joined at age 10, the normal age at which regiments accepted band recruits but a bit young for regular recruits.

Let us end the chapter by referring to Will Fairbairn's *Maffre Chart* one last time. The first and last parts of his brief entry appear to be correct. The Maffre family fled France when Toulon fell and the two sons ended up in London. These events didn't happen consecutively, however, and there is no hint that the family spent 2 years in Corsica and about 20 years in Lymington during which time Joseph Maffre was born, grew up, impregnated a local girl, married her, served a year in the West Indies, and then made his way to London in 1817 where his brother was now living.

MARQUIS OF WORCESTER.   LADY JERSEY.   CLANRONALD MACDONALD.   LADY WORCESTER.

THE FIRST QUADRILLE AT ALMACK'S.

Figure 4.1: The First Quadrilles at Almack's, 1815. The four people in the print are the Marquis of Worcester, Lady Jersey, Clanronald Macdonald, and Lady Worcester. It was Lady Jersey who introduced the quadrilles to London society after she learned the dance on a trip to Paris. From Wikimedia Commons but first published opposite the title page of "Reminisences of Captain Gronow" Second Edition by Rees Howell Gronow, 1872.

4

THE LONDON CONNECTION

Joseph Maffre and his family lived in the Somers Town district of London for the two and a half years between January 1817 and August 1819. This period was long enough for him to perform in three of London's musical seasons. His brother Francis also lived in this district and was married there. During his time in London, Joseph probably learned how to become a professional musician through his interactions with other performers at the nascent Royal Philharmonic Society and at Almack's Assembly Rooms, where the elite met to dance and dine.

Somers Town, London

In London, the Maffres lived at 25 Wellesley Street in the Somers Town area (Figure 4.2). This Street no longer exists but it was across Eversholt Street from the present-day Euston Train Station. It was only a few blocks from the St. Aloysius Catholic Church at which son Joseph Jr. was baptized.

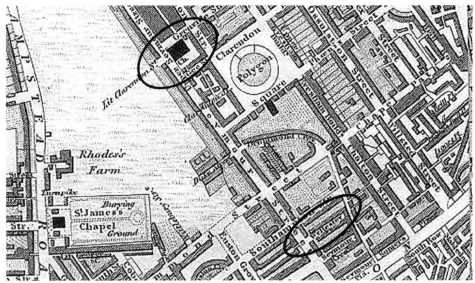

Figure 4.2: Map of Somers Town, London. The top oval shows the location of St. Aloysius Gonzaga Roman Catholic Chapel. The bottom oval shows where the Maffres lived at 25 Wellesley St. This is Greenwood's Map of London, 1827, from Genealogy Freepages by Rootsweb.

The French exiles who settled in England were united only in having been expelled by their native country. Most of them stayed where they landed because they were too poor or exhausted to continue. Many Normans and Bretons settled on the Isles of Jersey and Guernsey, located just a short distance from their homelands. The majority of exiles settled in London. The wealthiest settled on the edge of the West End. Most of them were from Paris or Versailles and were received by the English as aristocracy. The middle class settled in Soho, a traditional settling place for foreigners. The artisans and working class settled in the region surrounding the Polygon of Clarendon Square and used the church and yard of St. Pancras. The cheapest rents were found just south of the Polygon in Somers Town. Rents were cheap because of an excess of speculative building in the preceding decades. Finally, the destitute among the exiles settled in St. George's Fields, south of the Thames.

Joseph and Lucy's third child Joseph Ludwig Maffre (aka Joseph Jr.) was born in August 1817 and baptized in St. Aloysius Gonzaga Catholic Chapel, located a few blocks to the north of their home. The family sent notice of Joseph Jr.'s birth and baptism to Lymington and it was recorded in the Pylewell House Roman Catholic Church Register (see below), which is the only reason the record survives. St. Aloysius Gonzaga was built in 1808 to replace the eight French chapels that were in this area. After 160 years of use, the original St. Aloysius was torn down and the present St. Aloysius Roman Catholic Church opened in 1968, one block south of the original. The authors visited the church in 2005 and found that one corner of the interior contains a collection of artifacts relating to the earlier church.

Translations of Joseph Ludwig Maffré's birth and baptism certificates from the "Registers of Pylewell House, Lymington" chapter of The Catholic Register, volume 14, p. 311-312.

Certificate D.

[*Joseph Ludwig*] Maffré was born 10 August 1817, at 6 o'clock in the evening at Weselley [*Wellesley*] Street, number 25, in the parish of St. Pancras, son of Joseph Maffré and of Anne [*Lucy*] Thomas his wife, married in Lymington 1814. The father, son of the late Barthelemy Maffré and of Cecile Ordi, was born in Bastia in Corsica and baptized on the funds of the Cathedral of St. Omery [*St. Omer*] in October 1794. The Godfather was Jouan. The Godmother was [*crossed out*]. Of the Vine.

Certificate E.

Extract from the Baptismal Registry of the Chapel of St. Aloysius Gonzaga, in the canton of Sommerstown in the London district.

Born the 10th in the month August and year 1817, and the 12th same month and year baptized was Joseph Ludwig Maffre, son of Joseph and Lucy Maffre (formerly Thomas) married. Godfather was Mark Francois Jouan. Godmother designate was Mary Gree. Of the vine, by me J. Nevincka M.A. [*Missionary Apostle*]

I, Claude Guerry, priest, bear witness to the preceding extract in all things conforms to the Register: in whose faith this testimony my hand writes below. Sommer's town, the *Vigesimá Sectâ* month of August, year 1817.

C. Guerry, Priest.

On January 13, 1818, "Francis Maffray," bachelor, married Sarah Milon, spinster, in St. Pancras Church, Somers Town, London. Francis signed the certificate as "F. Maffrey" but his wife used a cross. The witnesses were Samuel Burkes and Sarah Jenkins. Assuming this is indeed Joseph's brother, Francis was 44 when he married.

In December 1818, Joseph's 3-year-old son Frank died and his burial took place in Lymington. Either Lucy returned home to Lymington, or young Frank had been raised by a relative in Lymington. Did he contract Yellow Fever in the West Indies and then die in Lymington of the lingering disease?

On February 3, 1822, "Francis Maffray" was godfather at the baptism of George Francis Scott in St. Aloysius Church, Somers Town, London. The godmother was Mary Manson.

In 1823, "F. Maffery" was living in Parkers Estate in Somers Town according to the London Land Tax Records. None of his immediate neighbors – Whitman, Gavell, Seal, Hill, Kirkland, and Cox – had French surnames. At the time of his death in 1837, William Parker leased dwellings on Northampton Street and on Essex Street, both in the St. Pancras area.

In the second quarter (April, May, and June) of 1854, "Sarah Maffrey" dies in the Marylebone district of London (Marylebone Civil Registration, volume 1A, page 316). She was living in the workhouse at the time. If this is the former Sarah Milon, then Francis must have died before this and his widow was working hard to pay her room and board.

Royal Philharmonic Society in the Argyll Rooms

In his August 1819 announcement in the *Leicester Journal*, Joseph Maffre tells us he had been a musician at Almack's and the Argyll Rooms. The vagueness of that statement could be a deliberate attempt by Maffre to obfuscate but it is certainly true that the Royal Philharmonic was the most prominent user of the Argyll Rooms even if they were not the only users. Nevertheless, we surmise that Maffre performed with the Royal Philharmonic during the 1817, 1818, and 1819 seasons since he favored the pieces they performed during those seasons throughout the rest of his career. Even if he performed with the Royal Philharmonic a few times, he probably soaked up as much knowledge from the leading musicians as he could. After all, someone had to direct him to the opportunities available in Leicester before August 1819.

London's musical season occurred in spring when Parliament was in session. As such, the Royal Philharmonic Society performed on every other Monday from late February to late May. Each concert began precisely at 8 o'clock and ended at about 11 o'clock. It was founded by leading musicians in 1813 who wanted to perform music by contemporary composers such as Ludwig von Beethoven and Wolfgang Amadeus Mozart. George, the Prince Regent, was among its founding patrons although he rarely attended. George became prince regent in 1811 when his father was declared incapable of ruling the kingdom and became King in 1820 when his father died. He died in 1830 at age 68. As Prince Regent, he was known as a patron of the arts who enjoyed a good time and allowed the politicians to run the country. The era of the dandy, a male who favored fashion and style above all else, arose during the Regency period on the strength of George Bryan "Beau" Brummel's personality and friendship with the Prince Regent. Male fashion changed quickly from the foppish wigs, white face, breeches, knee socks, and slippers to clothes resembling those of a well-dressed military man with pants, boots, tight-fitting jacket, cravat, and a clean and freshly shaved face.

During its first year in 1813, each of the Royal Philharmonic musicians paid £3 for the privilege to perform as a Member or Associate. The Members were the principal performers listed on the playbill whereas Associates performed the supporting parts. The number of Members was limited to fifty but there was no limit to the number of Associates. As Members vacated their positions, new Members were chosen from among the Associates. Another source of income was the £4 fee paid by the approximately 650 patrons who subscribed to the concerts. The income from the first year was used to pay £200 for use of the Argyll Rooms and £160 for the sheet music and transcriptions, leaving a large profit that was kept in reserve. The musicians were apparently uninterested in making money and used the concerts as a showcase of their talents. After Napoleon was defeated at Waterloo in 1815, however, so many musicians returned to their native countries that the Society had to begin paying for a few high-profile performers.

The Argyll Rooms began life as a mansion on Argyll Street in the Soho area of London in the early 1800's. The mansion was soon renovated into a venue for fashionable but lightweight entertainment. After Mr. Slade became its manager in 1813, it was selected as the venue for the newly founded Philharmonic Society, the first of its kind. After the 1818 season, the building was torn down when Regent Street was created and Mr. Slade was awarded the princely sum of £23,000 in compensation. He used the funds to build new rooms designed by John Nash on the northwest corner of Argyll Place, Soho, which reopened in time for the 1820 season. The Philharmonic Society renamed itself the Royal Harmonic Institution and consisted of 21 musicians. The Philharmonic boasts a number of 'firsts' including first use of a baton by a conductor on April 10, 1820. When a fire destroyed the building in 1830, the Philharmonic moved first to King's Theatre and then to Hanover Square Rooms.

During its first fifty years, the Royal Philharmonic most often performed pieces by Wolfgang Mozart (especially the overtures from *La Clemenza di Tito* and *Der Zauberflöte*, both published in 1791), Ludwig van Beethoven (especially the overture from *The Creatures of Prometheus* ballet of 1801), and Luigi Cherubini. In fact, Cherubini's *Anacréon* Overture (1803) was performed more than any other piece, being played at least once each Season but thrice during the 1818 Season. Maffre promoted enough events during the rest of his decades-long career that we can get some sense of his musical taste by noting which of these pieces he chose to perform when he controlled the playbill (see the Full Knowledge chapter). In 1823 specifically, he led a well-attended performance of the Leicester Musical Society, a group he resurrected. He advertised they would perform the overtures from *Clemenza di Tito, Zauberflöte*, and *Prometheus*, all three of which remain reasonably popular almost two centuries later. Maffre does not appear to have ever performed Cherubini's *Anacréon* overture, a piece that has since become much less well known.

Maffre paid several homages to Beethoven throughout his career and would certainly have heard about the Royal Philharmonic's negotiations with the composer. In June 1817, they mailed him an offer of £300 if he would direct two new symphonies for them. Beethoven responded with a request for £450, causing the negotiations to fade away by August. Beethoven never made it to England. Maffre's first homage to Beethoven came in August 1817 when he named his third child Joseph *Ludwig* Maffre. Secondly, one quadrille in his 1827 *New Set of Quadrilles* is called "La Beethoven." The final Beethoven-Maffre connection was initiated during the 1818 and 1819 Seasons, second and third concerts respectively, when the Royal Philharmonic performed Beethoven's "Quintett for 2 Violins, 2 Violas, & 'Cello." This was Beethoven's first composition for a string quintet and is more commonly called "Viola Quintet, Op. 29" (1802), or "Storm Quintet." Maffre used this piece as the basis for his 1829 "For a Military Band Beethovens Grand Quintetto No. 1 of String Instruments."

Maffre also paid homage to Giovanni Battista Viotti and may have become familiar with his work through the Royal Philharmonic. Viotti was a prominently featured Member during the 1813-1815 Seasons, just preceding Maffre's years, and even led performances of his own compositions. The second concert of the 1819 Season included Viotti's "Concertante for 2 Violins", which may be the inspiration for the first quadrille in Maffre's 1827 *New Set of Quadrilles* named "La Viotti."

Finally, the eighth and final concert of the 1819 Season included the "From Mighty Kings" song from George Frideric Handel's 1747 oratorio *Judas Maccabaeus*. Of course, Handel's works have been popular from the day they were written but it is an interesting coincidence that Maffre played the "See, the Conquering Hero comes" chorus from *Judas Maccabaeus* when Lord Durham boarded the *H. M. S. Hastings* for his journey to Canada in 1838.

Balls at Almack's Assembly Rooms

Maffre's subsequent career shows he was heavily influenced by the music performed at Almack's. The dances called the quadrille and the waltz were both introduced to English society at Almack's. Maffre composed five quadrilles and one waltz for his *New Set of Quadrilles* in 1827, published two separate quadrilles in the *Literary Garland* in 1840, and published six quadrilles for his

The Original Canadian Quadrilles in 1847. From 1847 to 1849, Maffre's Quadrille Band would play until the wee hours of the morning after a musical concert had ended.

The Balls at Almack's Assembly Rooms (Figure 4.3) took place every Wednesday from mid-April to mid-July so that they did not coincide with the Royal Philharmonic. The doors opened at 10 o'clock and the music began at 11 o'clock at which time the doors were secured. No one could gain late entry unless they were members of Parliament and even they were denied entrance if they weren't properly dressed. The musicians played continuously until 4 o'clock, at which time everyone left for home, exhausted.

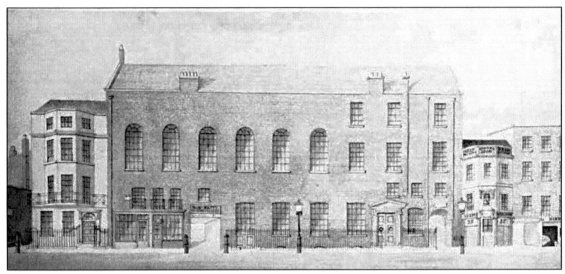

Figure 4.3: Almack's Assembly Rooms, about 1800. Although it was an undistinguished looking building, it was the center of the social scene for the upper class. Wikimedia Commons.

Almack's opened on King Street, St. James, London, on February 20, 1765 as one of the first clubs to admit both men and women. By 1790, it was the place to be seen because it was exceedingly difficult to gain admission. In 1814, Captain Gronow wrote "At the present time, one can hardly conceive the importance which was attached to getting admission to Almack's, the seventh heaven of the fashionable world. Only a paltry half dozen of the Guards' officers, out of some three hundred, were honoured with vouchers of admission to this exclusive temple."

Membership to the club, and therefore admission to the Wednesday evening Balls with supper, were governed by a select committee of six or seven "Lady Patronesses" (Table 4.1) who were not fond of the *nouveau riche*. The ladies would meet Wednesday afternoon to decide on the applications for admission and to make the arrangements for that evening's ball. The cost of one evening's subscription was £1 [*240 pence*] but decreased to seven shillings and sixpence [*90 pence*] after they stopped offering supper in about 1830. Since each season included ten balls, a Season's subscription was 10 guineas [*2500 pence*]. The men's tickets were non-transferable. Most of this information is from *Memorials of St. James's Street, Together with The Annals of Almack's* by Chancellor.

The quadrille was introduced to English society at Almack's by Lady Jersey in 1815 and quickly spread across the country (Figure 4.1). Its vibrancy replaced the Scottish reels and English country-dances that had been the norm. In 1816, Princess Lieven introduced the waltz and soon everyone was hugging their partner as they whirled around the dance floor.

Table 4.1: Lady Patronesses of Almack's in 1814

Lady Patroness	Brief biography
Lady Jersey, born Sarah Sophia Fane	Served the longest and was the most influential of the Lady Patronesses. She married the 5th Earl of Jersey in 1804 and became a Patroness in 1805. She reigned over London Society as "Queen Sarah" until her death in 1867. She introduced the quadrille to England in 1815 at Almack's.
Lady Londonderry, born Amelia Hobart	Was the wealthiest of the Patronesses, owning fine houses in London and on their Irish country estate. When her husband, Robert Stewart, known as Lord Castlereagh, became the 2nd Marquis of Londonderry in 1822, she became Marchioness.
Lady Cowper, born Emily Mary Lamb	Married the 5th Earl of Cowper in 1805. After he died in 1837, she remarried the 3rd Lord Palmerston. Both her brother and second husband served as Prime Ministers.
Lady Sefton, born Maria Margaret Craven	Daughter of the 6th Lord Craven. She married the 2nd Earl of Sefton, a dandy who was friend of the Prince Regent and companion of Beau Brummel.
Lady Lieven, born Dorothea Christorovna Benckendorff	Born in Russia and married to Lieutenant General Count Lieven. He became Russian Ambassador to the Court of St. James in 1811, at which time she became a Lady Patroness. She introduced the waltz to England in 1816 at Almack's. She was as politically active as her husband. In 1834, the Lievens were recalled to Russia, where her husband was created a Prince and she a Princess.
Princess Esterhazy, born Princess Theresa of Thurn and Taxis	Married Prince Esterhazy, the Austrian Ambassador to the Court of St. James.
Mrs. Drummond Burrell, born Clementina Drummond	Married Mr. Peter Burrell, a dandy who was friend of the Prince Regent and companion of Beau Brummel. In 1828, she became Lady Willoughby de Eresby when her husband succeeded to that title.

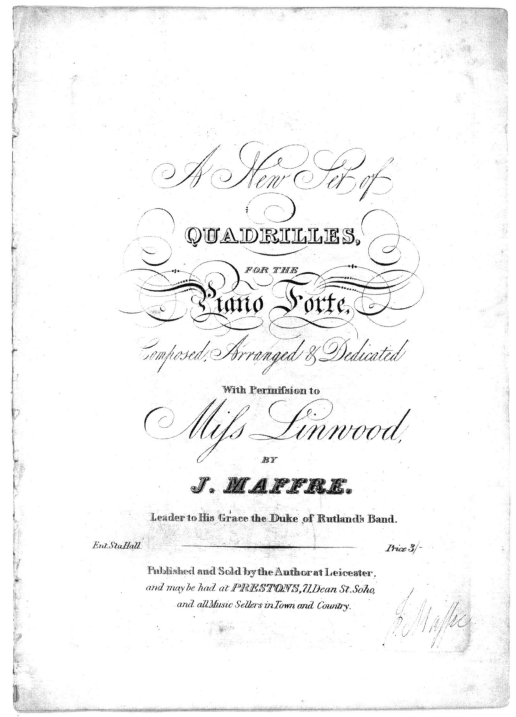

Figure 5.1: "A New Set of Quadrilles" Sheet Music Cover, 1827, signed "J Maffre" in the lower right corner. The authors' personal collection.

5

RESPECTFULLY DEDICATED

Joseph Maffre's career as a professional musician took off in Leicester. He moved there in late 1819 and was gone by late 1829. It is not known how he chose Leicester as his home base but it was a shrewd move. Leicester was small enough for him to make a big impact and it was centrally located to the many other cities in which he would perform. It was also during his Leicester period that he and Lucy completed their family of nine children. There is no information how the children were raised so we are left to imagine how Joseph taught them the family business.

1819

The earliest evidence of Joseph Maffre living in Leicester comes from the following advertisement in the *Leicester Journal.*

Leicester Journal
Friday, August 6, 1819, p. 3, c. 3, top item

J. MAFFRI,
Musician, from Almack's Argyle Rooms, London,
BEGS leave to inform the Nobility and Gentry of Leicester and its vicinity, that he intends teaching the German Flute, Violin, Clarionett, and Piano Forte.
Music provided for Balls and Quadrille parties in town or country on the shortest notice.
J. M. also teaches the French language.
Residence at Mr. Ireland's, Southgate street.

The unusual spelling of his name is either a typographical error or he was experimenting with his image. German flute is the archaic name for the flute and is used to distinguish it from the English flute, or recorder. Robert Ireland is a brewer living on Southgate Street according to the 1826 Poll Book.

1820

On February 1, 1820, Joseph and Lucy baptized their three-week-old daughter Charlotte at the Holy Cross Roman Catholic Church. They were probably living a short distance away on Holy Bones Lane. The red brick Holy Cross Church was completed in 1817 and was located between New Walk and Wellington Street. From October 12 to Christmas, the Holy Cross church featured Sunday performances of Haydn's First Mass, featuring an organist and choir. The names of the musicians are not given but the suspicion would be that Maffre had a hand in this promotion.

In June 1820, Maffre gave a Vocal and Instrumental Concert followed by a dance in Banbury, Oxfordshire. Banbury is located about three hours south of Leicester. The concert's patrons were Major George Frederick Stratton and the officers of the Bloxham and Banbury Yeomanry Cavalry. Stratton became sheriff of Oxford in 1806 and Yeomanry Cavalry were the precursors to the modern police force. To raise interest in the concert, the Bloxham and Banbury Yeomanry Cavalry paraded through Oxford one week earlier "accompanied with an excellent band of music." This is the first event known to have been created by Maffre and it set the model for the rest of his career.

1821

On November 1, 1821, Joseph and Lucy baptized their two-week-old daughter Maria at the Holy Cross Roman Catholic Church. Maria was their fifth child.

1822

By 1822, Joseph and his growing family are living on Holy Bones Lane, Leicester (Figure 5.2). The lane received its name because there was a butcher shop located near St. Nicholas' Church for centuries, and it generated quite a bone pile. St. Nicholas' Church was built about 1143 and was, of course, Church of England by the time Joseph moved in across the street. Today, the buildings located on the short street were all built in the late 1800's except for Leicester's Guru Namak Dev Ji Gudwara, or Sikh Temple honoring the Guru Namak Dev Ji, which moved into a former textile factory in 1989.

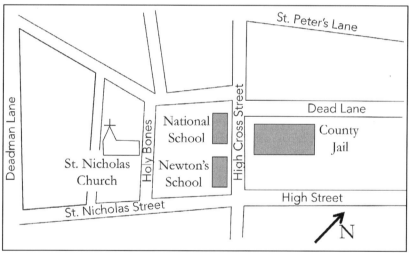

Figure 5.2: Map of St. Nicholas Church area of Leicester based on an 1857 Map. Illustration by Mark Griep.

In August 1822, Maffre and other local musicians perform at a benefit concert of sacred music for the family of Charles Jarvis, a local musician who died on June 15, leaving no provision for his widow Mary and their nine children. The concert was described in the *Leicester Journal*. The musicians and their instruments were John Ella (violin), Miss Maria Hewitt (organist), Joseph Maffre (clarinet), and John Waldrom (bassoon). The concert raised forty-five pounds. Maffre would later promote the singing ability of a Miss Jarvis, who must have been one of the daughters.

In October 1822, Maffre places an advertisement in the *Leicester Journal* thanking his supporters for their patronage during the past season. He ends by saying that he now possesses a complete collection of quadrilles and is living on St. Nicholas Street. This street intersects with Holy Bones Lane (Figure 5.2).

At some time before 1823, Maffre was 'Leader to His Grace the Duke of Rutland's Band.' During the Napoleonic Wars, the 5th Duke of Rutland John Henry Manners (1778-1857) was the Colonel of the third company of the Leicestershire Militia. The Militia likely formed and paid for its own band. The Leicestershire Militia was officially disbanded in 1815 when Napoleon was defeated. Afterward the band was known as the Duke of Rutland's Band, the Leicestershire Yeomanry Band, or even still the Leicestershire Militia Band. In fact, a concert review from December 1829 says Maffre is "formerly of the Leicestershire Militia." There is also Maffre's 1850 death notice in the *Leicester Chronicle* that says he was "formerly in the Duke of Rutland's band." Being the Leader to the Band was different from being the Bandmaster. It most likely meant that he kept the tempo for the band, most certainly while playing an instrument. A bandmaster would be responsible for all aspects of member training and performance. The Duke of Rutland's bandmaster during Maffre's time was Henry Nicholson Sr. who served in that capacity from 1816 (after Waterloo) until his retirement in 1854. According to Wade-Matthews' *Musical Leicester*, the Duke heard Henry Nicholson's band at the Battle of Waterloo and induced Nicholson to form a band in Leicester for the Duke's private use. Nicholson's band would play at the annual fireworks display, at the annual Race, and at the Duke's birthday celebration every January. Nicholson also formed his own quadrille band in 1820 with bassoonist John Waldrom. After Henry Nicholson died, the officers and men of the Leicestershire Yeomanry erected a double-arched Gothic monument over his grave.

1823

In the year 1823, Joseph Maffre demonstrates that he has a strong grasp on the musical taste and prestige of his era. He leads a Vocal and Instrumental Concert in Leicester and performs at one of England's Grand Music Festivals for the first time. During this era, cities would take turns hosting a Grand Music Festival in which the members of their local vocal society would provide the core members of the crowd-pleasing performances of one of Franz Joseph Haydn's great choruses that always ended the three- to four-day festival.

On January 26, 1823, the Maffres baptize son Henry in St. Nicholas' Church, indicating that Henry was baptized in the Church of England. This church was located across the street from their house on St. Nicholas Street. Three years later in 1826, they baptized their daughter Mary Anne in the same church.

In March 1823, Maffre is Leader of the Band for the most important Vocal and Instrumental Concerts that occurred in Leicester. The Leicester Musical Society, a group founded 1803, promoted the Concerts. The Society had become dormant so we can infer that Maffre resurrected it as a way of encouraging the best amateurs to perform and to raise interest in musical education among other citizens. The *Leicester Journal* glowingly reviewed the concert, saying that it came off with "great éclat."

In September 1823, Maffre performs at the Yorkshire Grand Music Festival (Table 5.1). His name is listed as "Maffey, Leicester" in the program and indicated he was "leader of a band." Henry Nicholson from Leicester was one of the lead flautists and gave a Flute Concerto on the third day.

Table 5.1: Grand Musical Festivals of the 1820's (plus 1835)

Musical Festival	Date	Notes
Birmingham 1820	Oct 3, 4, 5, 6	217 Performers (chorus 134, orchestra 83)
Chester 1821	Sept 25, 26, 27, 28	206 Performers (chorus 126, orchestra 80) Chester provided 41 of the chorus (33%)
Derby 1822	Oct 8, 9, 10, 11	Almost 300 Performers
*Yorkshire 1823	Sept 23, 24, 25, 26	*Maffre is one of the many violinists* 467 Performers (chorus 285, orchestra 182) York provided 30 of the chorus (11%) 3500 attended the first day & 5000 the second
Liverpool 1823	Oct 1, 2, 3, 4	
Birmingham 1823	Oct 7, 8, 9, 10	Under Royal Patronage
Norwich 1824	Sep 22, 23	251 Performers (chorus 150, orchestra 101) Norwich provided 101 of the chorus (67%)
Wakefield 1824	Sep 29, 30, Oct 1	185 Performers (chorus 98, orchestra 87) Performers were selected from those who were engaged at the 1823 Yorkshire Festival The only festival that ever lost money
Northumberland, Durham & Newcastle 1824	Oct 5, 6, 7, 8	117 Performers (chorus 62, orchestra 55) Durham Cathedral provided 15 of the chorus (24%) Newcastle provided 17 of the chorus (27%)
Derby 1825	Oct 4, 5, 6, 7	300 Performers
Yorkshire 1825	Sept 13, 14, 15, 16	614 Performers (chorus 374, orchestra 240) York provided 42 of the chorus (11%) 24,755 attended; £7,200 profit
*Market Harborough 1826	Sept 18, 19, 20	*"Principal Clarionet Mr. Maffre" is listed fourth* "The instrument Department will be sustained by a Concentration of the first Talent"
Birmingham 1826	Oct 3, 4, 5, 6	Patronized by the King; President was Rt. Hon. Earl Howe
*Leicester 1827	Sept 4, 5, 6	*Maffre is one of the many violinists* 288 Performers (chorus 188, orchestra 100) 1800 attended the first day, Leicester provided 91 of the chorus (48%)
Norwich 1827	Sept 18, 19, 20	341 Performers (chorus 222, orchestra 119) Norwich provided 166 of the chorus (75%)
Liverpool 1827	Oct 2, 3, 4, 5	(chorus 75) Liverpool provided 35 of the chorus (47%)
Derby 1828	Sept 9, 10, 11, 12	
Yorkshire 1828	Sept 23, 24, 25, 26	618 Performers 17,759 attended; £2635 profit
Manchester 1828	Sept 30, Oct 1, 2, 3	364 Performers (chorus 234, orchestra 130) Manchester provided 56 of the chorus (23%) Under Royal Patronage
Birmingham 1829	Oct 6, 7, 8, 9	Charles Darwin described it as the "most glorious" experience
*Yorkshire 1835	Sept 8, 9, 10, 11	*Maffre Sr. and Jr. are among the many violinists* Over 600 Performers; attendance and profits were very low; this was the last Yorkshire Musical Festival

* An asterisk has been placed next to the four festivals at which Joseph Maffre's presence has been confirmed. The newspaper entries for the other festivals do not list all the performer names, making it difficult to know whether Maffre was present. All Festivals except the one in Market Harborough are listed in Brian W. Pritchard's 1968 Ph.D. Thesis.

The other Leicester musicians were violoncellist Bankhart and vocalists Miss Jarvis, Mr. Fielding, and Mr. Handscomb. There had been many Music Festivals since the late 1700s but they were modest in size. Spurred on by the good economy of the 1820s, the Yorkshire Festival was the largest yet. It was held in the Yorkshire Cathedral, the largest building in England. With its 467 vocal and instrumental performers, the organizers recruited singers and instrumentalists from all over the provinces.

When the Yorkshire Festival proved successful, the other cities took notice and increased the size of their Musical Festivals (Figure 5.3). The largest cities - Birmingham, Derby, York, Norwich, and Liverpool - held their Festival on a triennial cycle. Industrial cities such as Leicester and Manchester apparently lacked the resources to offer more than one Festival.

Figure 5.3: English cities hosting grand musical festivals in the 1820s. Illustration by Mark Griep

As can be seen in Table 5.1 above, local choral societies comprised the largest portion of the choruses in the Grand Musical Festivals. In 1841, many years after the 1823 Yorkshire Grand Musical Festival, Maffre put forward a Prospectus for the Montreal Choral Society in which, "The Society will be conducted on similar rules with those of the Musical Societies of Birmingham, Manchester, Leicester, Sheffield, and York, in England." That is, he was familiar with those societies (Table 5.2). Since we know Maffre performed at the Musical Festivals in York (1823, 1835), Market Harborough (1826), and Leicester (1827), he may also have performed at the festivals in Birmingham (1823, 1826, 1829) and Manchester (1828). The Sheffield society sang in the Yorkshire Festivals of 1823, 1825, and 1828. Of these, the Birmingham Festival was considered to give the best performances and was the most prestigious.

Table 5.2: Choral Societies Associated with Grand Musical Festivals

Society	Choral Society Founded	Grand Musical Festivals
*Birmingham Oratorio	1806	1805, 1820, 1826, 1829
Derby Choral	1807	1806, 1822, 1825, 1828
Liverpool Choral	1821	1823, 1827, 1830
Norwich Choral	1824	1822, 1824, 1827, 1830
*Leicester Choral	1827	1827
*Manchester Choral	1828	1828

*Mentioned in Maffre's 1841 Advertisement

1824

From 28 October to 9 November 1824, Joseph Maffre played violin in five concerts in as many cities in Northamptonshire, located just south of Leicestershire. At each performance, the performers and vocalists were similar with a few variations. The conductors, leaders, pianoforte, and organ were traded between Mr. Muston, Charles McKorkell, and Mr. Barrett. The Principal Vocalists were Mrs. Muston and Miss A. H. Melville. The first event was a "Grand Concert" on 28 October at the George Inn Assembly Rooms in Northampton. The second event on 1 November was a "Musical Festival" at the Newport Pagnell Church. The third event was "Master Charles McKorkell's Concert" on 2 November at the Swan Inn Assembly Rooms in Bedford. In addition to his usual violin contribution, Maffre performed a piece he wrote titled *Concerto Clarionet*. Maffre ended the evening by leading the Ball with his Quadrille Band. The fourth event was a "Grand Concert" on 4 November at the Picture-Gallery in Daventry.

Maffre is billed as "Principal Clarinetist" in the fifth and last event called the "Moulton Grand Musical Festival" on 9 November at the Moulton church. It was not a true festival because it did not last more than a day. Even so, Maffre was highly lauded because he also performed principal violin at the last minute. According to the *Northampton Mercury* on 13 November 1824, "Gratias agimus, by the same performer [*singer Miss Melville*], was excellently accompanied on the clarionette by Mr. Maffre, who, in consequence of Mr. Muston's unavoidable absence, was kindly induced to take the principal violin, and he acquitted himself upon both instruments (notwithstanding the difficulty of such a transition) to the entire satisfaction of the orchestra and the audience."

In circa 1824, son Frederick Maffre was born in Leicester. We have not found a record of his baptism. He was their seventh child.

On December 7th, Miss Hewitt (probably Maria) promoted a Concert at the Leicester Theatre. Joseph Maffre was leader of the band. The vocalists featured Miss Melville, Miss Jarvis, Miss Russell, Miss Sharpe, Mr. Morris, and Mr. Handscomb. The musicians included Master McKorkell on the Harp, the Hewitt sisters (Maria and Elizabeth) on the grand piano forte, and Mr. Ella as Leader of the Band. The first act included a solo performance of Maffre's *Clarionet Concerto*.

1825

In July, September, and October of 1825, His Grace the Duke of Rutland's Band performed at a public balloon inflation, at the races, and at the fair, respectively. This was the first year the Band was advertised so prominently in the newspaper. Its prior appearances had been confined to the Duke's birthday celebrations. These news notes don't mention the musicians or leader or master. Nevertheless, Maffre may have performed with them at these events.

On December 20th, Miss Travis promoted a Concert of Vocal and Instrumental Music at the Leicester Theatre. Joseph Maffre was leader of the band. The vocalists featured Miss Travis, Miss Jarvis, Miss Sharpe, and Mr. Handscomb whose "bass is remarkable for its depth and smoothness." The musicians included the Hewitt sisters (Maria and Elizabeth) on the piano and Mr. Marshall from Warwick on the violoncello. The first piece to be performed was Beethoven's *Men of Prometheus* overture but there was no special performance of Maffre's *Clarionet Concerto*. The glowing review of the "delightful and unmingled enchantment" mentioned how many of the pieces were successfully executed including "The duet on the grand piano, by the Misses Hewitt, with the slight occasional accompaniment of Mr. Maffre, attracted particular attention, such was the correctness, that the three pair of hands seemed to be moved by only one volition." The Theatre opened in 1800 and was torn down in 1836 to be replaced by another building of the same name. Even though it was not designed for musical concerts, many of them were held there.

1826

By June 1826, the Maffre family is living on St. Peter's Lane, two blocks north of their previous address (Figure 5.2).

On August 6, 1826, Mary Ann, their eighth child, is baptized in St. Nicholas Church.

On September 18, 19, and 20, Market Harborough held a Grand Musical Festival. "Principal Clarionet Mr. Maffre" is listed as the fourth musician after the heading: "The instrument Department will be sustained by a Concentration of the first Talent." On Monday evening, the 18th, Maffre performed his *Clarionet Concerto*. The principal vocalists were Miss Jarvis from Leicester, Master Barker, and Mr. Robinson. On the Tuesday morning, Miss Travis sang *Gratias Agimus* while Maffre played the clarionet. On Tuesday evening, there was a Grand Miscellaneous Concert at which Maffre played First Clarionet.

In December 1826, François Fèmy (1790-1839) performed at a concert in Leicester. Maffre may have attended this concert and even trained with him. They may have met earlier when Fèmy performed in the third concert of the 1818 Season of the Royal Philharmonic Society in London. On November 20, 1828, Maffre wrote, "that he has availed himself of the skill of the celebrated Monsieur Fèmy, and now teaches the Violin according to the method used by the Conservatory of Music in Paris." In 1826, Fèmy was a member of the Russian Czar's orchestra but also traveled to participate in concerts in places such as Leicester. In fact, Fèmy had previously performed in Leicester in 1814 with his cellist brother Henri because their violinist father Ambrose Fèmy had met William Gardiner. François Fèmy is probably one of the "most eminent masters" that Maffre touted in his Montreal announcements.

Fèmy was taught violin by the renowned Luigi Cherubini (1760-1842). By 1784, Cherubini had already composed eight operas in the Italian style. In 1784, at age 24, Cherubini traveled to London where he received the honorary title of composer to the George III for one year. In June 1786, he traveled to Paris where he lived with Giovanni Battista Viotti for two years. Viotti was responsible for promoting Cherubini and earning him the patronage of the court of Marie Antoinette. Cherubini served as the Paris Conservatoire of Music's director from 1822 until his death in 1842.

1827

The 1827 Leicester Directory indicates that musician Joseph Maffre is living on St. Peter's Lane. He was located near an entertainment complex called Bowling Green, a popular venue for summer concerts because it had a garden and café.

There are eleven music-related entries in the 1827 City Directory (Table 5.3). Most of these people were active for decades even though their names don't appear in earlier directories.

Table 5.3: Music Professionals in the 1827 Leicester City Directory

Samuel Deacon	music warehouse on Gallowtree Gate
Frederick Dobney	musician and broker on Belgrave Gate
John Hewitt*	teacher of music on Southgate Street
Miss Jarvis	teacher of music on York Street
Ebenezer Tristam Jones	musician on Oxford Street
Joseph Maffre	musician on St. Peter's Lane
Charles Mavius	Professor of Music and music warehouse on Gallowtree Lane
Henry Nicholson	musician on New Walk
Thomas Sternberg	pianoforte tuner and repairer on New Walk
Miss Valentine	organist on Belgrave Gate
John Waldrom	musician and music seller on Market Street

*John Hewitt and his daughters, Maria and Elizabeth, taught music, especially piano. Daughter Elizabeth married Richard H. Cooke in 1821 but he died in 1828. John Hewitt was the Rugby Church organist for 20 years and died June 1, 1829 after a long, severe illness.

On the page of the 1827 City Directory that summarized Alderman Newton's School, Joseph Maffre is listed as its "singing master." The School's Master was Mr. Appleby. During the 1820's, the School had 84 pupils. According to Joan Stevens in *Leicester Through The Ages* (1995), this school was also known as "The Green Coat School" because the boys' uniforms were a bright green with scarlet facings and brass buttons, red cap, leather breeches, and grey worsted stockings. After seven years of instruction, the boys were to be given £5 to set them on the right track for life. It opened in 1785 with 35 pupils across the street from St. Nicholas' Church in a building that had been used by the town's butchers since 1682. It was founded with funds from Gabriel Newton (1683-1762), who earned his money as landlord of the Horse and Trumpet Inn. In 1732, Newton served one term as Mayor and was thereafter known as Alderman Newton. In 1760, Newton set up a substantial trust with the Town Committee to provide for the education and clothing of the sons of poor Anglicans. He died two years later and the School opened 23 years later in 1785. The boys were taught reading, writing, arithmetic, and psalmody.

On March 9 in the *Leicester Chronicle*, Joseph announced Maffre's earliest dated composition titled *A New Set of Quadrilles for the Piano Forte*. A copy is in the collections of the British Library, the Glasgow University library, the Oxford University library, and the St. Andrews University library. The British Library estimated a publication date of 1823 based on its location in their files but the advertisement was probably contemporaneous and indicates it was published in 1827. The six pieces have the following titles with the associated dance movements indicated in the parentheses (Table 5.4).

Table 5.4: Maffre's *A New Set of Quadrilles*, 1827

1 — La Viotti (Le Pantalon)
2 — La Beethoven (Figure L'Eté)
3 — La Pieltin (Figure La Poule)
4 — La Charmante (Figure La Trenice)
5 — La Maffre (Figure La Finale)
6 — Leicester Waltz

Maffre's first quadrille is named "La Viotti" for Giovanni Battista Viotti who was born 1755 in Italy and who died 1824 in London, only three years before this piece was published. Viotti was an influential violinist whose method of playing soon became the dominant type and whose compositions inspired many other composers including Beethoven and Brahms. Viotti spent the latter part of his career in London and was among the founders of the Royal Philharmonic Society. He was often listed as a performer and sometimes leader during its first three seasons, 1813-1815. Even though Maffre was in London for the 1817, 1818, and 1819 Seasons, it is possible he met Viotti or at least heard him perform during that time.

Maffre's second quadrille is named "La Beethoven" for Ludwig van Beethoven (1770-1827). Maffre performed selections of Beethoven's music throughout his career but was especially fond of the overture from *The Creatures of Prometheus* ballet of 1801. As mentioned in the London chapter, Maffre's affection for Beethoven is clear since he named his third child Joseph *Ludwig* Maffre.

Maffre's third quadrille is named "La Pieltin," which is most likely in honor of Dieudonné-Pascal Pieltain (1754-1833). Pieltain was a violinist and composer from southern Netherlands. It is not clear how Maffre came to know his work, given that Pieltain performed in Paris from 1776 to 1780 and in London from 1782 to 1792. By 1801, Pieltain was mostly retired and living with his daughter in Liège, Netherlands. Maffre may have been attracted to the Pieltain compositions that required a highly developed violin technique and which are described as "tuneful" in the *Grove Dictionary of Music*.

As mentioned earlier, the quadrille was danced in London for the first time in 1815 at Almack's Assembly Rooms. Originally, a "set" consisted of five pieces, each named to evoke its dance moves. La Trenise was added later to bring the total to six (Table 5.5). Note that Maffre's first four quadrilles had the same names as the traditional set.

Table 5.5: Traditional Set of Six Quadrilles

1. Le Pantalon	(trousers)
2. L'Eté	(summer)
3. La Poule	(hen)
4. La Trenise	(Viennese dance master Trenitz)
5. La Pastorelle	(shepherd girl)
6. Finale	

To dance a quadrille, four couples start at the corners of a square and then dance around and between each other. Since the dance sequences could be quite difficult to memorize, the master of ceremony (or the bandmaster) would call out the figures. For instance, in "Le Pantalon", the call for Figure No. 1 is "Right and left" and it requires 8 bars of music (Table 5.6). The first bar coincides with the first and third couples stepping forward with the right foot and simultaneously raising their right arms to receive the right hands of the opposite person. The second bar coincides with stepping forward with left foot coupled to a slight twist of the body to the right, letting go of the right hand each has just taken and then raising the left arm to receive the left hand of their partner. The movement proceeds in this alternating right and left fashion for the full eight bars.

Table 5.6: "Le Pantalon" Figures (or Dance Moves)

No.		Bars.
1.	Right and left, by the first and third couples	8
2.	Set to partners	4
3.	Turn partners round	4
4.	Ladies' chain	8
5.	Half promenade	4
6.	Half right and left	4
	The second and fourth couples repeat the same figures	

Maffre's byline on his "New Set of Quadrilles" indicates he was "Leader to His Grace the Duke of Rutland's Band" and that it was dedicated to "Miss Linwood." Miss Mary Linwood (1755-1845) ran a seminary for young ladies in Leicester and was a renowned needlework artist. She would have been age 72 in 1827.

Since the Sheet Music was "published and sold by the author", Maffre paid to have it printed and, therefore, speculated there would be a market. It was printed by Preston & Son, a family of music publishers from 1774 until 1836. In 1823, son Thomas Preston moved to 71 Dean Street, Soho, where he remained until 1836 when he sold the business. At its peak, Preston's was the most important music publisher in England, issuing vast quantities of music of all kinds.

In June 1827, Maffre begins training the Leicester Choral Society for their participation in the Leicester Grand Musical Festival of September 1827. To demonstrate they were ready, he held three practice concerts in St. Margaret's Church that drew large crowds. Prominent local musician William Gardiner organized the Festival and the newspaper suggests that Gardiner is the one who resurrected the Choral Society. Given the importance of this task, it is surprising that Gardiner does not mention Maffre once in his rambling, two-volume *Music and Friends; or, Pleasant Recollections of a Dilettante* that he published in 1838 and 1853. A large section in his book is devoted to the Festival.

In July 1827, Maffre plays a *Concerto Clarionet* of his own composition during the second part of the Kibworth Grand Concert. Mr. W. P. Cunnington, Professor of Music in Harborough, put the Concert together. It featured vocals by Miss Hughes, Miss Sharpe, and Master Watson. Maffre met Cunnington and many of the others at the 1826 Market Harborough Grand Music Festival.

The three-day Leicester Musical Festival in September 1827 was the first such festival in Leicester since 1774. Joseph Maffre was one of many violinists. Preparation began in the summer of 1826 and the first official meeting was held in October 1826. The two morning concerts of sacred music were in St. Margaret's church because it had a capacity of about 1500 people. A gallery was constructed to supplement the seats for an additional 320 guests. Two of the evening secular concerts were held in the "New Assembly Rooms" on Hotel Street. It had a capacity of about 650. William Gardiner was in charge of engaging musicians for the festival and selected a combination of nationally known and local musicians. The patrons who put forth the funds to engage these musicians included: the Earls of Denbigh, Chesterfield, Cardigan, Ayesford, Harborough, and Besborough; Earls Spencer,

Ferrars, and Howe; the Duke of Rutland, and the Bishop of Lincoln. In July 1827, the advertisements were printed and distributed. Earl Howe (Richard William Curzon) was the chief promoter of the Festival. He put forth extra funds to engage new singers when a few had to cancel at the last minute. Local musicians Samuel Deacon (double bass) and Charles Mavius (violin) agreed to fill in for late cancellations by musicians. The orchestra consisted of 300 musicians, many of them local. On the second morning of the Festival, William Gardiner led a performance of *Messiah* by the Leicester Choral Society. Its *Hallelujah Chorus* was "so well received that it had to be encored." The second evening of the Festival was a fancy dress ball with music by Litoff's Full Quadrille Band, which began at 8 pm and ended at 4 am.

Even though the Festival was a financial and social success, it was never repeated. Equally perplexing is that the Leicester music scene dried up in 1828 and Maffre joined the 19th Regiment as Bandmaster in 1829.

1828

In May 1828, Maffre was prominently advertised as appearing at the Annual Melton-Mowbray Harmonic Festival. He was the principal clarinetist and he performed his *Clarinet Concerto*.

In November 1828, Joseph published "A New Military March, Concertant, For the Piano Forte, with Violin or Flute ad lib." It sold for 2 shillings (Figure 5.4). His byline indicates that he was "Leader to His Grace the Duke of Rutland's Band." This piece was "Composed and Respectfully Inscribed to the Right Honble The Countess Howe." Countess Howe was the wife of Earl Howe, the principal promoter of the 1827 Music Festival. Richard William Curzon became Earl Howe in 1821 and was married to Anne Gore. The only known copy of this march is in the collection of the University of Cambridge library.

Joseph may have published "For a Military Band Beethoven's Grand Quintetto No. 1 of String Instruments." It is mentioned on the bottom of the second page of "A New Military March" that he will publish it shortly. We have not found an advertisement or copy of this piece.

Figure 5.4: English Half Crown (2.5 shillings), 1828, with the profile of "Georgius IV Dei Gratia" on the obverse. On the reverse, the words "Brittaniarum Rex Fid:Def" surround the English Coat of Arms. From the Robert Mikasen Collection.

1829

Maffre does not advertise any concerts in the *Leicester Journal* during the entire year of 1829. In fact, there are very few musical activities advertised by anyone in Leicester.

In early 1829, Joseph Maffre published a book titled *Method of Teaching Psalmody*, which he said was for use in the National Schools of England. According to *The New Grove Dictionary of Music and Musicians*, psalmody is a general term for music sung in Protestant churches in England and America from the 17th century to the early 19th century. By the time Joseph wrote his book, the term covered all kinds of music sung by amateur choirs. Many town churches had grammar schools for 'charity children' with statutes requiring that the students learn to sing psalms and to lead the singing every Sunday. They wore their uniforms and assembled on either side of the church's organ, which was usually located in the west gallery. In 1702, the first music written especially for these children was published in London. The published psalms grew from the custom of using the occasion of the annual 'charity sermon' to display the singing of the children. In Leicester, the National Society for Promoting Education for Poor Children in the Principals of the Church of England opened a school in 1812 on Holy Bones Lane across the street from St. Nicholas' Church on land ceded by the Crown for this benevolent purpose. A new school building was erected in 1814. The National School patron and superintendent was His Grace the Duke of Rutland. The school taught about 250 children and also engaged in the instruction of teachers for the surrounding villages. There are no known copies of Maffre's book.

1830

At the start of 1830, Joseph is in Barbados while Lucy is probably still in Leicester, pregnant and caring for eight children (Table 5.7). She has her hands full because only one child is a teen.

Table 5.7: Joseph and Lucy's Children in March 1830*

Child's Name	Age in 1830	Birth	Baptism
1. Ann [*Thomas?*] Maffre	16	October 3, 1813	November 17, 1813
2. Francis Maffre	died 1818	October 17, 1815	October 26, 1815
3. Joseph Ludwig Maffre	12	August 10, 1817	August 12, 1817
4. Charlotte Maffre	10	January 8, 1820	February 1, 1820
5. Maria Maffre	8	October 12, 1821	November 1, 1821
6. Henry Maffre	7	--	January 26, 1823
7. Frederick Maffre	6	circa 1824	--
8. Mary Ann Maffre	3	--	August 6, 1826
9. Alfred Maffre	1 ½	circa 1828	January 16, 1830
10. Francis Maffre	newborn	circa March 1830	--

*March 1830 was chosen so we could include their final child, Francis, on the list

In January 1830, son Alfred is baptized at St. George's Church. Based on the 1842 Canadian Census, he is probably about 2 years old. The family is living on Conduit Street in the south of town.

Their last child, Francis, is born about March 1830 in Leicester. He is named after his deceased brother and his uncle. His birth date is derived from his Army discharge papers, reproduced in the

"Notes on the Firm" chapter, where he says he was 30 years and 6 months on 8 October 1860. As an adult, he had dark brown eyes, dark hair, sallow complexion, and was 5 feet 8 ½ inches tall. We have not found a record of Francis' baptism. Given that Joseph Maffre is in Barbados in December 1829, he appears to have impregnated Lucy in June 1829 thereby fixing his departure month for Barbados.

Maffre's Career in Leicester

Nearly all of the information about Joseph Maffre's time in Leicester was obtained from newspapers. (The "Perfect Knowledge" chapter includes reproductions of the advertisements and reviews.) Since the entries were discovered using online newspaper search engines and since very few newspapers have been published online in their entirety, our list is incomplete. Even so, there is a large enough sample (Table 5.8) for making generalizations and comparisons.

Table 5.8: Maffre's Advertised Performances While Living in Leicester

Year	Event	Venue	Maffre's Roles
1820	Mr. Maffre's Concert & Ball	Banbury, Oxfordshire, White Lion Inn Assembly Room	Band Leader; Promoter
1822	Leicester Musicians' Benefit for Mrs. Jarvis	Leicester, Theatre	Clarinetist
1823	Leicester Musical Society's Concert	Leicester, Theatre	Band Leader; Promoter
1824	Leicester Musical Society's Concert	Leicester, Theatre	Band Leader; Promoter
1824	Grand Concert and Quadrille Ball	Northampton, George Inn Assembly Rooms	Violinist
1824	Moulton Grand Musical Festival	Moultan, Norths., Church	Principal Clarionet; Principal Violin
1824	Newport Pagnell Musical Festival	Newport Pagnell, Norths., Church	Violinist
1824	Grand Concert	Daventry, Norths., Picture-Gallery	Violinist
1824	Master Charles McKorkell's Concert	Bedford, Norths., Swan Inn Assembly Rooms	Violinist; Clarinetist; Leader of the Quadrille Band
1824	Miss Hewitt's Grand Concert	Leicester, Theatre	Clarinetist
1825	2 x Messrs. Marshalls' Concerts	New Assembly Hall, Rugby	Clarinetist
1825	Miss Hewitt's Grand Miscellaneous Concert	Leicester, Theatre	Band Leader; Clarinetist
1826	Market Harborough Grand Musical Festival	Market Harborough, Norths.	Clarinetist
1827	Concert and Ball	Ashby-de-la-Zouch, Leics., Queen's Head Inn	Clarinetist?
1827	3 x Grand Selection of Sacred Music	Leicester, St. Margaret's	Leader of the Band; Clarinetist
1827	Kibworth Grand Concert	Kibworth	Clarinetist
1827	5 x Leicester Musical Festival	Leicester, St. Margaret's & Assembly Rooms	Violinist
1828	Miss Sharpe's Concert	Leicester, Theatre	Leader of the Orchestra; Clarinetist?
1828	Melton Mowbray Harmonic Society Annual Concert	Melton Mowbray, National School Room	Principal Clarinet

These concerts were taken from advertisements reproduced in the "Perfect Knowledge" chapter.

Nearly every year, Maffre was the bandleader for one concert at the Theatre in Leicester. In 1823 and 1824, he led the concert by the Leicester Musical Society, a group that was founded years earlier but had become inactive. Maffre was able to revive it for at least two years.

In 1825 and 1828, it is possible that this Society's musicians performed at Miss Hewitt's and then Miss Sharpe's concerts. Even if they did not make an official appearance, most of the former amateur musicians of that Society would have still been living in the area and some are likely to have contributed. We have not yet found any advertisements for 1826.

The preparations for and performance of the three-day Leicester Musical Festival of 1827 undoubtedly soaked up the demand for performances of other types. As leader of the orchestra, Maffre helped prepare the amateur singers to perform in the Festival choir. To demonstrate they were ready, he held three practice concerts in St. Margaret's Church. During the Festival, William Gardiner led the choir while Maffre played the violin.

With the exception of 1827, Maffre performed as a musician at more concerts outside Leicester than within. In 1824 and 1825, he played the violin, or the violin and clarinet, at six venues, most of them in nearby Northamptonshire. At one of these concerts, he even performed principal violin and principal clarinet, which is no small feat. From 1826 to 1828, he played the clarinet and never the violin at four concerts outside Leicester.

Maffre's career is such an outlier as a musician that he is not among those captured on Deborah Rohr's list of 6,600 musicians in *The Careers of British Musicians, 1750-1850*. Rohr compiled her master list from three long lists of musicians, each of which strongly favored London performers. Nevertheless, it is informative to contrast Maffre's experience in the Midlands with these contemporaneous professional musicians. During this time period, the fathers of 80% of musicians were musicians, indicating they were following a family tradition. The fathers of the remaining 20% could be almost anything. There are numerous examples of boys from the lower social classes with a flair for music who found a sponsor to pay for a tutor. Since there is no evidence that Joseph Maffre's father had been a musician, we surmise he demonstrated an aptitude and was encouraged.

Most British musicians (56%) on Rohr's list had careers based in London, one third elsewhere in England (32%), and the rest were disbursed throughout Scotland, Wales, Ireland, Europe, and the Colonies. Amongst the third scattered throughout England, most were in Liverpool and Manchester, two large cities. Only 5.5% of musicians were in the Midlands, an area that includes Leicester. Public performances have long been known to be essential training experiences for emerging professionals. Since large cities have more opportunities to perform before the public, they offer the most training opportunities. In fact, Maffre was professionalized during his short time in London. Very few musicians (only 9 out of 6,600) began their public careers as members of military bands.

In terms of prestige, orchestral concert performances were the undisputed best, followed by benefit concerts with programs designed to appeal to the public, then military bands, and then dance bands at the absolutely lowest level. In terms of earning a salary, the majority of musicians were music instructors for some or all of their careers. One out of five musicians composed music but none relied on it for their sole source of income, suggesting that composing brought more prestige than income. The majority of compositions were religious, popular, or artistic. A mere 7% of compositions were dance or military pieces. During his time in Leicester, Maffre earned most of his money by teaching orchestral and choral students but he gained visibility and prestige by playing regional orchestral concerts, local benefit concerts, and composing dance and military music dedicated to prominent local people. Another way to think about this period of Maffre's life is that he pursued every musical angle at least twice. It must have worked because he tried them all again in Montreal in the 1840's.

Maffre and the Clarinet

During his time in Leicester, Joseph Maffre was often featured on the clarinet (Table 5.9) and favored performing two pieces — *Concerto Clarionet* and *Gratias agimus tibi*. He composed the first piece. The second piece is from Latin mass and one can imagine Maffre explaining to the audience that the translation was "We bless thee" just before he accompanied a young lady who would sing those words in high soprano. The mass has been adapted for chorus by numerous composers although Pietro Guglielmi wrote the version that was a perennial favorite on British concert programs.

Table 5.9: Maffre's Clarinet Performances during his time in Leicester

Date	Event	Named Piece	Billed Performer
Aug. 1822	Leicester Musicians' Benefit Concert	*Concerto Clarionet*	
Nov. 1824	Master McKorkell's Concert, Bedford	*Concerto Clarionet*	
Nov. 1824	Moulton Grand Musical Festival	*Concerto Clarionet; Gratias agimus**	principal clarionetist
Dec. 1824	Miss Hewitt's Concert, Leicester	*Clarionet* solo	
May 1825	Rugby Grand Concert	*Gratias agimus tibi**	clarionet
May 1825	Warwick Grand Concert	*Clarionet Obligato*	clarionet
Dec. 1825	Miss Travis's Concert, Leicester	*Clarionet Concerto*	
Sep. 1826	Market Harborough Grand Music Festival	*Concerto Clarionet; Gratias agimus**	first clarionet
Jun. 1827	Leicester Choral Society	*Gratias agimus**	
Jul. 1827	Kibworth Grand Concert	*Concerto Clarionet*	
May 1828	Melton Mowbray Harmonic Festival	*Concerto Clarionet*	principal clarionet

*Nov 1824 and May 1825: Miss Melville sang while Maffre accompanied on clarinet; Dec 1825: Miss Travis sang while Maffre accompanied on clarinet; Jun 1827: Miss Sharpe sang while Maffre accompanied on clarinet

Maffre does not appear to have published his *Concerto Clarionet* but he did publish one piece that included a solo for E-flat clarinet—*A New Military March, Concertant* in 1829 that may be based upon it. Another intriguing possibility is "La Maffre," one of the pieces from his *New Set of Quadrilles* of 1827. By naming it after himself, he may have been drawing attention to his familiar tune.

By choosing to focus on the clarinet, Maffre would have been communicating his roots in the military band tradition. Throughout the early 1800's, the clarinet was strongly associated with military bands for the simple reason that most British clarinetists were members of military bands. For instance, the Grenadier Guards had six clarinets in a band of sixteen players. They were not the only regiment with this many clarinetists but they were certainly the most prominent.

In their book, *Music & the British Military in the Long Nineteenth Century,* Trevor Herbert and Helen Barlow cite several reasons for the popularity of clarinets during the early 1800's. As background, it is important to realize that regimental bands arose from the essential need for drummers, who kept the troops in order during marches and were used to communicate troop movements during battles. In the mid-1700's, the fife was added as a tuneful accompaniment to the drums. By the late 1700's, the clarinet began to displace the fife because it is capable of carrying treble melodic lines. As such, the clarinet's melodic capabilities acted as a bridge from martial music to the use of bands of performers whose concerts helped define the self-image of the regiments. Concert music was used to improve the spirits of the troops when they were garrisoned in remote locations and to break the ice with the local citizenry. When the keyed trumpet became available in the 1830's, it slowly replaced the clarinet to the point where British military bands became known as brass bands by the 1870's.

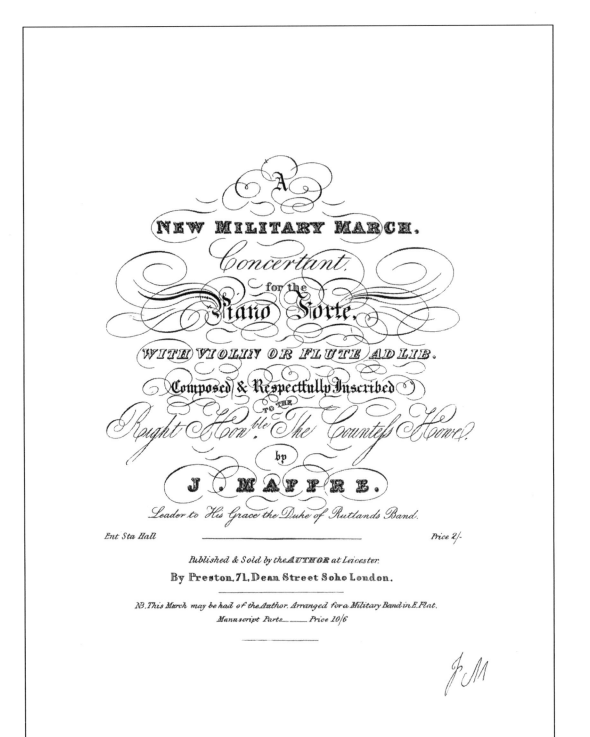

Figure 6.1: "A New Military March, Concertant" Sheet Music Cover, 1828, signed "JM" in the lower right corner. Reproduced by kind permission of the Syndics of Cambridge University Library.

6
A TROPICAL CLIMATE

Joseph Maffre left Leicester abruptly in 1829 to join the 19th Regiment of Foot just as it set off for the West Indies. His stint lasted about four years and began with a concert in Barbados. There is little information about his life during this period but we take this opportunity to summarize his 25 years in the military and speculate on how he may have been recruited to the 19th Regiment.

"Many years of this long period in a tropical climate"

As noted in the Barracks and Bastardy chapter, Joseph, Lucy, and their children spent a little over one year in the West Indies during his first 11 years with the Royal Foreign Artillery Regiment (Table 6.1). Specifically, they were deployed to the West Indies some time after November 1815 and returned home in January 1817. Within a few short years after returning from the West Indies, he was a full-fledged professional musician in Leicester thereby suggesting that Maffre was at least a member of the band when the Regiment was stationed in the West Indies.

Table 6.1: Maffre's Proposed Timeline in the West Indies

Start Date	End Date	# Years	Location	Regiment
after Nov. 1815	January 1817	1.3	West Indies	Royal Foreign Artillery
1829	1833	4	Barbados & West Indies	19th Regiment of Foot

Maffre's next stint in the West Indies appears to have occurred between 1829 and 1833, a period during which there is scant information of his whereabouts. A single news article says he was in Barbados (Figure 6.2) in December 1829. Maffre, "formerly of the Leicestershire Militia," led the Band of the 19th in a concert in aid of funds for a House of Industry in Bridgetown, Barbados. He must have traveled to Barbados with the 19th Regiment sometime between March and December 1829. The March date assumes he was in Leicester to impregnate Lucy nine months before his son Alfred was baptized in Leicester in January 1830, and that Alfred was baptized shortly after birth. This news article and the date of his son's baptism suggest Maffre's family did not accompany him to Barbados right away. In fact, his son Francis was born in Leicester in 1831 raising even more questions about his family's whereabouts and the frequency of his own travels back and forth from the West Indies. Unfortunately, a hurricane leveled Bridgetown's House of Industry in August 1831. The St. Ann's Barracks, where the troops were stationed, still exists and was designated a World Heritage Site in 2011 because its architecture is so well preserved.

The six service companies of the 19th Regiment were stationed in the West Indies (Figure 6.2) for eight and a half years from January 1828 to July 1836. Lieutenant-Colonel Hardy commanded three of the service companies while Major Timothy Raper commanded the other three service companies. In January 1828, these six companies sailed from Ireland to Barbados where they were stationed for two years. The British newspapers reported that the 19th suffered "opthalmia" on Barbados. Ophthalmia is inflammation of the eye and is now called pinkeye. In January 1830, Hardy's men removed to Grenada and Raper's men to St. Vincent. In 1833, Sir James Edward Alexander wrote his book *Transatlantic Sketches* in which he says Major Raper started a theatre during this time for which the troops performed a different play every two weeks. Surely, Maffre would have insisted upon playing an overture prior to each performance and "God Save the King" upon its conclusion. When Raper's companies left two years later, the *St. Vincent Gazette* thanked them heartily for their assistance after the 11 August 1831 hurricane.

In January 1832, Raper's companies removed to Tobago with six officers, twelve sergeants, three drummers, and 233 "rank and file" while Hardy's companies removed to Trinidad. They were stationed on these islands for four years during which time Hardy died at age 50 and Raper was promoted to Lieutenant-Colonel in charge of all the 19th Regiment service troops. In March 1836, the entire Regiment sailed back to Barbados. In July 1836, they sailed back to Ireland.

Figure 6.2: Map of Island Clusters in the Caribbean Sea. The Leeward Islands are downwind and the Windward Islands are upwind of the prevailing southeasterly winds. Illustration by Mark Griep.

Even though wives and children nearly always accompanied British married military men at their garrisons around the world, there is very little documentary evidence about the practice because very few regimental books have survived. The best analysis we've found is in R. N. Buckley's *The British Army in the West Indies*. The sole source of information about families rests on a return from July 1804 [*UK Archives Colonial Office (C.O.) 318/25 enclosure 2 in Myers to Camden*]. It gives numbers of men, women, and children. The list doesn't distinguish according to black or white troops, which is important because many West Indies troops were locally recruited or imported from Africa as slaves. The 1804 return indicates there were 12,633 men, 785 women, and 515 children garrisoned in the Leeward (St. Kitts, Antigua, Guadeloupe, and Montserrat) and Windward Islands (Dominica, Martinique, St. Lucia, St. Vincent and the Grenadines, and Grenada) (Figure 6.2). The numbers indicate that 6% of the troops were married but that there was less than one child per family. The small number of children is explained by two factors: (1) the extremely high mortality rate among infants and children; and (2) the high incidence of venereal diseases in the area that reduced fertility.

In most locations around the world, married British officers lived in a hut located adjacent to the barracks of the largest military installations. In the West Indies, such quarters were only available on Jamaica. Otherwise, living conditions for married troops in the West Indies "consisted of cramped space at the end of a long barrack room [*39 inches wide, enough for the iron bedstead and a space to walk past*], separated from the other soldiers only by a canvas screen or blanket behind which the couple contrived to make some sort of home. Children also inhabited these quarters. Some were actually born in the rooms under the intent gaze of half a dozen or so comrades. What life was like for these unhappy children can only be guessed. These squalid conditions obviously imposed terrible hardships and stresses on military marriages and families." This quote is from page 331 of Buckley's book.

From 1815 to 1868, soldiers of the British Army were paid 1 shilling [*12 pence*] per day from which 6 pence was deducted to pay for their rations. The standard diet consisted of one pound of bread eaten at breakfast with coffee, and three-quarters pound boiled meat at noon. The boiled beef or mutton was sometimes thickened into a broth by flour, rice, or yams, and accompanied by vegetables the men provided. The troops were also charged for laundry, hair cuts, cleaning materials, replacement clothing, lost or damaged equipment, medical treatment (9 pence per day), and barrack damages. Army regulations also specified, however, that troops must receive minimum 1 pence per day after deductions so they would be able to receive some funds on payday. This money was used for beer, cigarettes, prostitutes, and groceries. Some wives earned money by doing laundry and a few helped in the barracks kitchen or as nurses in the hospital. Children were commonly enrolled in the regimental school.

Since Maffre appears on the Newcastle voter rolls in 1833, we know he left the Army by that time. In 1834, the British government abolished slavery and the need for troops in the West Indies diminished. By September 1836, the 19th Regiment was no longer in the West Indies.

Figure 6.3: Nineteenth Regiment Officer's Uniform as of December 1828 from Ferrar's "History of the Services of the 19th Regiment" (1911). The white feather in the shako helmet was originally twelve inches tall but was reduced to eight inches in 1830 (as shown in the image above). The gilt star-shaped brass badge on the helmet was six inches across. Officers wore red double-breasted jackets with white epaulets whereas musicians wore all white.

25 Years in the Army

According to Joseph Maffre's 1842 letter to Colonel George Cathcart, he performed "a service of 25 years in the Army as Band Master and Many years of this long period in a tropical climate." Very little about Maffre's military career is definitive except this statement about 25 years so we will use it to clarify his military timeline (Table 6.2).

Table 6.2: Maffre's Proposed Military Timeline

Start Date	End Date	# Years	Location	Regiment
April 1806	after Nov. 1815	9.6	Lymington	Royal Foreign Artillery, Depot
after Nov. 1815	January 1817	1.3	West Indies	Royal Foreign Artillery
1828	1829	1	Leicester	Leicestershire Militia
1829	1833	4	Barbados & West Indies	19th Regiment of Foot
1833	1835	2	Newcastle	19th Regiment, Depot
1835	1843	8	Montreal	71st Highland Light Inf.

In 1842, Maffre said he had served a total of 25 years in the military. He left the military the next year giving 26 years as his total number of years of service.

As described in the Barracks and Bastardy chapter, Maffre began his service in 1806 at age 11 with the Depot Company of the Royal Foreign Artillery Regiment in Lymington. Then, he spent over a year in the West Indies with the Royal Foreign Artillery. There is no evidence he was in the Regular Army for the 11 years afterward. This period begins when he made his way to London in 1817 and ends when he joined the 19th Regiment of Foot in 1829. However, he was bandmaster of the Leicestershire Militia just before he joined the 19th. According to our speculation in the Respectfully Dedicated chapter, he was probably bandmaster of the Militia as early as January 1828. Next, Maffre was stationed in Newcastle with the 19th Regiment Depot from 1833 to 1835, during which time he performed in public as an independent musician in Newcastle. For some reason, he switched from the 19th to the 71st Highland Light Infantry in 1835 and traveled with them to Canada. He served a total of eight years with the 71st and was a professional musician in Montreal during his final six years.

Military Bandmaster Advertisements, 1822-1837

It is not clear how Maffre chose to join the 19th Regiment of Foot but it must have been word of mouth because it appears to have been rare for a regiment to advertise. We have found only six newspaper ads during Maffre's era, of which three were candid about the name of their regiment (Table 6.3). Even so, an examination of these ads can give us some insight into regimental needs. For instance, one of them mentions a requirement to enlist, three of them are sailing away forthwith, and four mention travel to the West Indies or East Indies. Several state or imply the need for evidence that the applicant is competent in the form of testimonials or other evidence. It is also telling that four ads were published in March and May, the end of London's musical season when musicians were undoubtedly searching for opportunities.

Table 6.3: Military Bandmaster Advertisements, 1822-1837

London's *Morning Chronicle* on 4 October 1822

WANTED, a MASTER for the BAND of an OLD REGIMENT of the LINE.—Ample testimonials of good conduct and abilities will be required.—Application by letter, postpaid, to be made to Mr. Key, Musical Instrument Maker, Charing-cross.

London's *Morning Post* on 14 May 1824

TO BAND MASTERS.—WANTED, for the 98th Regiment, a competent MASTER to FORM and TEACH a YOUNG BAND. He must be able to Compose and Arrange Music, and will be expected to enlist, and to go abroad with the Regiment if necessary. Application to be made, mentioning terms, &c. addressed, post-paid, to the Band Committee, 98th Regiment, Chichester.

Hampshire Chronicle on 13 March 1826

WANTED,—A MASTER and Nine MEN for a MILITARY BAND, on board an East Indianman, to sail forthwith.

Send terms and particulars, post paid, to Goulding and D'Almaine, 20, Soho-square, London.

London's *Morning Post* on 23 May 1832

BAND MASTER.—WANTED, for the 74th Regiment, a BAND MASTER. None but those whose character and abilities will bear the strictest examination need apply. Address (post paid) to the President, Band Committee, 74th Regiment, Templemore, Ireland.

London's *Morning Chronicle* on 12 January 1837

A BAND MASTER for INDIA.—A Band Master for the East Indies. WANTED to go out immediately, a YOUNG MAN who has a thorough knowledge of music and the management of a military band; he will be required for ten years certain, salary £80 per annum [*equivalent to about £4,000 today*] with quarters, and he will have an opportunity of doubling the amount by teaching and tuning. The most unexceptionable references will be required as to sobriety and general good conduct, and no person need apply whose character will not the strictest investigation. Apply by letter, post paid, to C. C., 47, St. Martin's-lane, Charing-cross.

London's *Morning Post* on 17 May 1837

WANTED, for the 3d, or KING'S OWN Regiment of Light Dragoons, about to embark for India, a Bandmaster. Application, with terms and references, to be made to the Officers of the Regiment, Canterbury Barracks.

In the earliest years, bandmasters were civilians funded by the regimental officers because British military bandmasters before the 1850's were not commissioned officers as they are today. There are very few surviving records relating to early military bands but Gordon and Alwyn Turner's three volumes of *The History of British Military Bands* provide a vast synthesis of sources to list the names the earliest regimental bandmasters and the types of instrumentalists in their bands. Another insight about early military bandmasters is that many were foreigners in part because they were perceived to be better musicians than the British (*The Careers of British Musicians, 1750-1850* by Rohr). It also helped that class divisions with foreigners were blurrier, thereby allowing for somewhat closer relationships between the officers and the bandmasters.

Although Bandmasters were able to bring much needed inspiration to bored troops and were often able to restore calm to restive civilians, there were dangers to this profession. As documentation, we reproduce this newspaper report about an assault on a Bandmaster *by the members of his own band*.

> *London Daily News*
> Monday, 16 August 1847
> MANCHESTER.—ATTACK BY A REGIMENTAL BAND ON ITS BANDMASTER.—On
> Friday, as the band of the First Royal Regiment was at practice in the Regent-road Barrack,
> all the members of the band, with the exception of the non-commissioned officers and one
> or two privates, made simultaneous attack on Mr. Castaldini, the bandmaster of the
> regiment. Throwing a sheet over him, so as to prevent his identifying any one in particular,
> they beat him with their fists severely about the head and body, though not so as to inflict
> any severer injury on his person than a sound thrashing. Of course all the offenders were
> immediately placed in confinement. Colonel Bell instituted an inquiry into the cause of this
> outrage; and it was alleged to have been provoked by a long series of harsh and offensive
> treatment to which the men had been subjected by the bandmaster. This was the more
> irritating to the band, as Castaldini is a civilian, and has therefore no right to abuse the power
> entrusted to him, as he has nothing to do with the discipline of the men, beyond the
> performance of his duty in teaching them music.

Finally, our most unusual find is an advertisement from a Regimental Band in search of performers. It compares the value of a good horn player versus a good clarionet and flute player.

> *Leamington Spa Courier*
> Saturday, 12 March 1831
> ## 59th REGIMENT.
>
> Wanted, PERFORMERS on the following INSTRUMENTS, for the BAND of the 59th
> REGIMENT:— 1st HORN, TWO CLARIONETS, and a FLUTE.
> To Performers on the above Instruments desirous of Enlisting, a Gratuity of £25. for *1st
> Horn*, and £20. for each *Clarionet* and *Flute*, will be given on attestation and approval by the
> BAND MASTER.—None need apply who are not Proficients [*sic*] on the respective
> Instruments.
> Letters (containing References as to Qualifications, and other necessary Particulars) to
> be addressed, Post-paid, to Mr. HEWETT, Librarian, UPPER PARADE, LEAMINGTON.

Newcastle, 1833-1835

Joseph Maffre appears in the Newcastle-upon-Tyne Polling Book records of 1833. He is living on William Street, which was lost to urban renewal long ago. The Depot Company of the 19th Regiment of Foot was stationed in Newcastle Barracks at this time and it seems that Maffre spent his time with them rather than with the regular troops in the West Indies.

In September 1835, the Yorkshire Musical Festival took place in the Yorkshire Cathedral. "Maffre" and "Maffre, jun." from Newcastle are listed among the principal second violinists. Twelve years earlier, Maffre had performed as a violinist in the 1823 Yorkshire Musical Festival. Over 600 performers participated in the 1835 event but the attendance and profits were so low that this became the last Musical Festival in York.

Figure 7.1: "Ball on Board the HMS Hastings" sketch by John Coke Smythe, on May 24, 1838. This pencil sketch is from the Library and Archives of Canada. Certain objects have their colors indicated as Spanish, red, blue, and green. The bottom of the sketch reads: "page 118; Ball on board the Hastings; by Coke Smythe." Most musicians on the poop are wearing a bearskin bonnet with an ostrich feather decoration but one musician is wearing the floppier piper's feather bonnet. The musician furthest to the right is facing the others and must be leading the band. Captain Francis Erskine Loch and his first mate are watching the band from the bridge. Library and Archives Canada, Acc. No. 1990-215-28.

7

HITTING THE HIGH C'S

Joseph Maffre became bandmaster of the 71st Highland Light Infantry Regiment in 1835 or 1836 and announced he was offering his musical services to the citizens of Montreal in 1841. In between those dates, Maffre led the band of the 71st on the ship that took Lord Durham and his family to Canada following the 1837 Rebellion. Upon their arrival, the band played music for Lord Durham's receptions and helped set exactly the right tone. Since Maffre was a bandleader who knew how to use music to impress and unite people, it is perhaps no wonder that he performed for the first six pre-Confederate Governor-Generals of British North America.

1836

Joseph Maffre Sr. and 18-year-old Joseph Jr. were musicians in Newcastle until late 1835 or early 1836 when they joined the 71st Highland Light Infantry (Figure 7.2). The date for Junior is based on Maffre Sr.'s letter of April 1842 in which he wrote that his son had served 6 years in the military.

Figure 7.2: "Seventy First Highlanders, Light Infantry" print from Cannon's "Historical Record of the 71st Regiment" (1852). According to Oatts (1969), the combination of scarlet jacket and Mackenzie tartan (green background with red and white stripes) dates from 1778 when the regiment was formed. The uniforms shown above were designed by the Prince Regent in 1815. The shako helmet has a small dark pom-pom and a brass emblem with "71" inside a horn's handle. Officers wore tight-fitting scarlet jackets with tails and gold epaulets with or without fringe depending on rank. The troops had a red-and-white checked band on their shako, white epaulets, and jackets without tails.

In early May 1836, the six service and four depot companies of the 71st left Edinburgh for Dublin, where they were stationed until June 1837. It is unusual that the depot companies accompanied the service companies to Dublin because their purpose is to recruit and train new soldiers. During their year in Dublin, the 71st Band performed for circuses, regimental skits, balls, and operas. The newspaper reviews poured on the accolades, calling them "the elegant Band of that distinguished Regiment."

On Saturday, June 18, the eight regiments garrisoned in Dublin, including the 71st, participated in a review in Phoenix Park in celebration of the King's birthday. A large crowd assembled to watch the proceedings. As soon as Constantine Phipps (Earl of Mulgrave, 1831-1835, and Lord Lieutenant of Ireland, 1835-1839) and Countess Mulgrave appeared, the bands of several regiments played "God Save the King." After an inspection of the troops, there were dramatic cavalry charges, precision formation of hollow squares, and artillery movements.

On November 25, the 71st Regiment celebrated the retirement of two sergeants with a ball and supper at which Colonel Grey proposed a toast to their health.

Charles Grey became the Colonel of the 71st in 1833 and served in that capacity until 1842 when he went to half-pay to begin focusing on political missions. He was the son of Charles, the 2nd Earl Grey, Secretary of State for War and Colonies but who had been the Prime Minister from 1830 to 1834. Charles' older sister Louisa Grey married John Lambton, better known as Lord Durham. In 1838, Charles Grey loaned the 71st Band and its bandleader Joseph Maffre to his brother-in-law John Lambton.

1837

The Band of the 71st Regiment performed at a five events in January and February that were advertised or reviewed in the Dublin newspapers. On January 9, the "band of the 71st regiment was in attendance [*at the Anniversary Ball for raising a roof on the parish chapel of Ballybohill*], and consequently the music was as good as could be desired." On January 26 (Thursday) and on January 28 (Saturday), Batty's Circus Royal (Figure 7.3) performed in Dublin under the "Patronage of Lieut. Colonel the Hon. C. Grey, and the Officers of the 71st Royal Highland Light Infantry, on which occasion the elegant Band of that distinguished Regiment will attend, and perform several select pieces of music." The second of these performances never took place because someone in the audience shouted "O'Connell" to provoke a scuffle. Apparently, a few audience members gathered up stones outside and returned inside to throw them. The soldiers intervened and "a very alarming riot ensued." A few people suffered broken bones and cut faces. Daniel O'Connell was the Irish political leader who, in 1829, was successful in asserting the rights of Catholics to sit in British Parliament. Between 1830 and 1836, O'Connell fought against the so-called tithe that Irish farmers had to pay to support the established, Anglican, church. On February 3 and 17, "By the kind permission of Lieut. Colonel Grey, the Band of the 71st Highlanders will assist in the Opera, to give greater effect to the Martial Music" during the performance at the Theatre Royal (Figure 7.3) of *La Donna del Lago* opera by Gioacchini Antonio Rossini that was based on Sir Walter Scott's *The Lady of the Lake*.

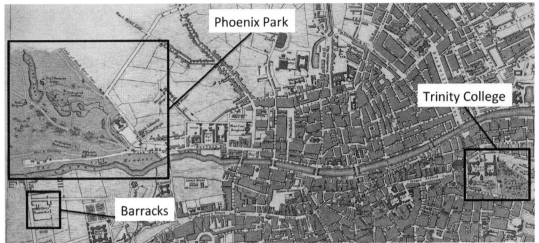

Figure 7.3: Map of Dublin showing the relationship between the Barracks, Phoenix Park, and the center of town as indicated by Trinity College. Map of Dublin by the Society for the Diffusion of Knowledge (1836). Illustration by Mark Griep.

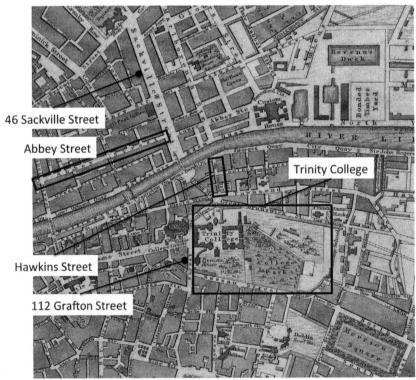

Figure 7.3 Detail: Map of Dublin showing where Joseph Maffre did business or performed. Johannes Logier's piano instruction and music business was located at 46 Sackville Street (now O'Connell Street) from 1829 until 1841. Batty's Circus performed on Abbey Street, just north of the River Liffey. Maffre performed at the Theatre Royal located on Hawkins Street just north of Trinity College. Maffre's sheet music was published by Samuel J. Pigott located at 112 Grafton Street, across from the Trinity College Prevost's House. Illustration by Mark Griep.

On Friday, May 26, the 71st Regiment of Highland Light Infantry was presented new colours in Phoenix Park (Figure 7.3) before a large crowd. At 2 o'clock, the troops of the 71st regiment marched in formation from the Royal Barracks to Phoenix Park. After they formed a line in front of the Chief Secretary's Lodge, "the excellent band of that regiment" played several "enlivening marches." At 2:30, Commander Sir Edward Blakeny and his staff rode onto the field and inspected the troops several times. The soldiers then demonstrated several maneuvers. At 3:30, the band played Lord Cromarty's March, at which point the soldiers presented arms and formed a hollow square. The new colours were then dramatically unfolded inside the square and the Commander gave a commendatory speech. The ensigns then presented the colours to Caroline Grey, wife of Colonel Grey. She was grateful for the honor, wished them well. and returned the colours to the ensigns who responded by cheering heartily. The old colours were retired and Colonel Grey gave a short speech. Afterwards, the 300 assembled guests enjoyed refreshments.

In Spring 1837, Maffre published his third composition, "A Set of Quadrilles." It was "most respectfully inscribed to the Hon[ble] Colonel C. Grey and Officers of the 71st Highland Light Infantry by I. Maffre, Professor of Music and Band Master of the Regiment" in Dublin. The author's initial of "I" is possibly a Romanized "J" but more likely an engraver's error. It may have been hurriedly published. The sheet music cost 3 shillings and was "Published for the Proprietor by S. J. Pigott, Harmonic Institution, 112 Grafton Street, Opposite the Prevosts." Samuel J. Pigott was a cellist and music publisher who removed to this location on December 12, 1836. The set of 5 quadrilles was labeled along the bottom according to the standard dance series: 1. La Pantalon (with a Solo Cornetto); 2. Le E'te; 3. La Poule; 4. La Trenise (with a Cornetto Solo); and 5. La Finale. The only known copy of this sheet music survives in the Irish National Library. It was part of the original collection of materials upon which the library was founded, indicating that it was collected contemporaneously.

By June 1837, the 71st Regiment had moved to Kilkenny in western Ireland, near Cork, where they spent another year. They performed at major events in Kilkenny from July 1837 to February 1838. On July 27, 1837, the Regiment celebrated the promotion of Serjeant-Major John Aiton to Ensign. They presented him with an engraved silver cup. On February 27, 1838, the 71st held a Grand Fancy Ball in their barracks in Kilkenny. It had been the topic of conversation for months. According to the newspaper review, the officers adorned their barracks simply but elegantly.

Joseph Maffre's career seemed to be doing well at this point but he entered the bubble of high society in Montreal through his participation in one of the defining events of Canadian history—Lord Durham's visit to Canada following the 1837 Rebellion. The Rebellion took place over a few weeks in November and December of 1837. The irritable and headache-prone Durham (John Lambton) was appointed to be the Governor-General of British North America to establish the causes of the Rebellion and then mete out a fair punishment for the Rebels. But Durham had to get there first, and it took him several months to prepare his family and suite for the sea journey. Three items about Durham's preparation were mentioned prominently in the English press. First, he decided to order a new set of silver plate and the ship couldn't sail until it was delivered. Next, he removed the chaplain from his entourage and placed him on one of the accompanying ships. Finally, and seemingly in place of the chaplain, Durham decided he wanted to bring a band to entertain his family and entourage during their 33-day ocean voyage. He was not able to procure the band of the Coldstream Guards because they had already sailed with their Regiment to Canada to help calm the situation. So, Durham settled for next best, which was the Band of the 71st Regiment. Lord Durham's need for a band on his journey to Canada is among his most defining actions and is even mentioned in *Lord Durham* (1961; John Howe director), the 28-minute film from the National Film Board of Canada that was shown to Canadian schoolchildren throughout the 1960's and 1970's.

1838

On April 24, 1838, the troops of the 71st sailed for Canada on three ships, the *Malabar*, the *Barossa*, and the *Hastings*. The *Barossa* carried 120 troops. The *Malabar* carried 520 troops including the Bugle Band, the Piper Band, 42 women, and 86 children. It seems likely that Lucy Maffre and her 8 children were among the accompanying families. The strongest supporting evidence is that the 1891 Census for daughter Maria Tate indicated she was in Canada since 1837, which is only off by one year. The men were quartered on the main deck. The women and children were assigned the lower deck from which all the cannons had been removed. Charles Grey and his wife Caroline were given the captain's cabin for the voyage. The *Malabar* and *Barossa* arrived in Quebec City on May 14, making it a 20-day journey for them.

The real focus of the journey was the *Hastings*, which carried Lord Durham's suite of 61 people (Table 7.1) and the 20 men of the 71st Band led by Maffre. From the first possible moment, the 42-year-old Maffre performed at his musical peak. As Lord Durham, her Ladyship, and family made their way on board, the band played "See, the Conquering Hero Comes" from Handel's 1747 oratorio *Judas Maccabaeus*. Durham's right-hand man, Chief Secretary Charles Buller, wrote that he had been ruminating about the journey when the family came on board and "on a sudden the band struck up its loud and slow strain, the sudden excitement brought tears at once to my eyes."

On April 25, the first day at sea, Buller wrote to a friend: "We pass our time as Britons usually do on such occasions; a large portion is spent in sleep, much in eating, some hours in tramping up and down deck, and but little in prayer. The band is agreeable, and when we hear it play we do not much regret the chaplain."

Table 7.1: Lord Durham's suite on the *Hastings*

1. Lord Durham was John Lambton, eldest son of William Lambton, Member of Parliament
2. Lady Durham was Louisa (Grey) Lambton, diarist and eldest daughter of Earl Grey, Prime Minister
3. Lord George Lambton, their child, born 1828, was age 10 in 1838
4. Lady Mary Lambton, their child, born 1819, was age 19 in 1838
5. Lady Emily Lambton, their child, born 1823, was age 15 in 1838
6. Lady Alice Lambton, their child, born 1831, was age 7 in 1838
7. Mr. Edward Ellice, Private Secretary, a principal owner of Hudson's Bay Company and grandson of Earl Grey's sister
8. Mrs. Jane (Balfour) Ellice, diarist, spouse of Edward, later taken by the Rebels in 1838, wrote a diary about her Canadian experiences
9. Miss Tina Balfour, sister of Mrs. Ellice, later taken by Rebels in 1838 and rescued by the 71st
10. Mr. Thomas Turton, Legal Advisor
11. Mr. Charles Buller, Chief Secretary, and later author of *Sketch of Lord Durham's Mission in Canada*
12. Mr. Arthur Buller, Commissioner of Inquiry into Education
13. Mr. Gervase Bushe, Attaché to Lord Durham
14. Mr. Edward Pleydell-Bouverie, Attaché to Lord Durham

15. Sir John Doratt MD, Private Physician to Lord Durham, who administered laudanum whenever Durham had a headache
16. Mr. Saddler, Tutor
17. Mr. John Coke-Smyth, Drawing Master, diarist, and author of *Sketches of the Canadas*
18. Lt. the Hon. Frederick Villiers, Aide-de-Camp and Lord Durham's cousin
19. Ensign William Cavendish, Aide-de-Camp
20. Capt. William Ponsonby, Aide-de-Camp
21. Cornet the Hon. Constantine Dillon, Aide-de-Camp
22. Lt. Stephen Conroy, Aide-de-Camp
23. Lt. Robert Clifford, Aide-de-Camp
24-43. Twenty band members of the 71st, including bandmaster Joseph Maffre
44-61. Eighteen Servants

Note: Lt. Col. George Couper, Military Secretary, is sometimes included as being on the *Hastings* but he actually traveled ahead to deal with the logistics of Lord Durham's arrival.

On April 28, Mrs. Ellice wrote "Besides the ship's own band, there is the band of Col. Grey's regt. on board. The Regt. is going to Canada & the band was allowed to come with Ld. Durham. Plenty of music."

On May 12, Mrs. Ellice wrote "The Band plays every morning & afternoon when it is fine—& we are all quick of two or three "Rule Britannias" before breakfast & "Roast Beef" before dinner. [*"Roast Beef" was a naval and army tune played by the drummer to announce dinner but, in this case, was apparently played by a full band*]. The Master of the Band [*Maffre*] sends up a card with the list of what he is to play every day. Ly. D[*urham*] says the Queen keeps all the *cards* of *her* band & every night puts them in a box made for the purpose. The same with her list of people who dine at the Palace every day, & she never goes to the play without putting the Play bill into a similar box. Such *order*, method & regularity even in trifles one seldom hears of."

On May 14, Mrs. Ellice wrote "After dinner we danced on deck to the amusement of all the company except Ly. Mary & Emily—they looked like *victims* rather than votaries of Terpsichore [*the Greek Muse of poetry and dance*]. Is it natural at their age to dislike dancing?" Although her two teenage daughters were shy according to this diary entry, the Lambton children befriended all the officers during their month-long journey.

On May 14, the *Malabar* and *Barossa* arrived in Quebec City with Col. Grey, Mrs. Grey, and all 700 men of the 71st Regiment. They immediately boarded the *British America* steamer for the final leg of the journey to Montreal. When the ship was within hearing distance of Montreal three days later on May 17, the Bugle Band of the 71st played three tunes in quick succession – *Voulez vous danser Mademoiselle, A la Claire Fontaine,* and *Auld Lang Syne*. The immense crowd of Montrealers who had gathered along the St. Lawrence cheered their approval. The troops disembarked and crossed to St. Helen's Island the next morning May 18, where they were stationed for a few months. When Lady Durham arrived in Quebec City a week later, she was disappointed to find that her brother Colonel Grey was already in Montreal.

On May 24, when the *Hastings* was in sight of the Canadian shore, the passengers celebrated the Queen's Birthday. Victoria had been crowned only the year before at age 18. The Aide-de-Camps fired 21 rounds into the air and the suite had a grand dinner during which Lord Durham gave three short speeches. Lady Durham wrote, "In the evening the Officers got up a Ball on the Quarter Deck [*at the stern where the naval officers gather*] which was very prettily arranged with flags, &c the dancing was very gay." The artist John Coke-Smyth wrote that he "went onto Quarter Deck, found it cover'd in with Ensigns and Colors, very pretty and making a capital Ball Room. Highland Band on the Poop, and female Household had up to dance, capital fun." Then, he made a sketch called "Ball on Board the HMS Hastings" (Figure 7.1). Note that the person on the poop nearest the chandelier is facing the band, presumably to conduct. This is the only known image of Maffre. The two men on the main deck are probably the ship's captain Francis Erskine Loch and his first mate.

When the *Hastings* sailed into Quebec City at 2 p.m. on May 27, the paper reported, "The fine band of the 71st Light Infantry was on the quarter deck, and, as the ship passed the town, played the air of 'Rule Britannia' with powerful effect." Historian Bruce Curtis used this occasion of the band's performance as a prime example of Durham's spectacular and tightly scripted official landings and departures. Similarly, Coke-Smyth wrote they "found the *Malabar* 74 [*the size of warships was measured by the total number of cannon ports*], *Pique*, [*Inconstant*] 36, and *Race Horse* Corvette here. The wind was right up the River carrying us in about 10 knots an hour with studding Sails set. We had the Band of the Highlanders 71st Regiment on the Deck and the officers in full Dress, making the Scene one of great interest to us Entering for the first time a Country of which we expected the Arrival of his Lordship would create considerable sensation." From the shore, Rev. Henry Scadding wrote, "During the morning service the Hastings frigate arrived, bringing Lord Durham and suite—crowds upon all the walks commanding a view of the river. Band playing on board, but his Lordship does not land till to-morrow at 2." They actually disembarked two days later because it rained the next day.

On May 29, Mrs. Ellice wrote "Landed in due form with Ld. D. *et toute sa boutique*. Music playing, colours flying. Cannons roaring, streets lined with Grenr. Guardsmen amongst whom I recognized many friends. The Streets are very steep & I thought no horses could ever pull us up." Once Durham's suite reached the top of the hill and was inside the Castle of St. Louis, he did three things that made him very popular in the hearts of French and British Canadians: (1) he refused to continue the appointments of the Executive Councilors as every Governor General before him had done; (2) he ordered that the names and charges against all political prisoners be brought before him for review; and (3) he issued a proclamation asking all Canadians to forget "all party and sectarian animosities, and unite with me in the blessed work of peace and harmony."

On May 31, Colonel Grey in Montreal writes, "Heard yesterday of the arrival of the Hastings — 33 days passage from Portsmouth, having sailed on the 24th April, the same day that we did. Sent Sir Hew Dalrymple down [*river*] to look after our Band, which is come out in her."

On June 4, Colonel Grey in Montreal writes, "Sir H Dalrymple returns with the band. From what he says I am certainly going somewhere, so in all probability it is to Washington." Grey's guess was a good one. The next day, he and Mrs. Grey traveled to Quebec City, where they spent a few days with the Durhams. On June 9, Grey traveled to DC to soothe U.S.-Canadian tensions in a meeting with President Martin Van Buren. Grey was back in Quebec City on June 22.

On June 26, Lord Durham proclaimed a general amnesty for all those implicated in the 1837 Rebellion with the exception of the eight leaders. Showing considerable mercy, he banished them to Bermuda instead of hanging them.

On June 28, Coronation Day, the Special Council appointed by Durham ratified his June 26th ordinance. Canadians strongly approved of his decision to leave Canadian politicians out of this decision so that old wounds could heal. Nevertheless, this ratification by a non-Canadian body was the action criticized in England that ultimately caused Durham's recall. It would take weeks, however, for his letters to reach England and then for the British Government's response to reach him.

On July 2, 1838, a detachment of 60 men of the 71st under Sir Hew Dalrymple escorted the eight imprisoned 1837 rebel leaders from Montreal to their exile in Bermuda. They took the steamer *Canada* to Quebec City, and on July 3, set sail on the ship *Vestal.* They reached Bermuda on July 24. Since Dalrymple was in Montreal on July 27, he must not have accompanied them. It is very unlikely the 71st Band accompanied the prisoners to Bermuda.

Everything was going well for Durham so he decided to embark on his tour of Canada. On July 4, 1838, after one month in Quebec City, Lord Durham and suite boarded the *British America* steamer for the journey to Montreal. Colonel Grey left one day earlier to have things ready for their arrival.

On the morning of July 5, 1838, the steamer *British America* arrived in Montreal. Colonel Grey took them by boat to St. Helen's Island to enjoy an outdoor meal under the shade trees. It rained and everyone got soaked. When Durham appeared in public the next day, Montrealers turned out to applaud his political actions of the previous month. In fact, the public demonstrations grew increasingly favorable every day of his tour. On July 10, the Durhams left for a tour of Cornwall and Kingston.

On Friday July 13, the Rev. Scadding wrote that he returned to Montreal from St. Johns on this day and mentioned he saw "The Glengarry officers and the 71st Band on the Champs de Mars" (Figure 7.4). On three consecutive Fridays, August 24, 31, and September 7, Colonel Grey wrote about the band: "Walk on the Champ de Mars to hear the Band"; "Walk with Caroline [*his wife*] on the Champ de Mars to hear the band;" and "Walk with Caroline on the Champ de Mars to hear the Band play." It appears that the 71st band performed on the Champ de Mars every Friday.

Figure 7.4: Champs de Mars was Montreal's military parade ground. It was a popular place for citizens to stroll. It was 680 feet long by 340 feet wide, or 5.3 acres, and edged with Lombardy poplars. Across the center of this image facing west, there is a soldier on a horse, 17 soldiers lined up facing the reader, 12 band members facing left, and 17 more soldiers lined up perpendicularly along the right. Onlookers are scattered around the edge. At the end of the field on the far left is the spire of St. Gabriel Church. The tall building of dressed stone was Lawyer David Ross's home at 11 St. Gabriel Street. From Bosworth's Hochelaga Depicta, 1846.

Figure 7.4 Detail: The twelve band members are wearing light pants, a dark jacket, and shako helmets decorated with a tall feather, indicating they are not from either the 19th or 71st Regiments. The first band member holds a rifle and must be the leader. The second member plays a trombone, the fourth, fifth, and sixth may hold French horns, the eighth is playing a clarinet-like wind instrument, and the last four members are playing percussion. The last member is playing a side drum.

In August 1838, Montreal celebrated the first anniversary of Queen Victoria's Coronation Day. Throughout September, Lord Durham was in Quebec City and received news about the attacks against him in the British Parliament. It was claimed that he overstepped his bounds by having his proclamation of amnesty approved by the Special Council he put into place. By September 19, he resolved to resign as Governor General even though Canadian citizens were indignant about the attacks on his character and besieged him to stay. On September 30, Durham submitted his official resignation. On November 1, Durham and his suite left Quebec for England on the ship *Inconstant*. According to New's biography, the ship "ran aground once, was on fire twice, sailed through twenty-five days of continual gale and storm, and reached Plymouth harbour, November 26, in weather too rough to permit a landing for four days. Lord Durham could not find peace on either land or sea."

On November 2, Colonel Grey received intelligence that the rebels had taken Beauharnois and made prisoners of Mr. Ellice and others. Beauharnois was the house belonging to Mr. Ellice's father, one of the founding members of the Hudson Bay Company. It was located 10 miles south of the eastern end of Montreal. Soon, Mr. Ellice and the other prisoners were taken to Châteauguay while Mrs. Ellice and her sister Tina Balfour remained captives at Beauharnois. The next day, the local priest brought them to the presbytery where they slept with other harmless prisoners.

On November 7, the 71st Regiment began their march to St. Johns, 30 miles southeast of Montreal. It seems unlikely the full band was with them. On the evening of November 9, the Grenadier Guards, the 71st, and the 7th Hussars arrived outside Napierville, the rebel headquarters, and halted for the night. By the morning of Saturday the 10th, most of the rebels had flown so these three regiments were able to take possession easily. As they entered the town, however, a soldier of the 71st was killed by gunfire from the rebels. This was the only military casualty during the 1838 Rebellion, although three were wounded.

On Sunday, November 11, the rebels in Châteauguay decided to take Mr. Ellice to an even more remote village but he escaped when they were arguing amongst themselves. The 71st began their march from Montreal to Beauharnois where they arrived on the 14th and quickly freed Mrs. Ellice, her sister Tina Balfour, and the others. The 71st remained in Beauharnois for about one month while they disarmed the inhabitants, arrested the instigators, and made all others swear an oath of loyalty to the crown. On November 15, the Ellices sailed back to England for good.

On December 19, 1838, the 71st marched to L'Acadie because there were reports of unrest. Such reports persisted for months and kept the 71st on the move. L'Acadie is located 20 miles from Beauharnois but even further from Montreal. Colonel Grey quickly grew tired of the place because there never was any rebel activity. He began spending long weekends in Montreal with his wife.

1839

By May 13, 1839, the 71st Regiment was stationed in Montreal once again.

On July 5, the Greys left Montreal to travel throughout the United States. They stopped in Boston, New York, Philadelphia, and Baltimore. On August 20, they sailed from New York City and reached England about September 13. They returned to Canada in November 1840 and visited the Eastern Townships in June 1841. In August 1841, they returned to England for the last time. In England, Colonel Grey's rank increased and he became Prince Albert's private secretary in 1849. When Prince Albert died in 1861, Grey became private secretary to Queen Victoria. In 1866, he was additionally appointed joint keeper of the Privy Purse.

1840's Montreal and the Governor Generals

With his former Regimental commander out of the picture, Maffre hit the ground running in bilingual and ethnically diverse Montreal. This city was a perfect fit for his affable personality, background, and talents. He was born to French parents so he spoke French fluently but he was raised entirely in England and spoke excellent English. His wide travels had taken him to southern England, central England, northern England, Scotland, Ireland, and the West Indies. He was raised Catholic but married a Protestant wife. During the 1840's in Montreal, he performed at the churches serving French Catholics, Irish Catholics, and English Anglicans. Even better, Montreal was a city with a rising middle class of both French and English speakers. Many of them had children who needed all types of musical instruction to be properly educated.

In March 1841, Maffre advertised his intention to teach music in Montreal. Within months, he formed the Montreal Musical and Choral Society and soon his amateur performers were presented to the public and received excellent reviews from the newspapers. Maffre also organized more professional concerts than any other local musician and was often called upon to lead the band for visiting performers. One way to show his prominence is to describe his encounters with the five Governors General who came after Durham.

The second Governor General was Lord Sydenham (Charles Poulett Thompson). One day in June 1840, Sydenham traveled to St. Johns to review the troops of the 71st Regiment. At first, Military Commander Colonel George Cathcart had his troops march around and then he took Sydenham on a short steamer ride. As they came to a bend in the river, a second barge carrying the band of the 71st materialized out of nowhere while the band began playing a jaunty tune. The very dramatic entrance delighted Sydenham.

The third Governor General was Sir Charles Bagot. The Band of the 71st played during one of Lady Bagot's receptions in August 1842. Mary Charlotte Wellesley married Charles Bagot in 1806.

The fourth Governor General was Lord Metcalfe (Charles Theophilus Metcalfe). In January 1845, Maffre advertised his latest sheet music titled *Notes of the Forest; or, Eastern Township Melodies*. It was "dedicated (by permission) to—His Excellency Sir C. T. Metcalfe, Bart., G C B., Governor General, of British North America, &c. &c. &c."

The fifth Governor General was Earl of Cathcart (Charles Murray Cathcart). We know from newspaper notices that Cathcart attended at least two of Maffre's Vocal & Instrumental Concerts in late 1846 and early 1847. Maffre led the band during these public performances.

The sixth Governor General was Earl of Elgin and Kincardine (James Bruce). As mentioned earlier, James Bruce had married Lady Mary Lambton, Lord Durham's daughter. Maffre had met her nine years earlier during their joint voyage on the *H.M.S. Hastings*. The first Montreal appearance of Elgin and Lady Mary was at the Annual Soiree of the Mechanics' Institute in February 1847, where Maffre was the featured performer. Afterwards, Maffre performed at several events sponsored by either Elgin or Lady Mary. The most significant manifestation of their closeness is that Maffre dedicated *The Canadian Quadrilles* to the Countess of Elgin in November 1847. There is evidence that Maffre performed it many times for the public.

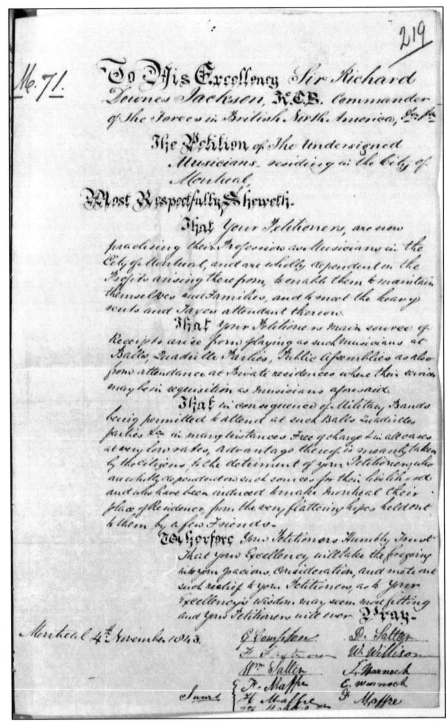

Figure 8.1: Petition for Relief from Military Band Competition, November 1843. Library and Archives Canada, RG8/C76, Microform c-2643, p. 446.

8
MONTREAL MELODIES

Joseph Maffre rose to the top of Montreal's musical scene between 1840 and 1848 by doing everything he could to raise the public's interest in all types of music. He taught many instruments and singing, led military and dance bands, founded musical societies, gave charity concerts, and published sheet music. One reason it worked for him was that Montreal was an excellent fit for someone fluent in English and French and who had something to offer families. He appealed to the Anglo Canadian politicians and military because he was a royalist and British military man. He appealed to the French Canadians because of his French heritage, because they were already more culturally refined than the British, and perhaps most of all because he favored playing the quadrille, which was derived from French country dance music. In the later years of this period, he even planned musical events that were designed to unite the diverse populations of Montreal. Maffre also brought his children into the family business as they came of age and this helped him expand his influence.

1840

As the hard feelings of the 1837 and 1838 Rebellions began to fade, Maffre worked to become better known among the cultural elite of Montreal. In May and November 1840, he published two quadrilles for beginning pianists in *The Literary Garland*, a monthly art magazine published by John Lovell in Montreal from 1838 until 1851. The bulk of the magazine was devoted to fiction, poems, and other literary material but every issue also included one musical score on the fifth page from the end (Figure 8.1). Beginning with the first issue in December 1838, the musical contributions were managed by William Henry Warren, organist at Montreal's Christ Church. Three-fourths of the 150 published pieces in the *Garland* were songs, marches, and dance music by other composers that Warren scored. Warren made a few original musical contributions, as did Joseph Maffre (see 18 & 23) and Charles Sauvageau.

Table 8.1: Selection of the music published in *The Literary Garland*

Issue	Date	Title	Contributor	Explanation
1	Dec. 1838	*Favorite Waltz*	W. H. Warren	"as performed by the band of the First Royals; presented by a gentleman of this city [*Warren*], who has kindly consented to superintend the Musical Department"
15	Feb. 1840	*C'est La Belle Francaise*	W. H. Warren	"Canadian Melodies, No. I"
16	Mar. 1840	*Le Fils du Roi*	W. H. Warren	"Canadian Melodies, No. II"
18	May 1840	*Quadrille*	J. Maffre	"Professor of Music, and Director of the Band of the 71st Regiment"
21	Aug. 1840	*The Canadian: A French Air*	Anonymous	This piece was also known as *Vive la Canadienne*. Maffre performed it at the 1843 St. Jean Baptiste Parade and it as the basis of his 5th Canadian Quadrille.
22	Sep. 1840	*Waltz and Trio*	W. H. Warren	This is possibly Warren's first original contribution.
23	Oct. 1840	*Quadrille, No. II*	J. Maffrae [*sic*]	"Professor of Music and Director of the Band of the 71st Regiment"
24	Nov. 1840	*Gallopade*	J. Clarke	"7th Hussars." This is an original composition.

In 1840, son Joseph Maffre Jr. arrived in Canada as a member of the 71st Highland Light Infantry, two years after the rest of the family. In late 1840 or early 1841, Maffre Sr. helped secure his son's transfer to the prestigious King's Dragoon Guards Cavalry Corps band by writing to Col. George Cathcart, commander of that company.

1841

At age 46, Joseph set up his business in bilingual Montreal in March 1841 by advertising his intention to teach music. He is a Professor of Music and wants to make sure the public knows he had been bandmaster of the 71st Regiment. Although he says he is the "late Master of the Band," he did not sever his ties to the 71st Band completely and led them in public concerts until 1843. His home and place of business was 11 Sanguinet Street, located near Champs de Mars (Figure 8.2). He enlisted the help of his second oldest son Harry but it wasn't enough help so he soon paid for the discharge of son Joseph Jr. from the Kings Dragoon Guards.

> *The Montreal Transcript, March 6, 1841 (Repeated on March 11)*
> MUSICAL TUITION.
> MR. MAFFRE, PROFESSOR of MUSIC and late Master of the Band of the 71st Highland Light Infantry, most respectfully begs leave to announce to the Public, that by the request of several families he has been induced to settle on Montreal, for the purpose of following his profession, and trusts that his terms as well as his abilities will meet their approbation. Mr. M. has had the advantage for a series of years to study the Art under the most eminent masters, and has a perfect knowledge of the following Instruments: —Pianoforte, Organ, Violin, Viola, Violoncello, Clarionet, Flute, Oboe, and all WIND INSTRUMENTS—also teaches the ELEMENTS OF SINGING, and thorough BASS, with the art of SCOREING MUSIC for ORCÆSTRA or MILITARY BAND. Mr. M. will attend any Ladies or Gentlemen as accompanying master, with the Violin, thereby inculcating a perfect knowledge of time and Musical expression. Seminaries and Schools punctually attended to. For terms, &c. apply at Mr. M.'s Residence in Sanguinet Street, near the Champs de Mars.
> Mr. M. has for disposal, a choice collection of the most recent ITALIAN OPERA MUSIC, arranged for a MILITARY BAND, the list of which may be perused at MEAD'S and HERBERT'S MUSIC STORES, where may be had, A NEW SET OF QUADRILLES, for the PIANOFORTE, lately composed by J. M., and also his METHOD of TEACHING PSALMODY to the children of Free and Parochial Schools, as adapted by him for the use of National Schools in England.
> Montreal, March 6, 1841

On April 23, 1841, Maffre proposed forming the Montreal Musical and Choral Society. The Society would consist of amateur musicians and singers. They would give three annual Grand Concerts of Vocal and Instrumental Music and three annual Miscellaneous Performances of Sacred Music. It took one and a half years to train a group of amateurs for their first concert on October 5, 1843.

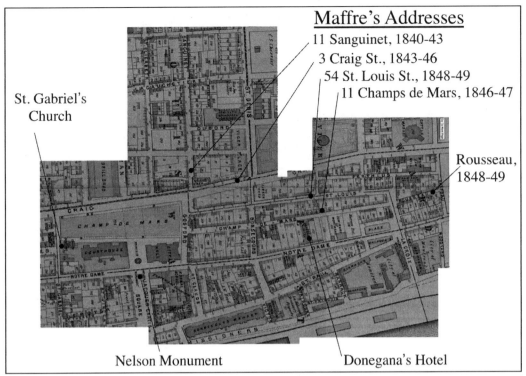

Figure 8.2: Joseph Maffre's Addresses in the East Ward of Montreal. The labeled house numbers are from "Atlas of the City and Island of Montreal" by Henry Hopkins, 1879. Illustration by Mark Griep.

In mid-July 1841, Maffre paid for his son's discharge from the King's Dragoons Guards Cavalry Corps saying that he needed him for his musical business. The Army did not act quickly until finally, on September 30, 1841, Colonel Cathcart placed Joseph Jr.'s name in the 30-day Consideration List for possible discharge. In mid-October 1841, Joseph Jr. obtained leave to visit Montreal to see his father. On Junior's return to regiment, the roads were bad, he was drunk, and he arrived three hours late. His name was then placed in the Defaulter's Book for being drunk and late. From the tone of subsequent letters, Joseph Jr. failed to inform his father that he had been drunk. To be placed in the Defaulter's Book meant the discharge would be delayed six months. In November 1841, the Discharge payment was returned to Maffre.

1842

On March 27, 1842, Maffre once again gave the regiment's Pay Master the amount required to purchase his son's discharge from the Kings Dragoon Guards. However, Maffre was confused about the timing. He thought the six-month delay started from the time Joseph Jr.'s name was put on the Consideration List rather than in the Defaulter's book.

On April 2, 1842, "Joseph Maffre—Professor of Music" at 11 Sanguinet Street wrote a letter to Colonel Cathcart requesting the release of his son Joseph Jr. from the King's Dragoon Guards. He had been writing to Cathcart for six months. In this final letter, he wrote a long and highly revealing sentence about himself and his family:

Your memorialist begs for them to state to your Excellency that his son being a good Musician (and educated as such at Memorialists expence [sic]) it will be evident to Your Excellency that there is a desire to retain his sons services, and to prevent him from obtaining his discharge, which would be a great loss to memorialist being desirous of having his assistance in Memorialists profession to enable him to support a large family of eight children, as Memorialist is advanced in years and declining in health from a service of 25 years in the Army as Band Master and Many years of this long period in a tropical climate.

Joseph and Lucy had ten children, one of whom died in England. Given that Joseph Jr. traveled separately to Canada, the remaining eight children must have accompanied Joseph and Lucy in their journey to Canada. In April 1842, therefore, the family living at home included: Joseph 47 "advanced in years and declining in health", Lucy 50, Ann Thomas 29, Charlotte 22, Maria 20, Henry 19, Mary Ann 15, Frederick ~14, Alfred 12, and Frank ~11.

In mid-April 1842, Joseph Jr. was discharged from the British Army, exactly six months after his name was placed in the Defaulter's Book.

On June 13 and 17, Maffre's concert band accompanied Miss Jane Sloman at both of her well-advertised performances at Rasco's Hotel (Figure 8.3). At the "Soiree Musicale", Maffre's band opened the evening with an "Introduction." After the intermission, they performed a "Sinfonia." Governor General Bagot attended the first performance during which Jane Sloman gave a piano recital of the "greatest compositions of the most eminent composers." She was probably the daughter of Mr. and Mrs. Sloman, who were in Montreal to perform vocally at the Theatre Royal. In their review of the first performance, the *Transcript* was astonished at Miss Sloman's "surprising power and command over the instrument." They also noted, "it is but justice to Mr. Maffree [sic] and the other instrumental performers to add that they performed their parts with spirit and effect." This is the first time Maffre's performance was reviewed in Montreal.

Figure 8.3: Rasco's Hotel on St. Paul Street. Rasco's was the city's largest hotel. It opened in 1836 and could accommodate 150 guests. The young author Charles Dickens stayed at Rasco's when he visited Montreal in 1842. From Bosworth's Hochelaga Depicta, 1846.

On August 2, 1842, "Jos[h] Maffre" was enumerated in the Canadian Census (Table 8.2). He and his family were renting a house on Sanguinet Street in the St. Lawrence Ward. His profession or trade was "Prof Music." His neighbors were all tradesmen—on the same page of the census there were 4 Joiners, 2 Traders, 2 Shoemakers, and 2 Pensioners but one each of Grocer, Boatman, Mason, Merchant, Cabinet Maker, Coach Maker, Shop Keeper, Painter, Confectioner, and Bailiff. None of the other professions were related to the arts, indicating that Maffre was renting far from other performers. There were eight family members residing in the Maffre home, and none were "temporarily absent." After accounting for Joseph and Lucy, this means there were 6 children at home. The eldest children must have moved away. One member of the household, undoubtedly Joseph, was a member of the "Church of Rome" while the seven others were "Church of England." One family member, undoubtedly Lucy, was a Native of England, 1 was a Native of France, Joseph, and "6 French origin not native of Canada," indicating the children. It seems that Joseph and his children were considered to be natives of France, even though none of them was born there. There was 1 alien not naturalized which could be either Joseph or his son Joseph Jr. The family had been in the province for 2-4 years, which is consistent with an arrival date of 1838 for Joseph and his family but 1840 for son Joseph Jr.

Table 8.2: Maffre's 1842 Canadian Census Entry

Census entry	Proposed ID	Known age	Interpretative Notes
1 married male 30-59	Joseph	47	correct
1 married female 14-44	Lucy	50	incorrect by 6 years
3 single males 18-20	3. Joseph Jr.	24	incorrect by 4 years
	6. Henry	19	correct
	7. Frederick	~17	age chosen to fit
1 female 6-13	8. Mary Ann	15	incorrect by 2 years
1 single male 14-17	9. Alfred	14	correct
1 male 6-13	10. Frank	12	correct
[no entry]	1. Ann	28	must be living elsewhere
[no entry]	2. Francis	died 1818	died at age 3 in England
[no entry]	4. Charlotte	22	must be living elsewhere
[no entry]	5. Maria	20	must be living elsewhere

The most disappointing part of the 1842 census is that it does not name the family members but only their age ranges: 1 male age 6-13, 1 female age 6-13, 1 single male 14-17, 3 single males 18-20, 1 married male 30-59, and 1 married female 14-44. The three eldest daughters are living elsewhere.

On September 13 and 15, "The Lion" performed twice at the newly renovated Theatre Royal. Among his exploits was that he caught a cannonball just after it was discharged from a cannon. The advertisements noted, "By kind permission of Major [*William*] Denny, the Band of the 71st Regiment, directed by Mr. Maffre, will execute overtures and other pieces of music during the evening."

On September 23, violinist Jean Nagel and tenor August Nourrit performed their third concert at Rasco's Hotel. John-Chrystosome Brauneis Jr. and Leonard Eglauch assisted on the piano at all three concerts and were favorably noted in the *Transcript*. The advertisement for the third concert also says, "By special permission, the Band of the 71st Regt., under Mr. Maffre's direction, will attend the Concert." The playbill indicates that Maffre's band will play the *Elligio E Claudio* Overture by Mercadante, an Overture by Beethoven, and a Set of Waltzes by Labitzky. Brauneis Jr. was born in 1814 Quebec City where his father was a musician, music teacher, and music merchant. Brauneis Jr.

was musically trained in Europe from 1830 to 1833 and then returned to Canada to become the organist for Notre Dame Cathedral from 1833 to 1844. He performed at several concerts with Maffre in 1842 and 1843, which was when he began to teach music on the guitar, harp, violin, and theory. Eglauch was born about 1820 in Germany. He immigrated to Kingston, Upper Canada (Ontario), in 1842 and performed several concerts with Maffre during 1842 and 1843. In 1845, Eglauch was the organist at Notre Dame after Brauneis Jr. vacated the position.

On November 25, guitarist Dolores de Goni and cellist Gustav Knoop performed a postponed concert at the Theatre Royal. The advertisement noted, "The Band of the 71st Regiment, by permission, will be in attendance, and, under the direction of Mr. Maffre, will perform music from the latest Opera of the most approved masters." In their review of November 29, the *Transcript* described the nature of the extensive renovations to the newly reopened Theatre. Doña Dolores de Goni was from Spain, performed before English royalty in early 1840 and then toured throughout North America until the early 1850s. She was very popular and began performing with German-born cello virtuoso Gustav Knoop, whom she married in 1845. Historian David Bradford wrote in 2009 that, "she was perhaps the most accomplished musician among the many European guitarists that immigrated to America in the 1840s."

Figure 8.4: Theatre Royal on St. Paul Street had the largest theatrical stage in the city. The Theatre was built in 1825 and was owned by John Molson. From Bosworth's Hochelaga Depicta, 1846.

Beginning in December 1842, the "Gentleman Garrison Amateurs" performed a weekly light farce at the Theatre Royal. Mrs. Gibbs assisted by singing. The first ad of December 17 states that pianist Berlin and flautist Francis Walcott [*Woolcott?*] have been engaged for the season and that the 71st Band will be under the direction of Mr. Maffre. The Amateurs were members of the various British Regulars who were garrisoned in the City. Mrs. Gibbs was born Miss Graddon in 1804 in Taunton, Devon. In 1824, she debuted on the London stage but then married Mr. Gibbs who was the wealthy son of a dyer. They immigrated to North America and spent the years from 1842 to 1844 in Montreal, performing at several events with Maffre. We haven't found much about Berlin or Walcott, suggesting they were local amateurs.

1843

Joseph Maffre was Chapel Master of Récollet Church (Figure 8.5) from 1843 to 1848 and of

St. Patrick's Church (Figure 8.6) from 1847 to 1848. As a Chapel Master, he led the singers and played the organ. From the 1830's to the 1850's, the greatest number of immigrants to Canada and Montreal were from Ireland. In the early years, most of these Anglophone Catholics were displaced from Ireland by its rising population, farm mechanization, and the Industrial Revolution. Starting in 1847, nearly 2 million Irish left their homeland because of the Irish Potato Famine brought on by a fungal blight. Since the cost of the ship's journey was less expensive going to Canada than to the ports of the United States, most of them chose to go to Canada. In Montreal in 1841, there were 6,500 Anglophone Catholics. They were served by Récollet Church but it could only hold about a third of that number so plans were begun to build St. Patrick's Church in 1843. Perhaps Maffre helped design the musical features of St. Patrick's. Its completion in 1847 was fortuitous because the potato famine resulted in 30,000 Irish in Montreal in 1848.

Figure 8.5: Récollet Church on Notre Dame Street. The front of the church was rebuilt in 1830. It was connected to an Orphan Asylum and a Catholic School. From Bosworth's Hochelaga Depicta, 1846.

Figure 8.6: St. Patrick's Church on Lagauchetiere Street. When the church opened in early 1847, it could seat 7000. From Bosworth's Hochelaga Depicta, 1846.

On January 27, 1843, the 71st Regiment held a ball for the other regiments that was attended by 460 ladies and gentlemen. According to the *Transcript*'s glowing review of the event, "The bugles cease, and the more lively tones of violin and clarinet, with deeper bass, resound along the hall", which brings to mind Maffre Jr. on the violin and Maffre Sr. on the clarinet. There were two bands, one on each side of the room, and both played quadrilles until midnight when dinner was served. Afterward, dancing "continued till grey morn warned the stars to sleep."

On February 7, Mr. Anderson held a benefit concert of secular music at Rasco's Hotel for "The Ladies Benevolent Society" and "The House of Industry." The concert featured Mrs. Gibbs, the City Amateur Glee Singers, the Band of the 71st Regiment, and John-Chrystosome Brauneis Jr. at the piano. Maffre is not mentioned in the ad but he probably led the 71st Band.

On February 17, Mr. Fax held a benefit concert of vocal and instrumental music at Rasco's Hotel for "The Montreal General Hospital." It featured vocalist Mrs. Gibbs, pianist Leonard Eglauch, Joseph Maffre leading the 71st Band, and glee singers Brown, S. Fax, and D. Fax. The 71st Band played "several favorite Overtures" and Eglauch played "some splendid and difficult pieces." Simon and David Fax were tailors in 1843, working at separate locations in Montreal.

On March 17, St. Patrick's Day began with a well-attended Mass at Récollet Church where the sermon concerned the need to serve the poor. The *Transcript* reported that, "Besides the united Choirs of the Récollet and Bonsecours Churches, the Band of the 71st Regiment was present, and contributed much to the harmony and effect of the services." The service was followed by a procession through the city streets to the Bank of Montreal where cheers ended the day.

On May 29, Matthew Wall, the Blind Harper, gave a concert of vocal and instrumental music at Rasco's Hotel. Wall emigrated from Ireland to New Brunswick in 1830 and had a long career as a harpist. In Montreal, Wall was assisted by Brauneis and Eglauch on the piano, Francis Woolcott on the flute, and Swain and Whitty as vocalists. Mr. Maffre led the Band of the 71st.

At some date in June, Maffre and a group of individuals wrote the constitution for the Montreal Choral Society, a copy of which is still in the City of Montreal Archives. The constitution's first line is, "Rule I. That this Society be called "The Montreal Choral Society," and shall have for its object: improvement in and the cultivation of a taste for the science of Music and shall confine itself exclusively to the practice and performance of Sacred Music." The Society had considerable success in 1843 but the last time the Montreal Choral Society was mentioned in the newspapers was for a practice in January 1845. The Society was revived in 1858 by Rev. J. S. Sykes and again in 1923 but didn't last long either time.

On June 24, St. Jean Baptiste Day began with a well-attended Mass at Notre Dame Cathedral (Figure 8.7), the first time it was held there. According to the *Transcript*, "The Band of the 71st Regiment was stationed near the Organ, and played several national airs." The service was followed by a procession through the city streets, during which the band of the 71st Regiment played the air of *Vive la Canadienne*. Following the band were people holding two-sided banners with St. Jean Baptiste on one side and a Canadian Habitant on the other. Both images were "surrounded with a wreath of maple leaves and buds." Joseph Bourret, the Mayor, and his wife, the Lady Mayoress, were part of the march, which ended by returning to the Cathedral. *Vive la Canadienne* and *A la claire fontaine* were the earliest unofficial Canadian National Anthems. The maple leaf was the official emblem of French Canada since 1834.

Figure 8.7: Notre Dame Cathedral on Place D'Arms showing a funeral procession. Construction began in 1824 and was complete in 1829. It could accommodate 8000 people. The organ was located in the gallery over the front entry. From Bosworth's Hochelaga Depicta, 1846.

On June 28, 1843, Joseph Maffre Jr. married Julie Marie Théophile Perrault at Trinity Memorial Anglican Chapel. Julie was Catholic and had been baptized in Notre Dame Cathedral. The witnesses were a military friend and two Maffre siblings. The original Trinity Anglican Church was built in 1840 near Bonsecours Market and the Quebec Gate Barracks. It was attended by military commanders such as Colonel Wetherall, Colonel Gore, and Captain Maitland.

Table 8.2: Marriages for Joseph and Lucy's Children*

Marriage	Witnesses	Church	Date
Joseph Maffre Jr & Julie Théophile Perrault	Private W. Brown, Marie Maffre, Henry Maffre	Trinity Memorial Anglican Chapel	Jun 28, 1843
Maria Maffre & William Tate	Joseph Maffre Jr, Charlotte Maffre	Trinity Memorial Anglican Chapel	Feb 27, 1845
Mary Anne Maffre & Thomas Buckley	E. Heard, E. Pillar	St. Thomas Anglican Church	Feb 26, 1847
Frederick Maffre & Mary Mullen			~1848
Charlotte Maffre & George McDonnell			~1849

*We have not found the marriages for Ann, Alfred, or Francis.

On July 2, Mrs. Bailey held a Grand Concert of vocal and instrumental music at Rasco's Hotel. She sang "selections from the admired Operas of *La Somnambula, Norma, Marino, Faliero, L'Ambassadrice, Le Preaux Clercs*, and *Fra Diavolo*; with Scotch and Irish Ballads." William Henry Warren was pianist and the Band of the 71st assisted and performed some of the pieces. We have not been able to find much information about Mrs. Bailey.

On July 29, two advertisements were published in the *Transcript* that cited "Mr. Maffre, Professor of Music, Sanguinet Street." In the first, Mrs. Charles Hill announced she had just opened an academy to teach dance and callisthenic exercises to young ladies. She conducted such academies in London, Bath, Cheltenham, and Newcastle. In the second ad, Miss Rock announced she was now giving instruction in the harp, guitar, and singing according the manner she used successfully in Dublin, Edinburgh, Liverpool, and the principal cities of the United States. Both women encouraged families to apply at Mr. Maffre's, Mr. Martell's in the Quebec suburbs, and Mr. Herbert's music store. Mrs. Charles Hill began life as Anne Fairbrother in London. She learned to act from her father and to dance from her older sister. In 1826, Anne married fellow actor Charles Hill and left her family's troupe to travel the circuit of Bath, Cheltenhem, and Newcastle. They returned to London when she began having children. By 1833, she was a very popular dancer on the stage and was proving very good at training other dancers. By 1840, the Charles Hills left for North America where they traveled up and down the eastern seaboard. In 1843, they joined John Nickinson's troupe at the Theatre Royal in Montreal but left the next year when the Theatre burned down. For the rest of their lives, they performed in the small and large towns of Canada and the U.S.A.

In September, a request was made to Mayor Joseph Bourret to use the second floor of St. Ann's Market (Figure 8.8) for the first public performance of the Montreal Choral Society. The Mayor approved the request on September 22. Apparently, the organizers expected that the inaugural performance would attract an audience larger than any commercial space could handle. On October 5, the Montreal Choral Society gave its First Public Concert during which Maffre led over 100 vocalists and 25 instrumentalists. Nearly 1000 people attended the concert, making it an enormous success. In their review of this inaugural concert, the *Montreal Transcript* wrote: "On the whole, we think this public must have been taken by surprise, and we confess that we were. We had formed no idea that, in so short a space of time [*they were founded three months earlier*], such a Society could have been formed, and it is only another proof of what the combined efforts of a few persons can do."

Figure 8.8: St. Ann's Market was a substantial building made from cut stone. The ballroom was on the second floor and was 46 feet by 58 feet, rising as high as 46 feet in the center. On the first floor, there were customized stalls on the east end for vegetables and poultry, in the middle for 32 butchers, and on the west end for fish. When Montreal became the capital in 1844, the second floor of St. Ann's was renovated for use by the Parliament. In 1849, citizens who were upset with the Rebellions' Losses Bill burned down the building. From Bosworth's Hochelaga Depicta, 1846.

The next practice session for the Montreal Choral Society was announced for October 18 in preparation for a concert on December 29th. Before their second concert, however, the competing Harmonic Society was formed. Even though the Choral Society's second concert on 29 December was well attended and satisfying for everyone, the Harmonic Society's performance in January 1844 did not go very well and seems to have soured the public. When the Choral Society gave their third concert, a Grand Concert of Sacred Music, on March 24, 1844, it was not well attended even though the review said the music was the best managed to date. Despite this hiccup, the Choral Society lived on until January 1848 but then faded away until Reverend Sykes revived the Montreal Choral Society in 1858. This time, it must have lasted quite a few years because Borthwick's *History and Biographical Gazetteer of Montreal to the Year 1892* mentions that Montreal architect and builder William Kennedy was a member and librarian of the Montreal Choral Society starting in 1865, "which was organized under the direction of the late Mr. Maffre, the Society giving many concerts at which they rendered the compositions of the old masters."

On November 4, eleven musicians signed a petition (Figure 8.1) to the army authorities pointing out that it was difficult for Montreal musicians to make enough money when the army bands made themselves available "in many instances Free of charge & in all cases at very low rates." Joseph Maffre probably wrote the petition even though he has not signed it. Military Historian Elinor Kyte Senior poked fun at this petition in her book *British Regulars in Montreal* by noting that Maffre knew of what he spoke since he had held the position of military bandmaster for so long. The petition was addressed to Lt.-Gen. Sir Richard Downes Jackson, who had become commander of the Canadian forces in November 1839. The eleven signers (Figure 8.9) were probably members of Maffre's Quadrille Band and the first six signers are underlined, suggesting they were the primary authors. The very first signer is G[eorge] Compton, the only petitioner besides Maffre who had professional credentials – he was listed as a musician in the 1848/9 Montreal Directory. Compton died in 1869 and is buried in Mount Royal Cemetery. D. Sallter and Wm. Salter are probably two of the many children of Richard Salter who married in 1814 in Montreal when he was a Sergent in the 49th Regiment. The 1820 City Directory lists Richard Salter's occupation as musician and grocer. The 1844 City Directory gives Richard Salter's address as 29 Champs de Mars, located very near Maffre's. Richard's first son, David Salter, was baptized in 1815 in the Anglican Garrison Church. David Salter became a tinsmith and was living on Lagauchetiére near Campeau Street in the 1843-4 Lovell's Directory. David Salter was enumerated in the 1881 Canadian Census as a widowed tinsmith aged 66. David Salter would have been 28 when he signed the petition. His brother William was baptized in 1821 in Christ Church Anglican Cathedral and was buried in 1899 in Mount Royal Cemetery. He would have been 22 when he signed the petition. J. Warnock could be either John Warnock, a carpenter in the 1842 census, or James Warnock, a cabinet-maker working in Perrault's buildings on St. Gabriel Street in the 1844-5 Lovell's Directory. We have found no information about H. Fastrois or W. Willison. They must have been laborers by day and musicians by night. The five "Jun[io]rs" are C. [or E.] Warnock, who is probably the son of J. Warnock, and four Maffre boys: F[rederick, age 20], H[enry, age 21], Jos. [age 26; his signature was partially obliterated when the petition was trimmed many years ago], and F[rancis, age 13]. The senior Joseph Maffre did not sign the petition.

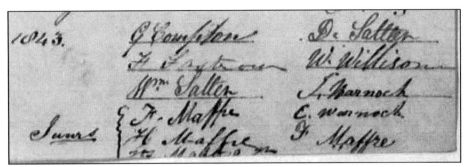

Figure 8.9: Signatures on the 4 November 1843 "Petition for Relief from Military Band Competition." Library and Archives Canada, RG8/C76, Microform c-2643, p. 446.

On December 29, the Choral Society gave their second public performance. It was at St. Gabriel Street Church (Figure 8.10) with proceeds going to the Ladies' Benevolent Institution. According to the *Transcript*, the concert "was very well attended, and went off much to the satisfaction of every one present."

Figure 8.10: St. Gabriel's Church was located at the western edge of Champs de Mars. It was the first Presbyterian Church in Quebec when it was built in 1792. It could accommodate 750 people. From Bosworth's Hochelaga Depicta, 1846.

1844

In 1844, Joseph Maffre moved his business a few blocks to 3 Craig Street (now St. Antoine) according to the 1844/5 Montreal Directory.

On March 7, Maffre advertised in *La Minerve* that he has opened an Academy of Music on Craig Street, near Champs de Mars, and that he will use the system of Mr. Johann Bernard Logier. "Mr. Maffre can affirm by his personal observation in the academies of Mr. Logier, there examining its numerous students, that this system is invariably successful." Maffre says the system can be used to teach the piano and harmony to children as young as 6 years old. For two days a week, he will teach piano. For another two days, he will "give lectures on harmony, thorough-bass, and composition." He also offered lessons to those who are already advanced, and offered lessons in French, German, or English.

Maffre had three opportunities to observe the Logier method in action. The earliest possibility dates to November 17, 1817, in London when members of the Philharmonic Society and leading musicians attended a public examination at Samuel Webbe's music school in London. Logier patented his chiroplast, or hand-director, in 1814 after he had found it useful when teaching his daughter.

Logier's piano method used a device that constrained the pupil's fingers so they would hit only the keys directed by a piece of paper that indicated which piano key was associated with which note. He soon drew high fees from the many teachers who used it throughout Britain and the United States. However, a number of London Philharmonic members were expressing dismay about the method, especially that it might reduce the number of pupils they would be hired to teach. In September 1817, Mr. Logier invited members of the Philharmonic to hear pupils who had learned how to play using his method at Mr. Samuel Webbe's School in London. The performance was supposed to take place at Argyll's on November 6 at noon but only five of the 43 members agreed to attend: Bishop, Horsley, Bridgetower, Potter, and Naldi. By November 12, Bishop sent a note on behalf of many other members of the Philharmonic asking for a private performance at which they could freely examine the pupils. The performance was set for Monday, November 17. The committee included Philharmonic members Attwood, Ayrton, Bishop, François Cramer, Crotch, Dance, Dizi, Griffin, Horsely, Kalkbrenner, Latour, Neate, Ries, and Sir G. Smart. The non-philharmonic attendees were J. B. Cramer, Beale, Ferrari, Fionillo, Charles Knyvett, William Knyvett, and Mazzinghi. The professors who attended were Ashe, Bellamy, Cutler, Clifton, Dragonetti, Immins, Novello, Spray, and Wilkins. The amateurs who attended were Alsager, Broadwood, Fred Collard, Davis, Buckholz, Hastings, Hunter, Berkeley Paget, Pocock, Gosnell, and others unnamed. Even if Maffre didn't attend the demonstration, he would have been aware of the method at this early date and would have known it was useful for training multiple students at once. After the demonstration, two of these men wrote testimonials in favor of the Logier's method, Johann Baptist Cramer and Friedrich Wilhelm Kalkbrenner. In fact, Kalkbrenner was so taken by the method that he negotiated to open a Logier school of his own. Others were not so enthusiastic and brought their views back to a meeting of the full Philharmonic, which chose to publish an advertisement denouncing the method as being unsuitable even though some of them had expressed approval of the pupils' performance during the exhibition. After this successful demonstration, Logier wrote an account titled *An Authentic Account of the Examination of Pupils* that he published in 1818.

Maffre would most certainly have observed the Logerian method when he lived in Leicester. The two Miss Hewitt sisters and their father John Hewitt specialized in using Logier's method to teach piano to children aged seven to fourteen. Maffre often performed with the sisters as a quartet between 1822 and 1825. At these concerts, one sister performed on the piano, the other on the organ, John Waldrom performed on the bassoon, and Maffre played violin.

The third opportunity that Maffre had to learn about the Logerian method was when the 71st Regiment was stationed in Dublin in 1836 and 1837 (Figure 7.3 Detail). This was the city in which Logier invented his method and in which he ran his very successful music school.

On March 22, the Montreal Choral Society gave their third public concert. It was again at St. Gabriel Street Church but with no mention of a charity. According to the *Transcript*, the "orchestra was not so well filled as on former occasions, nor was the attendance so numerous; but there was, certainly, no fall off in the execution of the different pieces. On the contrary, the choruses were better managed than we ever heard them, and there was, in all other respects, a marked improvement in the performers, both instrumental and vocal."

On April 8, Maffre held a grand musical event at the Theatre Royal. It was advertised in *La Minerve* and the *Transcript* using the phrase "For the benefit of Mr. Maffre." Today, that phrase would suggest a charitable event on behalf of Maffre in which he might not even participate. In the early 1800's, "benefit concerts" meant the opposite. According to scholar Simon McVeigh, they were "a single one-off event organized by an individual musician as an annual reward for good service, whether to a musical society or to his patrons in general." Maffre led an orchestra of 40 people in the performance of his own arrangements of Weber's *Der Freischutz* Overture and Kotzwara's *The Battle of Prague*. The 40 members of his band were probably chosen from the best pupils in his Academy of Music. They were assisted by Christ Church's organist Mr. Warren, Montreal's leading flautist Mr. Woolcott, and frequent singer and concert organizer Mr. Anderson. There was also singing by amateur vocalists and a glee by the Fax brothers, the Montreal tailors. After the music, there was dancing and the event concluded with "a popular drama." The performance was not reviewed in the papers.

On December 10, the Montreal Choral Society gave another public concert; it was probably their fifth. This time it was held in the Wesleyan Methodist Chapel on St. James Street (Figure 8.11). According to the *Transcript*, the "pieces selected for the occasion were excellent, and the performances of a superior order. The audience was large and respectable, and evinced their satisfaction as far as the nature of the place would allow. The Choral Society has strong claims on the public, as it has enabled them to pass their leisure hours in a pleasing and rational manner."

Figure 8.11: The Wesleyan Chapel on St. James Street was erected in 1821. It could accommodate 1000 people. From Bosworth's Hochelaga Depicta, 1846.

In April 1844, Joseph and Lucy's first grandchild was born (Table 8.3). He was christened Leopold Alfred Maffre and he continued the family musical profession to a greater degree than any other grandchild. Their first seven grandchildren were baptized between 1844 and 1850 at churches dictated by their children's spouse's religious affiliations.

———

103

Table 8.3: Baptisms for Joseph and Lucy's First Seven Grandchildren

Grandchild	Parents (and Sponsors)	Church	Date
Leopold Alfred Maffre	Joseph and Julie Maffre	Notre Dame Cathedral	Apr. 1844
Lucie Hermelinde Maffre	Joseph and Julie Maffre	Notre Dame Cathedral	Jul. 10, 1845
William Wilberforce Tate	Maria and William Tate (sponsor Thomas Tate)	Trinity Memorial Anglican Chapel	Dec. 21, 1845
Julie Virginia Maffre	Joseph and Julie Maffre	Notre Dame Cathedral	Sep. 10, 1846
Georgiana Australina Maffre	Joseph and Julie Maffre	Notre Dame Cathedral	Dec. 29, 1847
Frederick Maffre Jr.	Frederick and Louisa Maffre; privately baptized [*which suggests he was ill*]	Christ Church	Mar. 15, 1850
Lucy Jane Tate	Maria and William Tate (sponsors Henry Tate, Jane Tate, Charlotte McDonnell [*recorded as McDonnald*])	Christ Church	Jul. 31, 1850

Figure 8.12: "View from Snowdon Cottage" oil painting by Lucy Doris Maffre Snowdon (1897-1996) in 1965 of Sally's Pond in the Eastern Townships. Doris was a descendant of Joseph Maffre Sr. but was not aware of his accomplishments or that he had published any sheet music. She learned to play the piano when she was young and took up oil painting when she was 60 years old. Photo taken by the authors.

At some date in mid-1845, Maffre published his arrangements of John Crispo's *Notes of the Forest; or, Eastern Township Melodies*, a set of music comprising two sets of quadrilles, six waltzes, and five marches. There are no known copies of this work. It was dedicated to the Governor General Sir Charles Theophilus Metcalfe, indicating that Maffre was familiar with his third Governor General. Prior to its publication, Maffre sought subscribers by placing a series of advertisements in the *Montreal Gazette* and *Montreal Transcript* between December 1844 and March 1845. We don't know what happened past April because the *Transcript* issues from April 1845 to May 1846 are missing.

Composer John Crispo emigrated from England to Canada with his parents, two brothers, and three sisters. Their father left his career as a Lieutenant in the British Royal Navy and, in July 1835, the family started working a small Land Grant in Warwick, Quebec. In 1837, the Crispos moved to a larger farm in Compton Township, about 10 miles from Sherbrooke. They found life in the bush to be dangerous and challenging but made it tolerable with music. In the evenings and at parties, the father and his three boys performed pieces by "celebrated composers," especially Mozart. John Crispo composed *Notes of the Forest; or, Eastern Township Melodies* during the five years the family lived in Compton. In April 1843, the Crispos quit farming and moved to Montreal where John and an unnamed friend gave weekly lectures on "The Charms of Music" to family members. John died suddenly in July 11, 1847 of typhus he contracted while helping Irish emigrants. When the family quit farming, John's sister Elizabeth returned to England to live with a maternal uncle and his wife. On April 17, 1845, Elizabeth Crispo married in London to Henry Laird Cox, a naval surveyor on the *HMS Fearless*. There are miniature paintings of Elizabeth and her husband by William Egley in the National Maritime Museum, Greenwich. In 1850, Elizabeth published her 80-page "Reminiscences of Canadian Life" and her brother John's 8-page "The Charms of Music" in *The Christian Treasury* (see excerpts of both in the Perfect Knowledge chapter).

The Montreal Transcript
Tuesday, January 7, 1845

PROSPECTUS.

WILL be PUBLISHED shortly, the first MUSICAL WORK ever printed in Canada, to be entitled

Notes of the Forest;
OR,
EASTERN TOWNSHIP MELODIES;

being a collection of (original) AIRS, set of Quadrilles, Waltzes and Marches; composed by J. CRISPO, and arranged for the Piano Forte, by Mr. Maffre, Professor of Music; to be dedicated (by permission) to—His Excellency Sir C. T. Metcalfe, Bart., G C B., Governor General, of British North America, &c. &c. &c.

The WORK will contain two sets of Quadrilles, six Waltzes and five Marches; and will be published at 5s. [*$0.60*], in neat coloured stiff covers; and about 8s. 6d. [*$1.02*] or 10 s. [*$1.20*], if half bound, or bound in cloth, with gilt lettering on the outside.

The ad for *Notes of the Forest* describes it as "the first musical work ever printed in Canada." No matter how you parse it, this statement is not true. In 1981, scholar Maria Calderisi listed all of the known printed music in Canada that was published before 1867. Leaving aside the problem that Crispo's *Notes of the Forest* is not on her list and considering only sheet music and not the music published in newspapers or magazines, the first sheet music was published in 1833 (Table 8.4), twelve years before *Notes of the Forest*. Even though the publisher is unknown, it is reasonable to propose that it would have been John Lovell of Montreal, whose business was thriving at this time.

Table 8.4: Earliest Sheet Music Printed in Canada

Sheet music title	Composer	Year	Publisher
Caroline	Anonymous "for Mrs. L. Gosselin"	1833	Leclère & Jones, Montreal
The Merry Bells of England	J. F. Lehmann, Ottawa	1840	Lovell, Montreal
Le dépit amoureaux	Charles Sauvageau	1840	Aubin & Rowen, Quebec City
Deux valses	Charles Sauvageau	1840	Aubin & Rowen, Quebec City
Chant canadien	Charles Sauvageau	1840	Aubin & Rowen, Quebec City
Troix marches canadiennes	Charles Sauvageau	1840	Aubin & Rowen, Quebec City
Notes of the Forest	John Crispo & Joseph Maffre	1845	Canada

All of these except *Notes of the Forest* are listed in Calderisi's *Music Publishing in the Canadas, 1800-1867*.

On March 19, Maffre played the pianoforte and conducted the instrumental music for a Grand Concert of Sacred Music, given at St. Paul's Church. He conducted the 93rd Highland Regiment Band. Mr. Simon Fax led the choir and was "assisted by the principal singers of the city."

On July 7, there was an ad by Miss St. Clair to teach polka dancing in a few lessons during her short stay in Montreal. She asks that correspondence be sent to "Mr. Maffre, Professor of Music, Craig-Street, near St. Denis-Street; or, Miss St. Clair, Quebec Hotel, adjoining Rasco's." She was the third professional female dance or music instructor that Maffre helped promote in Montreal.

1846

On October 6, 1846, "Mr. Maffre's splendid quadrille band" was engaged for the Independent Order of Odd Fellows Annual Soiree. This appears to have been their first Soiree and was held in New Market Hall (Figure 8.13), which had been recently completed. The promenade concert included Mr. Davis playing his new Boehm flute, Mr. Labelle playing the piano, and then Miss Livingston and Mr. Anderson singing a glee. Maffre's Quadrille Band concluded the event with dancing. Prior to the event, the *Transcript* wrote, "Mr. Maffre's splendid quadrille band has been engaged." In the review after the event, the *Transcript* wrote, "Then came singing, now solos, now duets, and now good lively glees, varied by the harmonious roarings of Mr. Maffre's famed band, who surrounded themselves, as often before, with an immortal halo of musical glory." After one adventurous couple began to waltz, everyone else joined in. "Henceforth the triumph was Maffre's, and nobly we understand he acquitted himself, playing with his band of heros to 'past four o'clock in the morning,' when exhausted nature and legs gave in."

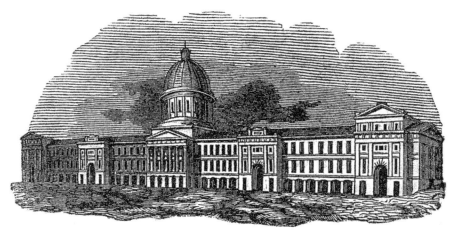

Figure 8.13: New Market Hall on the riverbank between St. Paul Street and Commisioners Street was completed in 1846. The central vestibule enclosed two grand staircases that led to a circular gallery on each floor. The ballroom could have been one of the two magnificent 230-feet long rooms on the third floor, or it could have been the smaller circular hall beneath the dome that was 48 feet in diameter. The dome was lighted by 16 windows and commanded the best views of the city. The building had a concrete base but was otherwise made of stone. The first floor housed separate markets for fruit and vegetables, pork, poultry and eggs, grain, and skin (or hide). The second floor housed the Butcher's Market in the center, the Clerk of the Market on one end, and the Police on the other end. From Bosworth's Hochelaga Depicta, 1846.

On December 26, Maffre led the first of three Grand Concerts of Vocal and Instrumental Music. It was given at Donegana's Hotel (Figure 8.14). Maffre's frequent associate, William Henry Warren, presided at the piano. According to the *Transcript*, the performers were local amateurs and the affair was under the patronage of the Earl of Cathcart who supported "their really deserving scheme." It also indicates that Maffre knew his fourth Governor General in a row. The review in the *Transcript* indicated it was poorly attended except for the

Figure 8.14: Donegana's Hotel. From Wikimedia Commons.

"elite of the city" and that "The band, under the leadership of Mr. Maffre, was all that could be desired." The *Transcript* urged more people to attend the second and third subscription concerts. This seems to be the first time that Maffre performed at Donegana's, an early hotel frequented by American tourists. Over the next three years, he would perform here more than any other venue in the city and, in fact, he performed his final concert at Donegana's.

1847

In 1847, Joseph Maffre once again moved his business – this time to 11 Champs de Mars.

On January 5, Maffre led a Military Band at a Charitable Soiree for the benefit of the Montreal Lying-In Hospital. It was given at Daley's Hotel in association with Donegana's Hotel. According to the *Transcript*, "The dancing was kept up until two o'clock with great spirit. The Quadrille was under the direction of Mr. Joseph Maffre, and it had a most potent charm on the trippers of the light fantastic toe. In fact, the music was excellent."

On February 1, Maffre led the second of the Grand Concerts of Vocal and Instrumental Music, this time in the Odd Fellows' Hall on Great St. James Street. "After the concert, Mr. Maffre's full Quadrille Band will be in attendance." In touting the event, the *Transcript* wrote, "Mr. Maffre's second Concert of Vocal and Instrumental Music takes place on Monday evening. The Concert is under the immediate patronage of the Earl of Cathcart. Mr. Maffre's abilities are too well known, and appreciated, to doubt his having an overflowing house, more especially, as the proceeds, after deducting expenses, are to be applied to charitable purposes." It was one of Cathcart's last public functions. He had resigned two days earlier on January 30th. Lord Elgin arrived ten days later.

On February 11, Maffre's Quadrille Band performed at the Annual Soiree of the Mechanics' Institute of Montreal. At least 2,500 people attended the event at the Bonsecours Market including the Earl of Elgin (James Bruce), the new Governor General. After a short speech of introduction, Miss Livingston sang. Next, Mr. Anderson and his Glee Party sang. Then, Elgin gave a short speech and examined the machinery. As soon as the Quadrilles began, the Governor General retired. The bands of the Rifle Brigade and the Light Infantry were also in attendance. The music didn't stop until 5 a.m.

On February 25, the performance of February 11th was repeated. The Mechanics' Institute was induced to leave their decorations so there could be a Grand Soiree in aid of the funds for the relief of the suffering poor of Ireland and Scotland. This is the first hint that the Irish Potato Famine of 1847 had begun. Over the next decade, nearly 2 million destitute Irish citizens would immigrate to all continents. Mr. Tate opened the assembly of over 1000 people by speaking on the issue. Mr. Anderson and his Glee Party sang. Mr. Cordae spoke on this issue. Miss Livingston and Mr. Anderson sang a duet. There were other speeches followed by refreshments from Mr. Keilor. From half past 11 until the early morning, "The band of the Rifle Brigade, the Light Infantry Band, Mr. Maffre's Quadrille Band, were in attendance" and "everything passed off with the greatest harmony."

On February 25, 1847, Mary Anne Maffre, the youngest daughter of Mr. Joseph Maffre, married Mr. Thomas Buckley in Montreal. We found a notice that Thomas Buckley, age 36, "late of Montreal" died in New Orleans on September 30, 1847; he may have been her husband.

On March 8, Montrealers celebrated St. David, the patron saint of Britain, for the first time. The ball and supper took place at Mayo & Flagg's Exchange. About the dancing, the *Transcript* wrote, "Maffre's band appeared really inspired by the graces their music brought into action, and, with little intermission, kept the whole in motion till many hours "ayont the twal'."

On April 6, the second Elgin Assembly was another reason for a dance. This one took place at Hall's Ottawa Hotel on Great St. James Street. This hotel was built in 1831 and could accommodate forty guests. Torrential rain lowered the attendance to only 80 ladies and gentlemen but Maffre's Band kept them dancing until 5 a.m. "in their customary correct and excellent manner."

In November, Miss Maffre advertised in *La Minerve* and the *Montreal Transcript* that she had formed a Dancing Academy for the instruction of young ladies and gentlemen. Requests were to be made at her residence of 77 Rousseau Street, near Dalhousie Square. This address was probably transcribed incorrectly and was more likely 11 Rousseau, her father's address. Her first year must have been successful. She held two Dancing Balls for her pupils in February and March 1848.

"Miss Maffre" was most likely to be Charlotte. It is possible to eliminate two daughters because they were already married in November 1847. Maria Maffre married William Tate two years earlier and would be Mrs. Tate. Mary Anne Maffre married Thomas Buckley, was widowed, and would be Mrs. Buckley. There is no information about Ann Thomas after April 1842. Perhaps she married a soldier and sailed back to England. On the other hand, there is evidence that Charlotte stayed close to the family in Montreal. Charlotte was unmarried in 1845 when she witnessed her sister Maria's wedding as "Charlotte Maffre" but she was married as "Charlotte McDonnell" on July 31, 1850 when she sponsored the baptism of her sister Maria's daughter Lucy. Charlotte's marriage to George McDonnell in 1849 or 1850 would provide an explanation for the absence of the Dancing Academy in the newspapers of 1849 and 1850. It should also be noted that family historian Will Fairbairn wrote that Charlotte died in 1849 and that Henry was a dance master, information he may have obtained from his Aunt Maria Tate. We believe Fairbairn (or Maria) confused Charlotte's and Henry's lives. Charlotte was the dance mistress and Henry died in 1848.

In November 1847, Maffre published *The Original Canadian Quadrilles* (Figure 1.1). Inside, the set is called 'Canadien Quadrilles' but none of the five pieces has an individual name. Each quadrille has the words 'Aria Nativa' meaning 'based on a native air.' From listening to the pieces, we have surmised that the fourth quadrille is based on *À la Claire Fontaine* and the fifth on *Vive le Canadienne*. In Maffre's advertisement for the work in the *Montreal Transcript*, he wrote "These quadrilles are founded on old Voyageur Airs that have enjoyed an extensive popularity in Manuscript, amongst our resident population, and have been universally admired by all strangers visiting our city. They are beautifully got up, with a characteristic title page."

The *Encyclopedia of Music in Canada* indicates that *The Original Canadian Quadrilles* is perhaps the most Canadian of all compositions because its cover page features a beaver surrounded by maple leaves. It was the first piece of Canadian music adorned with either of those icons. The maple leaf was the official emblem of French Canada since 1834. The beaver had been an emblem since the early 1600's but was in the Montreal coat of arms only since 1832. The work was dedicated to the Countess of Elgin, formerly Lady Mary Lambton, whom Joseph had met when she traveled to Montreal with her parents on the *H.M.S. Hastings* in 1838. She returned to Montreal in 1847 as wife of the Earl of Elgin (1811-1863), who served as Governor General of Canada between 1847 and 1854. A copy of this piece is in the collections of the National Library of Canada, U.S. Library of Congress, and Johns Hopkins University Library.

The publisher of *The Original Canadian Quadrilles* was J. W. Herbert of Montreal (active from the 1830's to 1861) and the printer was Firth & Hall of New York. Just two years later this publishing company (as Firth, Pond, & Co.) signed the World's first publishing contract with Stephen Collins Foster, the first person to earn his living solely from his compositions. Prior to 1849, composers earned very little money from their works. Foster changed that with his enormously popular minstrel-inspired music and lyrics.

Endicott, the New York City lithograph company, created the sheet music cover image of the beaver and maple leaves for *The Original Canadian Quadrilles*. Endicott was among the most successful lithographers of its time. It published its own line of framing prints as well as taking on a wide range of commercial subjects. It was producing images for Firth & Hall as early as 1836. Although the beaver and maple leaf image is not signed, it seems likely that the artist was Frederick Swinton because he was at Endicott from 1842 to 1851 and is known for his calm style, proficiency with shading, and ability to draw animals, fossils, and scientific imagery.

1848

On January 1, son Henry Maffre died of consumption at age 24. Consumption is a wasting disease now called pulmonary tuberculosis. It is caused by a bacterium that lives in lung nodules (originally called tubercles). This disease is spread by coughing and was common in the 1800's when large numbers of people were living in close quarters in cities. Henry was Joseph and Lucy's second child to die. Henry had been one of the musicians in Maffre's Quadrille Band and was a co-signer of the 1843 Petition. In the news entry, Henry is listed as "son of Mr. J. E. Maffre", indicating that Joseph Sr.'s middle name started with an E.

On February 1, Miss Maffre sponsored the first Ball for her pupils. It took place in the Odd Fellows' Hall on St. Gabriel Street. Odd Fellows' Hall opened in 1832. Its second floor ballroom was 34 feet wide by 65 feet long with 15-foot ceilings. The building's first floor housed shops and the third floor housed the Odd Fellows meeting rooms. Miss Maffre's confectioner was Mr. D. W. Crerar who often advertised he could give dancing instruction in the newspaper. Even though it wasn't mentioned in the newspaper, Maffre's Quadrille Band was surely in attendance.

On February 10, the Independent Order of Odd Fellows (I.O.O.F.) held their annual celebration. It appears to have been their second and over 400 people were present at Donegana's Hotel. The long review of the event in the *Transcript* ends with a description of the dancing: "soon a hundred feet tripped merrily over the floor, to the exhilarating sounds of Mr. Maffre's Quadrille Band." The second review of the event in the *Gazette* includes a description of the dancing: "At opposite ends of the room were erected two orchestras, occupied respectively by Maffre's Quadrille band, and the band of the Montreal Light Infantry, both of which acquitted themselves to admiration."

On February 15, the Mechanics' Institute held their annual festival in the Bonsecours Market, where "the Halls will be thoroughly cleansed and heated in every part." Concerning Maffre, the *Transcript* wrote, "About midnight the hall was cleared for dancing, and to the music of Maffre's quadrille band, a thousand couples gaily tripped in giddy mazes through the length of the room in alternate reels and waltzes, till daylight dissolved the magic of the scene." The *Gazette* painted a similar scene, "two thousand feet were speedily in motion to the strains of Maffre's Band. The fun now "grew fast and furious." Dancing was kept up till a late, we should rather say early, hour, with right good spirit. People seemed half daft with the "Polka" and the jolly "Sir Roger.""

On March 17, Miss Maffre sponsored the second and final Ball for her pupils. Again, it took place in the Odd Fellows' Hall on St. Gabriel Street. This time, coffee and tea were included in the price of the ticket and it was clearly stated that, "Mr. Maffre's full Quadrille Band will attend."

On May 4, Maffre's Quadrille Band and the Band of the 77th Regiment played at the Annual Soiree in aid of the funds of the University Laying-In Hospital, held at Donegana's Hotel. It was patronized by the Countess of Elgin, wife of the Governor General. Maffre had dedicated his *Canadian Quadrilles* to her six months earlier.

Maffre's Career in Montreal

Now that we have gathered the particularities of Maffre's career through his numerous advertisements, compositions, and letters (see the "Perfect Knowledge" chapter), his career can serve as a case study for the life of a mid-nineteenth century musician living in Montreal. After Maffre decided to settle in Montreal in 1841, all of his performances took place in Montreal. The demand for music and musical instruction in this city bustling with international commerce probably arose because it was the capital (1844-1849) during most of the years he lived there. Unlike his career in Leicester, however, there is no database of other musicians against which he can be compared. This is mostly because there were vastly fewer musicians in Montreal, making it hard to draw generalizations, but also because detailed information about the other musicians is minimally available.

One striking observation about his public Montreal performances (Table 8.5) is that he was almost exclusively operating as Leader of the 71st Regiment Band in his first two very active years of 1842 and 1843. The 71st Band provided the orchestral backup to a variety of visiting musicians. When the 71st left Montreal for the West Indies in October 1843, Maffre had to develop a new band but before he did that he wrote a petition to the military in an attempt to prevent any of the other Regiment Band Leaders from following in his footsteps.

Table 8.5: Maffre's Advertised Performances While Living in Montreal

Year	Event	Montreal Venue	Maffre's Roles
1842	Miss Sloman's Soiree Musicale	Rasco's Hotel	Band Leader
1842	Lady Bagot's private party	Lady Bagot's party	Band Leader of the 71st and 43rd Regiments
1842	The Lion, The Monster (Feats of Strength, etc)	Theatre Royal	Band Leader of the 71st
1842	The Lion, The Monster (Feats of Strength, etc)	Theatre Royal	Band Leader of the 71st
1842	Nagel and Nouritt's Grand Concert	Theatre Royal	Band Leader of the 71st
1842	De Goni and Knoop's First Concert	Arcade Hotel Saloon	Band Leader of the 71st
1842	De Goni and Knoop's Second Concert	Rasco's Hotel	Band Leader of the 71st
1842	De Goni and Knoop's Third Concert	Theatre Royal	Band Leader of the 71st
1842	St. Andrew's Society Celebration	Mack's Hotel	Band Leader of the 71st
1842	De Goni and Knoop's Farewell Concert	Theatre Royal	Band Leader of the 71st
1842	Gentlemen Garrison Amateurs	Theatre Royal	Band Leader of the 71st
1843	71st Regiment Ball	Montreal	Band Leader of the 71st; Clarinetist
1843	Mr. Fax's Grand Concert of Vocal & Instrum. for Benefit of the Montreal General Hospital	Rasco's Hotel	Band Leader of the 71st
1843	St. Patrick's Day Parade	Montreal	Band Leader of the 71st
1843	Mr. Wall, The Blind Harper's Concert	Rasco's Hotel	Band Leader of the 71st
1843	St. Jean Baptiste Day Mass	Notre Dame Cathedral	Band Leader of the 71st
1843	St. Jean Baptiste Day Parade	Notre Dame Street	Band Leader of the 71st
1843	Mrs. Bailey's Soiree Musicale	Rasco's Hotel	Band Leader of the 71st
1843	Montreal Choral Society's Grand Concert	St Ann's Market	Leader of the Orchestra
1843	Montreal Choral Society's Grand Concert [2nd]	St Gabriel's Church	Leader of the Orchestra
1844	St. Patrick's Parade	Recollet Church to Notre Dame Cathedral	Band Leader of the St. Patrick's Amateur Band and 89th Regt.
1844	Montreal Choral Society's Grand Concert [3rd]	St Gabriel's Church	Leader of the Orchestra
1844	Musical and Dramatic Entertainment for the Benefit of Mr. Maffre	Theatre Royal	Leader of the Orchestra
1845	Concert of Sacred Music	St Paul's Church	Conductor; Pianist
1845	Concert Under the Patronage of His Honor the Mayor	New Oddfellows Hall	Leader of the Orchestra; Violinist
1846	IOOF Public Soiree	New Market Hall	Quadrille Band Leader

Year	Event	Venue	Role
1846	Mr. Maffre's Grand Concert of Vocal & Instrumental, First Season Subscription	Donegana's Hotel	Orchestra Leader; Promoter
1847	Charitable Soiree to Benefit the Montreal Lying-In Hospital	Daley's Hotel	Band Leader; Promoter
1847	Mr. Maffre's Grand Concert of Vocal & Instrumental, Second Season Subscription	Odd Fellows' Hall	Orchestra Leader; Promoter Quadrille Band Leader;
1847	Mechanics' Institute Festival and Exhibition	Mechanics' Institute	Quadrille Band Leader
1847	Grand Soiree to Benefit the Poor of Ireland and Scotland	Mechanics' Institute	Quadrille Band Leader
1847	St. David's Ball & Supper	Mayo & Flagg's Exchange	Quadrille Band Leader
1847	Second Elgin Assembly	Hall's Ottawa Hotel	Quadrille Band Leader
1848	Miss Maffre's Dancing Academy First Annual Ball	Odd Fellows' Hall	Quadrille Band Leader
1848	Celebration of the IOOF	Odd Fellows' Hall	Quadrille Band Leader
1848	Mechanics' Institute Festival and Exhibition	Montreal Mechanics' Institute	Quadrille Band Leader
1848	Miss Maffre's Dancing Academy Second & Final Ball	Odd Fellows' Hall	Quadrille Band Leader
1848	Annual Soiree to Benefit the Montreal Laying-In Hospital	Donegana's Hotel	Quadrille Band Leader
1849	Montreal Musical Society's Grand Concert of Vocal and Instrumental Music	Donegana's Hotel	One of 12 Professor Performers
1849	Mechanics' Institute Grand Annual Festival	Bonsecours Market	Quadrille Band Leader
1849	Annual Soiree to Benefit the University Laying In Hospital	Donegana's Hotel	Quadrille Band Leader
1849	Mr. Maffre's Montreal Professional Musical Society's Concert of Vocal & Instrum. Music	Donegana's Hotel	Quadrille Band Leader; Promoter

These representative concerts were taken from advertisements reproduced in the "Perfect Knowledge" chapter. They are not a complete set of his concerts because there are many issues, and even entire years, of missing Montreal newspapers. IOOF is the International Order of Odd Fellows.

From 1844 to 1846, Maffre was most often listed as Leader of the Orchestra. We don't know the names of the musicians but he may have handpicked some of them from among his students or from among the people who joined the Montreal Musical and Choral Society. He created that organization in 1841 but it was soon defunct. There may not have been a sufficient number of amateur instrumentalists because, in 1843, he formed the Montreal Choral Society, which was active until at least January 1845. The band during these years probably consisted of his son, Joseph Maffre Jr., and an ever-changing group of amateur and professional musicians.

From 1847 until 1849, the focus was on Maffre's Quadrille Band. This Band had serious chops and was capable of performing from 8 p.m. until 6 a.m. The popularity of this band was unmatched according to the numerous accolades piled upon by the press.

Maffre favored five venues: Theatre Royal (7 times); Rasco's Hotel (5); Odd Fellows' Hall (5); Donegana's Hotel (4); and the Mechanics' Institute (3). These venues could accommodate 100 to 200 paying customers. The events at the Odd Fellow's Hall and Mechanics' Institute took place after these organizations built or renovated their building so they would have been nicely outfitted. In addition, the reviews seem to suggest that Maffre even had a hand in planning several newly inaugurated Annual Soirees. He gave only one performance at four other hotels: Arcade Hotel; Daley's Hotel; Hall's Ottawa Hotel; and Mack's Hotel. It has not been possible to learn much about these hotels suggesting they were smaller or at the end of their useful lives.

Finally, an analysis of highest ticket prices (Table 8.6) shows that Maffre's performances with the 71st Band in 1842 and 1843 averaged 69 and 40 cents. After the 71st Regiment left Montreal, he led orchestral concerts for three years (1844-1846) offering the top ticket price of only 30 cents. By 1847, nearly all his performances involved Maffre's popular Quadrille Band and he was drawing an average 58 cents as the highest ticket price. Even though leading an orchestra was prestigious, he earned more money with his Quadrille Band.

Table 8.6: Maffre's Montreal Ticket Prices

Year	Average Price (pence)	Price for the Most Expensive Ticket
1842	69	$1, $1, $1, $1, 2s6d, 3s, 5s, 5s, 5s, 5s, 5s, 5s
1843	40	1s3d, 1s3d, 2s6d, 5s, 5s, 5s
1844-1846	30	1s2d, 1s3d, 2s6d, 2.5s, 5s
1847-1849	58	5s, 5s, 3s6d, 5s, 6s3d, 2s6d, 6s3d

There were 12 pence (d) in a shilling (s) and 20 shillings in a pound to give 240 pennies in a pound. Since there are 100 pennies in $1, there are 8s4d in $1.

Bank of Montreal, Penny Bank Token (33 mm), 1842. The obverse shows the bank building. The reverse shows a belt encircling the Montreal Coat of Arms. The four fields inside the belt include a thistle for Scotland, a rose for England, clover for Ireland, and a beaver for Canada..

Bank of Upper Canada, Half Penny (23 mm) and Penny (32 mm), both Bank Tokens 1850. The obverse shows Saint George slaying a dragon. The reverse shows a crown and two entwined cornucopia surrounding three overlapped military symbols: a sword for the army, an anchor for the navy, and a hatchet for the first nations warriors. All three coins are from the Robert Mikasen Collection.

Figure 9.1: Sir Hew Hamilton Dalrymple, 1861, taken at the Notman Studio, Montreal. McCord Museum I-1808.1.

9

CHOLERA IN THE CITY

Joseph and Lucy Maffre died in the 1849 cholera epidemic that began among the troops occupying the city. Joseph probably contracted cholera when he visited the 19th or 71st Regiments during the month after what would turn out to be his final concert in June 1849. These two Regiments were garrisoned in the city because a mob had burned down the Parliament House after Lord Elgin assented to the Rebellion Losses Bill. The roots for that Bill date back to the reason Maffre and the 71st Regiment came to Canada in the first place – the 1837 and 1838 Rebellions.

The Military in the City of Montreal in 1849

One way to understand how much the British Regulars affected the everyday life of Montreal between 1832 and 1854 is to summarize the number of troops quartered in the city. Keep in mind that there were many more troops stationed within a day or two, such as in St. Johns (now St. Jean sur Richelieu). The number of troops in the city increased from 500 to 2000 within one year after the 1837 Rebellion (Figure 9.2). This first wave of troops was primarily from the 1st, 24th, 32nd, and 83rd Regiments. By 1842, the number of troops had reached a maximum of just over 3,000. They were primarily from the 23rd, 74th, 85th, and Royal Canadian Rifle Regiments. Three thousand is quite a large number considering that the population of Montreal was about 40,000 in 1842. From this peak, the number of troops dropped to 1,500 in 1845 and remained constant until 1853. The population was rising rapidly and was about 50,000 in 1850. Throughout the entire period, no Regiment was in the city for more than two years at a time with the exception of the approximately 80 troops from the Royal Artillery who stood guard at government buildings. By 1855, the military presence was reduced to only a couple hundred troops, primarily the Royal Canadian Rifle Regiment.

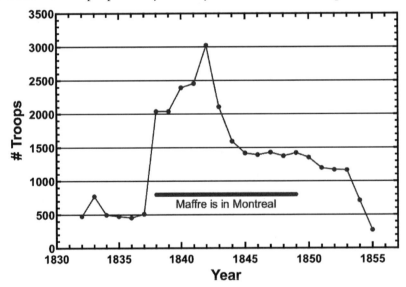

Figure 9.2: Number of troops serving in Montreal, 1832-1855, on January 1 of each year from Appendix B of Kyte Senior's British Regulars. *Illustration by Mark Griep.*

The impact of these young, unattached men on the city is still felt today. As Robert Jones argued in his *History of Agriculture in Ontario*, demand from these soldiers created the success of

Molson's and many other breweries and distilleries. Elinor Kyte Senior goes further in her *British Regulars in Montreal* by featuring a section titled "The Cultural Dimensions of the Garrison" in which she describes their social activities, sports, religious activities, and fraternal and cultural relationships with the townspeople, although she does begin with tales of drunken soldiers.

One of the most dramatic events in early Canadian history was burning of the Parliament House after Lord Elgin approved the Rebellion Losses Bill. There were actually two bills that dealt with compensation for the economic harm brought on by the 1837 and 1838 Rebellions. In June 1840, the first commission awarded almost £50,000 to Loyalists whose property was damaged or whose goods were pillaged by any combination of military authorities, the insurgents, or individuals who took advantage of the lawlessness of the moment. By December 1845, there were 2,176 additional claims, nearly all from French Canadians. Therefore, a second commission was formed that found many of the claims to be legitimate. However, no one was reimbursed while a dozen of those claims were debated for years in Legislative Council and discussed at length in the press. The contentious claims were put forward by former Patriote leaders, some of whom had confessed to their roles and been exiled for several years as a result. Several claimed their property had been just as damaged during the altercation but a few submitted claims for lost economic productivity while they were in exile. The argument in their favor was that Lord Durham's proclamation had absolved them of responsibility and, ultimately, their convictions were declared illegal.

Parliament House was located on William Street between McGill Street and St. Peter Street (Figure 9.3). When Montreal became the Provincial capital in 1844, it precipitated the need for a Parliamentary meeting place. St. Ann's Market (Figure 8.8) was chosen because it was the largest building. After renovation, the second floor west wing was capable of holding about 500 people. The wing was officially called the Chamber of Legislative Assembly. The building served its function for five years until it was burned down in April 1849.

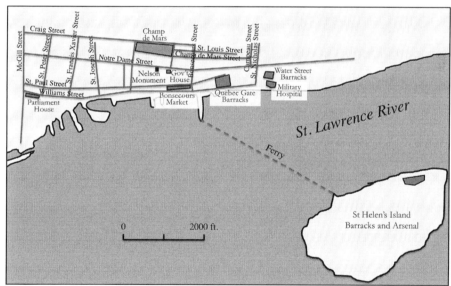

Figure 9.3: Montreal's major buildings and streets in 1849. This map is based on the "Topographical and Pictorial Map of Montreal" by James Cane, 1846. The Water Street Barracks was a 1-mile march from Parliament House. Illustration by Mark Griep.

After four years of debate, the Legislative Council passed the Rebellion Losses Bill on March 15, 1849. Most officials did not expect it to be approved for payment. Instead, it was widely expected that Governor General Lord Elgin would forward this issue to Earl Grey for payment by the Empire. At this time, Grey was Secretary of State for War and Colonies. Therefore, it is perplexing that Elgin did nothing with the bill for six weeks during which time tensions began to rise. The National Film Board of Canada produced a 29-minute film titled *Lord Elgin: Voice of the People* (1959; Julian Biggs director) that proposes he waited because he did not want to upset his wife, the former Mary Louisa Lambton, in her final month of a troublesome pregnancy. What is known is that Lord Elgin rode to the Parliament House late on April 25 without alerting the military or police and then gave assent to thirty bills, including the Rebellion Losses Bill. On his carriage ride home, Elgin was cheered and hissed. Then, the angry members of the crowd began pelting him with eggs and sticks and stones. Within the next few hours, a mob assembled and set fire to Parliament House. One hundred troops of the 19th Regiment were called in from the Water Street Barracks to restore order. They arrived just as the building was fully ablaze. They set about preventing the crowd from getting too close to the conflagration, helped the fire fighters deal with the blaze, and attempted to prevent the fire from spreading to adjacent buildings. Soon, the remainder of the 19th was called in to help.

The 19th Regiment had arrived in the city of Montreal one year earlier, in May 1848, after spending six years in Barbados. Its 580 troops were quartered in the Water Street Barracks. Two years earlier, in 1846, the Army spent nearly £1200 converting a commercial building into these barracks. The low ceilings and poor latrines were perennial problems as indicated by a terse March 8, 1849 report that states "effluvia from the privies offensive in summer."

Three days after the Bill passed and Parliament burned, troops from the 71st Regiment arrived from St. Johns. They were quartered in Bonsecours Market, where mobs of people had been congregating for the past few days. Bonsecours was very hurriedly converted into a barracks and had an insufficient number of privies and cooking facilities. Five days after the Bill and fire, Elgin returned to the city to receive a vote of confidence from the Assembly. This time, he was escorted by 63 troops from the Queen's Light Dragoons to Government House, where Sir Hew Dalrymple (Figure 9.1) and the popular 71st Highland Light Infantry were stationed. After his business was completed, Elgin was once again showered with stones. Dalrymple ordered the 71st to charge the rioters but the crowd gently fell back and cheered the soldiers. This defused the tension temporarily but then some of the crowd caught up with Elgin and began pelting his entourage with stones again. Elgin and the others in the carriage were hit, his carriage was badly damaged and the Dragoons suffered numerous injuries. Even though the horses took the brunt of it, Elgin did not return to the city for the next four months.

With the presence of the 71st Regiment in Bonsecours Market, the excitement died down and April and May were peaceful in the city. In fact, on May 4, for the third year in a row, Maffre's Quadrille Band and the Band of the 77th Regiment performed at the Annual Soiree in aid of the funds of the University Laying-In Hospital, held at Donegana's Hotel. For the second year in a row, the Countess of Elgin patronized the event although it is not clear whether she actually attended the performance. After all, she was still recovering from the troublesome birth of her first child.

Maffre's Musical Activities in 1849

In the midst of considerable political unrest, Maffre and the other musicians continued to perform and even to innovate. On February 13, the Governor General Lord Elgin sponsored the Annual Festival at Bonsecours Market of the Mechanics Institute during which the country's latest technology was put on display. In attendance were the 19th Regiment Band, the Montreal Light Infantry Band, and Maffre's Quadrille Band.

On March 20, the newly formed Musical Society of Montreal offered their first Grand Concert of Vocal and Instrumental Music at Donegana's Hotel. This Society was composed of a dozen music professors of which the two most prominent were William Henry Warren and Joseph Maffre Sr. Warren was the Society's President. The Society's second concert was led by Maffre indicating that he was in charge of their public performances. From 1841 to 1851, Warren taught organ, piano, harp, guitar, violin, cello, and voice in addition to performing and editing the music section of the *Literary Garland*. From 1841 until his death in 1849, Maffre taught piano, organ, violin, viola, cello, flute, clarinet, oboe, and voice. Most of the Society's other members were well known. John Follenus taught music from 1841 until 1864 in the High School Department of McGill College. Leonard Eglauch taught piano from the 1840s to the 1860s. John-Chrystosome Brauneis Jr. taught piano, harp, guitar, and voice in Montreal from 1833 until his death in 1871. For many years, Eglauch and Brauneis accompanied visiting performers as dual pianists. Frederick Veit was a music teacher from 1843 until 1851. F. Seebold (piano) and Edward Hird (piano) were in Montreal from 1848 to 1851 and Mr. Arthurson was active in 1848 and 1849. Carlo (or Charles) Guaita was born in Spain but married in Montreal to Mary Bull Mackett in 1847. Guaita is a portrait painter according to the city directories of 1848 and 1849. Antoine Zeigler is in the 1849 Montreal City Directory but no occupation is given.

On June 15, Maffre's final concert took place "under the patronage of Sir Hew Dalrymple" and included a performance by a Mr. Smyth. Dalrymple was the colonel for the 71st Regiment and Mr. Smyth might very well have been James Smyth who became Bandmaster for the 19th Regiment in 1841 at age 23. James joined the 19th band when he was a boy. Maffre undoubtedly visited Dalrymple and Smyth in their Barracks in the weeks prior to the performance. One suspects he intended to use the power of music to unify the citizens and to entertain the troops for their hard work.

The Montreal Gazette
Friday, June 15, 1849, p. 2

Mr. Maffre's Concert comes off to-night, at Donegana's, under the patronage of Sir Hew Dalrymple. The following is the Programme:—
PART I.
1.—Overture, "Zampa" ....Herold
2.—Concerto—Flute—(Lindenberg)
3.—Glee
4.—Oboe—Solo ....Mr Maffre, jr.
5.—The Drum Polka, in which will be introduced 20 Drums. This Polka, lately performed by Jullien's celebrated band in London, will be played from the author's Score, including all the original effects.
PART II.
1.—Overture,...Mr. Maffre
2.—Solo—On Irish and Scotch Melodies—Violin.................................Mr. Maffre
3.—Glee
4.—The Sleigh Polka—Written for "The Montreal Sleigh Club,"..........Mr. Smyth
5.—God Save the Queen,
    Tickets only 2s 6d. Doors open at Eight o'clock.

An earlier advertisement called this a Grand Concert of Vocal and Instrumental Music and said Maffre would lead the Montreal Professional Musical Society. This was probably the second performance by this Society. It must have also included the combined Bands of the 19th and 71st Regiments so that he could assemble an Orchestra of 50 musicians. The advertisement also indicated that, "After the Concert, an Excellent Quadrille Band will be in attendance for the amusement of the Company." Sadly, there was no review of the important concert.

The playbill for Maffre's final concert opened with what might have been a familiar standard, the Overture from *Zampa* Opera Comique (1831) by Louis Hérold. The overture probably took 30 minutes to perform. It was followed by a Flute Concerto and a Glee, each of which were probably 20 minutes. An Oboe Solo by his son Joseph Maffre Jr. was next. The finale of the first part was the new and flamboyant "Drum Polka" by Louis Jullien, the great showman of London. Jullien didn't publish this piece as sheet music until 1850 so Maffre must have used a manuscript copy. After the intermission, every concert program during the early 1800s led off with the most important piece of the evening. In this case, Maffre's performance was the feature. He chose to play an unnamed Overture and then a Violin Solo on Irish and Scotch melodies. After another glee, the band performed a Sleigh Polka written by Mr. Smyth. When the concert ended, the Quadrille Band probably played until the early hours of morning.

In late June 1849, a cholera epidemic broke out in Montreal. It was the second of the nine global cholera epidemics since 1832. This one began in Asia, spread to Canada, and then to Philadelphia and New York. Cholera is a water-borne disease that breaks out when wastewater mixes with drinking water. This bacterial infection of the small intestines leads to severe dehydration due to the symptoms of watery diarrhea and vomiting. If not treated within hours, the infected person has a 50% chance of dying. It was a mysterious disease in the 1800s and, even today, there are still no good vaccines against it. We now know the best plan of action is to boil water before drinking and to wash food before eating or cooking. The long-range solution to preventing cholera is to install water and wastewater treatment facilities. Montreal didn't have these facilities until the late 1800s.

The epidemic reached its peak in mid-July but may have emerged from the Water Street Barracks. Apparently, Lt.-Col. Charles Hay of the 19th wrote one of the earliest complaints about illness in late June: "My Regiment has suffered more from sickness in these barracks than at any time the last six years, which embraces the whole period the Regiment was in the West Indies." Then, he requested to move his troops out of the city because they were located where liquor was cheap and easily procured. At first, his request was denied but then suddenly granted on June 30th, at which time they moved to St. Helen's Island along with the 71st. There is no explanation why they were allowed to move out of the Barracks or why the Water Street Barracks were not used after 1850 but it is reasonable to suppose that cholera played a role in the decision. On July 16, the 71st Regiment returned to their quarters in St. Johns.

From late June until August 10 (Table 9.1), there were 483 cholera deaths of Montreal citizens and 21 cholera deaths among the troops garrisoned in the city. Since the total number of deaths during this period was 986, it meant cholera caused the death rate to nearly double.

Table 9.1: Montreal Cholera deaths in 1849

Week	Deaths
Prior to July 9	25
July 9 to July 16	97
July 17 to July 23	154
July 24 to July 30	136
July 31 to Aug 6	53
Aug 7 to Aug 10	18
Total Cholera Deaths	483

These statistics were assembled from several issues of the Montreal Transcript.

Lucy died on July 26 and Joseph died three days later. They died during the second deadliest week of the summer. Joseph's obituary in *La Minerve* says he was ill for only a few days before he died, which is consistent with the abruptness of their deaths from an infection. Seven months later, the *Leicester Chronicle* published an obituary that clearly states they died of cholera. It also states that, "Mr. Maffre was well known in Leicester as a clever musician," which is remarkable given that he left Leicester two decades earlier but was still fondly remembered.

> *Montreal Transcript*
> *August 2, 1849*
> The late Mr. Joseph Maffre, was formerly Band Master of the 19th Regt., and subsequently of the 71st. He was son of a French loyalist, and, when a child, was, upon the evacuation Toulon by the English in consequence of Napoleon's capture of one its principal outworks, taken by his parents to England.

> *Leicester Chronicle*
> *Saturday, March 2, 1850*
> **DEATHS.**
> At Montreal, Canada, on the 26th [*actually 29th*] of July, 1849, Mr. Joseph Maffre, formerly in the Duke of Rutland's band, and on the 30th [*actually 26th*], Mrs. Maffre, both deaths were from cholera. Mr. Maffre was well known in Leicester as a clever musician. He was the son of a French emigrant, formerly in the service of that nation but driven from his country in the Reign of Terror.

Lucy died at age 57 and her service was held at St. Gabriel's Presbyterian church. The witnesses on her burial record are John Fisher and George Douglas, neither of whom we've been able to identify. St. Gabriel's was located on Champs de Mars and would have been the closest Protestant church to their home on St. Louis Street.

Joseph was 56 when he died one month after his last performance. The obituary in the *Transcript* gave a surprising amount of his biography in two sentences but no hint about his career in Montreal. Apparently, the readers knew who he was. We do not know where his services were held except that it was not at St. Gabriel's or Notre Dame. It has not been possible to check the records at St. Patrick's Basilica.

According to the Mount Royal Cemetery records, Joseph and Lucy were buried in the "Papineau Avenue Cemetery", also known as the "New Burial Ground", which accepted burials from 1816 until 1869 and that existed until 1944. It was the city's second Protestant cemetery and was located at Garrison Street and Papineau Avenue, immediately adjacent to "The Military Cemetery" that operated during the same years. All of the city's older cemeteries were mostly forgotten after the opening of more modern cemeteries, such as the Mount Royal Cemetery in 1852. Over the decades, many of the headstones were broken and moved from their original locations. In 1902, the Imperial Order of Daughters of the Empire was founded to care for the city's neglected, military cemeteries. In 1912, a group of individuals vandalized many of the headstones, including the obelisk for General Benjamin D'Urban in the Papineau cemetery. He had been Supreme Commander of the Her Majesty's forces in British North America and had died a few weeks after Maffre during the 1849 cholera epidemic. In 1915, the city repaired some of the damaged headstones including D'Urban's obelisk. In 1942, the city purchased the burial grounds from the federal government and gave the funds to the Last Post Fund to begin planning for the transportation and rededication of the remains to Pointe Claire. In 1944, Sydney Ham compiled a list of 1,797 *military* burials at the Papineau cemetery based on records from the Court House, church records, and as many headstones as he could decipher [available as *Family History Library film 1643110*]. Since the Maffres are not on this list, it strongly suggests they were buried on the civilian side of the cemetery. In July 1944, the remains of 1,100 individuals from both cemeteries were re-interred in the Field of Honor at the Pointe Claire cemetery. The centerpiece of the Field of Honor is D'Urban's obelisk encircled by 54 headstones from Papineau. Three of the readable stones are for Lieutenant George Weir who died in 1837, Commissariat Conductor James Poole who died in 1845, and Captain John Hornby Phipps who died in 1848. Years later, the Papineau Avenue Cemetery location became an entry ramp for the Jacques Cartier Bridge.

Maffre's Personal Music Collection

Some of Joseph Maffre's personal music collection is housed in the Music Library of McGill University, Montreal. Two were works that he probably brought with him from England and the third was published after he came to Canada. It seems likely that his son Joseph Jr. is the one who donated this material to the Library because his handwriting is on them. During the 1800's, most libraries were collections that individuals had amassed and then donated to a library.

In 1960, Marvin Duchow gave a luncheon address during which he described the Canadian Music Libraries. He had this to say about the holdings of McGill University, where he was Dean of the Faculty of Music: "The accident of our Faculty's recent move to new quarters has brought to light an interesting accumulation of such 19th century material progressively acquired since the inception of the McGill Conservatory in 1904. Still uncatalogued, as previously noted, this material had long been hidden in musty basement storerooms...The earliest inscribed date noted is 1847. Superscribed we find what is presumably the owner's name, Joseph Maffre, and the place Montreal. It is, quite characteristically, a volume of violin duets, containing works by Mazas, Viotti, and others. Another volume, bearing the same owner's name and dated 1853 at Montreal, contains a collection of sacred music published in London in the year 1806. It contains works by C. P. E. Bach, Caldara, Mozart, Hasse, the Haydns, Pergolesi, and others. The supposition is that Maffre may have been a choral director as well as a violinist."

The McGill Library actually has three bound volumes with a Maffre name inscribed on them.

1. "Collection of Sacred Music from the Works of some of the Most Eminent Composers of Germany and Italy" included selections by C. P. E. Bach, Handel, Haydn, and Mozart. It was published in London in 1806 by C. I. Latrobe. This large volume is signed "Joseph Maffre, Montreal 1853" in Joseph Jr.'s handwriting.

2. "Collection Progressive, Six Duos Brillants pour deux Violons dédiés Aux Amateurs" was composed by Jacques Féréol Mazas and is his opus 40. The sheet is not dated but this piece was first published in 1834 by the Schott brothers of Brussels, London, Liepzig, Vienna, and Rotterdam. This small volume of three pieces is signed "Joseph Maffre Jr, 9 October 1847, Montreal." The cover of the bound volume is signed as "Duets, Violino Secondo, The Property Of, Joseph Maffre, 1862."

3. The third volume has two sets of sheet music. The first set is titled "Collection de tous les Duos concerta pour deux Violons." It was composed by Giovanni Battista Viotti and published by C. F. Peters in Liepzig. There is no date of publication. The cover page is signed "H[enry] Maffre Esquire, Montreal." Therefore, this set of sheet music pre-dates Henry's death on January 1, 1848. The writing on the title page says "Violino Primi" and "The property, Of Joseph Maffre, 1862." The second set of music is the same as number 2 above. Its cover page says "Joseph Maffre Jr, 1847, Montreal."

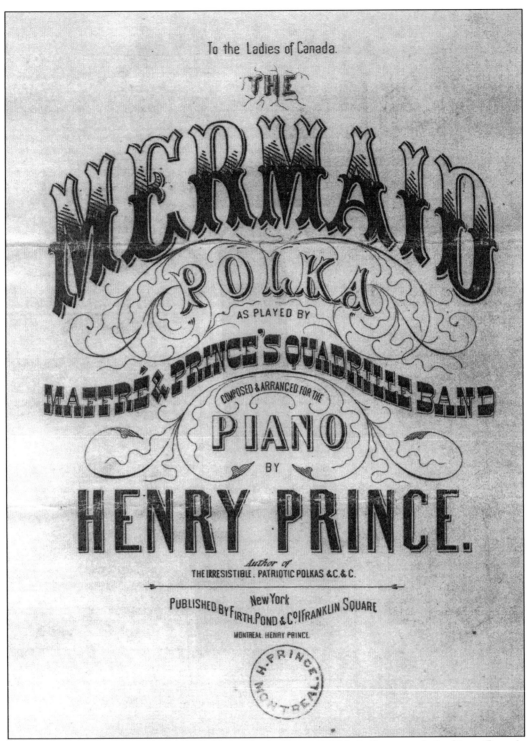

Figure 10.1: "The Mermaid Polka" Sheet Music Cover, 1855. Library and Archives Canada.

10
NOTES ON THE FIRM

The majority of Joseph and Lucy Maffre's children (Table 10.1) stayed in Quebec when they reached adulthood and several stayed in the family business. Eldest son, Joseph Jr., was the most successful at continuing the Maffre musical legacy and even passed it on to his son Leopold Alfred. Son Henry was also a musician but he died as a young man. Joseph and Lucy's younger son Alfred became a Professor of Music but we have not been able to trace his activities past the year he earned his musical degree. One of their daughters, probably Charlotte, taught dance but gave it up after her parents' sudden deaths. Charlotte married a pawnbroker and then died suddenly herself in Toronto a few years later. The fate of eldest daughter Ann is unknown whereas daughter Maria married a very successful businessman who ran the largest dry dock in Montreal. Maria's descendants sold the dry dock to the City of Montreal so it could widen the Lachine Canal. Mary Anne married a man who died shortly after they moved to New Orleans. Frederick and Francis became carpenters.

Table 10.1: Joseph and Lucy Maffre's Ten Children

Child	Birth Year	Marriage Age	Spouse's Name	Death Year	Death Age
Ann Thomas	1813	?	?	after 1842	?
Francis	1815	--	--	1815	3
Joseph Ludwig	1817	25	Julie Perrault		
		40	Jeanne Carruthers		
		48	Theresa Leseuer	1881	64
Charlotte	1820	about 29	George McDonnell	1853	33
Maria	1822	24	William Tate	1907	86
Henry	1823	--	--	1848	24
Frederick	about 1824	about 24	Mary Mullen	about 1848	?
Mary Anne	1826	21	Thomas Buckley	after 1851	?
Alfred	about 1828	?	?	after 1871	?
Francis	1830	?	?	after 1861	?

1. Ann Thomas Maffre

Ann Thomas was born October 3, 1813 to Lucy Thomas in the Lymington Poor House and was then baptized November 17, 1813 at St. Thomas Church, Lymington. She is the child for whom the bastardy bond was written in November 1813 and in which Joseph Maffre admits he is her father. Since her parents were married after her birth, she was not legally a Maffre but customs about such things were more lax during this time period and she may well have been known as Ann Maffre.

Ann must have accompanied her family to Montreal in summer 1838 since her father claimed to have eight children living at home in April 1842 when he wrote his letter to Colonel Cathcart about releasing Joseph Jr. from the Army. A few months later, in August 1842, she was not enumerated with her family in the Canadian Census. Her whereabouts after this time remain a mystery.

2. Francis Maffre

Francis Maffre was born October 17, 1815 in Lymington, and was baptized October 26, 1815 in Pylewell House Roman Catholic Chapel, near Lymington. His baptismal entry translates as follows: "The 17th of October 1815 born, the true 26th of the same month and year baptized was Francis Mafre, son of Joseph and Lucy Mafre, formerly Thomas, married. Godfather was Francois Maffre. Godmother Roza Carmine. By me John Browne, Missionary Apostle."

Francis died December 17, 1818, at age 3, with last services at Lymington's St. Thomas Church even though his parents were likely residing in London at this time.

3. Joseph Ludwig Maffre (aka Joseph Maffre Jr.)

Joseph Maffre Jr. was born August 10, 1817 in Somers Town, London, and was baptized August 12, 1817 in St. Aloysius Gonzaga Roman Catholic Church, Somers Town.

In early 1836, at age 18, Joseph Jr. joined the First Battalion of the 71st Highland Light Infantry as musician and private while it was stationed in Dublin, Ireland. The year is from his father's letters to the military authorities saying that his son had served in the military for six years ending in April 1842. The 71st Regiment was shipped to Montreal in 1838. In early 1841, Joseph Jr. transferred to the 1st King's Dragoon Guards when they were stationed in Chambly, Québec. His father was instrumental in getting his transfer to this prestigious regiment. It was a Cavalry Corps and Joseph Jr. continued to serve as a private in the band.

In early 1841, his father, Joseph Sr., was starting his private music practice in Montreal and needed his son's help. His father started a letter writing campaign to the military authorities to purchase his son's discharge and he was ultimately successful.

Joseph Maffre, Jr., age 25, married June 28, 1843, to Julie Theophile Perrault, age 23, in Trinity Chapel Anglican Church, Montreal. The church record reads: 1843; 28th June; Maffre; & Perrault; Married; Joseph Maffre, of this City of Mtl, Bachelor, and Julian Perrault, of the same place, Spinster, were married by license the twenty eight Day of June, Eighteen hundred and forty three; by me Mark Willoughby, COC; in the presence of: Pvt W Brown; Marie Maffre; H Maffre; Contracting Parties; *Joseph Maffre jn, Julia Perrault*. Maffre's best man was in the military and the other witnesses were his sister and brother.

According to Will Fairbairn's family history, Julie met Joseph while walking down the street. It turns out they could hardly have avoided each other because both families were living on Sanguinet.

Julie Perrault was born August 7, 1819 in Montreal, and baptized October 10, 1825 at Notre Dame de Montreal. Her father was a day worker and her uncle owned a quarry. She had deep French Catholic roots in Quebec. Her baptism entry reads: Julienne Perrault Le dix Octobre mil hund cent vingh cinq le Octre soupsigné ai baptize Julienne nee hier du legitimée marriage a Henry Perrault journalier et de Marie Raiza de cette paroise Marrain Henry Perrault et Marraine Mari Perrault qui oinse que lee pere present out declare—re savoir signé.

From 1844 to 1857, Joseph and Julie lived at 58 Sanguinet Street, close to his father and the music business. During this time, they had seven children (Table 10.2), only three of whom survived to adulthood. The last died during childbirth, one month before Julie died.

In July 1849, Joseph Jr.'s parents died. For the first time, Joseph Jr. lists himself as Professor of Music in the 1850 Montreal City Directory rather than simply as Musician as he had been doing. In 1851, Maffre's Quadrille Band performed in at least three major charitable events. In January, it was the third annual Young Men's St. Patrick's Soiree held at Corse's New Building. In March, they performed at the St. John's Ball at an unknown location. In November, it was in the St-Jean-Baptiste parade and at the Soiree afterward at Hays House.

Table 10.2: Children of Joseph Maffre Jr. and Julie Perrault

Child	Born	Spouse	Married	Died	Age at Death
Leopold Alfred*	1844	Sarah Ellis	1870	1891	47
Lucie Hermelinde	1845	--	--	1846	8 mos.
Julie Virginia	1846	--	--	1850	3
Georgiana Australina*	1847	William Fairbairn	1870	1937	90
Charles Henri	1850	--	--	1831	2
Charles Antoine	1852	--	--	1857-1863	5-11
Frederick Arthur*	1853	Alice Carruthers	1878		
		Maria Louisa Gurney	1886	1939	86
unnamed daughter	1857	--	--	1857	0

*L. A. and Sarah Maffre had two children. Georgiana and William Fairbairn had four children. Frederick Maffre had one child with his first wife Alice and five children with his second wife Maria Louisa.

On July 9 and 10, 1852, there was a fire that destroyed nearly 400 houses in Montreal, one of which was Joseph Maffre's. Afterward, his public musical performances never reached the same prominence. On April 5, 1854, tenements owned by Joseph Maffre on Peel Lane in Montreal were seized by the Sheriff in response to a complaint from the Mutual Fire Insurance Company, of Montreal. These buildings probably suffered fire damage so that Maffre had trouble collecting enough rent to pay the insurance.

L. A. Maffre, 1880
L. A. Maffre was 36
McCord Museum II-59341.2

Miss Maffre, 1866
Georgiana Maffre was 18
McCord Museum I-21728.1
Detail

Frederick Arthur Maffre, ca. 1900
Fred Maffre was about 40
Family Photo

Figure 10.2: Photos of the Adult Children of Joseph Maffre, Jr., and Julie Perrault. From the Notman Archive in the McCord Museum.

In 1855, Henry Prince published the *Mermaid Polka* (Figure 10.1) that reads "as played by Maffré & Prince's Quadrille Band." The full title page reads: To the Ladies of Canada; The Mermaid

Polka; As Performed By; Maffré & Prince's Quadrille Band; Composed and Arranged for the Piano; by Henry Prince; Author of The Irresistable, Patriotic Polkas, & C&C; New York; Published by Firth, Pond, & Co., Franklin Square; Montreal Henry Prince. The copy of the sheet in the Canadian Archives is stamped: H. Prince Montreal. The *Encyclopedia of Music in Canada* used this music to indicate that Joseph Sr. led a quadrille band with Henry Prince in 1855 but Sr. was deceased by this time so it is certainly Joseph Jr. We don't know how long Prince and Maffre performed together. Henry Prince acquired a music business from Mead, Brother and Co. in 1854 and began selling instruments and sheet music under his own name. He published sheet music from 1854 to 1878, but it was always printed and copyrighted in the USA. He composed numerous quadrilles, polkas, and other dance music. He remained in business until 1888, at which time it is thought he died.

Julie died July 16, 1857 in Montreal due to tuberculosis at age 38. Her funeral service was held at Notre-Dame Cathedral but we have still not located her burial site. After Julie's death, Fred, 4, Charles Antoine, 5, and Georgiana, 10, were raised by their 64-year-old great-aunt Marie Julie Couvrette. Mme Couvrette's nickname was Ta-Ta which is possibly childspeak for *tante*, which means aunt. By this time, Mme. Couvrette's husband had died and she was living with the family. Oldest son Leopold Alfred, 13, was attending Schools of the Christian Brothers in the St. Lawrence suburbs at the corner of Lagauchetiere and Cheneville Streets. In May 1856, his early musical talent was specially noted in the *True Witness and Catholic Chronicle* when the editor happened to hear him during a visit to the School.

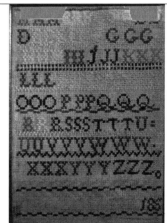

Figure 10.3: Georgiana Maffre's Sampler
The bottom line reads "GEORGIANA 185_."
Photo taken by the authors.

Daughter Georgiana attended Ville Marie Convent in Montreal and became an accomplished pianist. In 1870, she married John Fairbairn, a produce broker and a widower with two daughters. The Fairbairns eventually moved to Chicago and then to Minneapolis. Their son, Will Fairbairn, assembled the first Maffre family history in the 1930's to 1950's.

Joseph Jr., age 41, married a second time on April 22, 1858 to Jean Carruthers, age 47, in St. Stephen's Church, Montreal. The marriage entry reads: Maffre's; Marriage; Joseph Maffre of the City of Montreal, Widower, and Jeanie Carruthers Spinster of Sainte [*Hilaire?*] were married by license on the twenty Second day of April one thousand eight hundred and fifty eight by me, [*unreadable signature*]; This Marriage was solemnized between us: *Joseph Maffre; Jeanie Carruthers;* In the presence of Charles Therbatin and Mary M. Ann Liston who have hereunder signed their names: *Charles Therbatin; Mary Ann Liston.*

Jean Carruthers was born December 13, 1811, in Gorbals, near Glasgow in Scotland. She was baptized a few weeks later in the local Presbyterian Church. In 1820, her family immigrated to Quebec. In 1824, her father was granted land in North Georgetown, Quebec, where he farmed. Her younger sister Annie Carruthers married William Pillar (1805-1886) who is buried in Mount Royal Cemetery near Joseph and Jeannie's baby Jane Pillar Maffre.

In July 1859, their twin daughters Anna Pillar Maffre and Jane Pillar Maffre were born in Montreal. In May 1860, Jane Pillar Maffre died at 8 months. She was buried in Mount Royal Cemetery near her cousin James Pillar who died in 1854 at age 3.

In the 1861 Canadian Census in Montreal, "Joseph Moffre" is a musician living in a four-story building (possibly a hotel). He is married but has no family is living with him. In the 1861 and 1862 directories, he was living at 111 Fortification Lane and, from 1862 to 1872, he is living in an apartment building at 72 St. Maurice Street.

In 1863, Jean died after only 5 years of marriage. Her burial was from North Georgetown Presbyterian Church. Her entry says "Carruthers Jane (wife Maffre)." Their daughter Anna was adopted the next year by Raphael and Laura Cook of Brockport, New York. Anna later married Mades Lenk and they adopted a daughter named Esther. Joseph's other children at this time were L.A., 20, Georgiana, 17, and Fred, 11. Charles Antoine had died by this time.

In January 1865, Joseph, Jr., age 48, of Knowlton, married Theresa Leseuer (or Lessard), of Montreal, in St. James Anglican Church, Montreal. Theresa was born in 1843 and hailed from near Cowansville. The 1881 Census indicates that her heritage was "Indigenous."

In February 1865, Joseph Jr. announced he would teach pianoforte, violin, wind instruments, and vocal music in Knowlton (Figure 10.4).

Advertiser and Eastern Townships Advocate
February 2, 1865, p. 4

CARD.

MR. JOSEPH MAFFRE, at the suggestion of some of his old friends and pupils, would announce that he has returned to WATERLOO, where he intends making his permanent residence for the future. He will give instruction upon the Pianoforte, Violin, and Wind Instruments, and select classes in Vocal Music, as formerly. He will attend his classes at Knowlton, Tuesdays and Fridays of each week, where he will be happy to meet his old pupils and instruct others who may desire it.

Orders for Mr. MAFFRE at Knowlton, may be left with J. MCFARLANE, Esq., and at Waterloo, at REYNOLDS' HOTEL or ALLEN, TAYLOR & CO.'s Store.

Waterloo, Feb. 1, 1865.

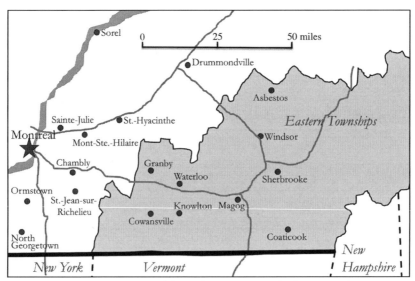

Figure 10.4: Map of Quebec's Eastern Townships showing the location of major cities and modern highways. Illustration by Mark Griep.

In Spring 1870, Monsieur Maffre led a group of musicians to the Eastern Townships where they performed concerts as a way to create interest in music instruction. Monsieur Maffre is probably Joseph Jr. and not his brother Alfred or his sons L. A. or Fred. The Eastern Townships are due east of Montreal past Chambly and St. Jean (Figure 10.4). The towns visited by Maffre include Cowansville, Granby, Waterloo, Magog, and Sherbrooke.

The 1871 Census places father Joseph Jr. and his sons L. A. and Fred in Waterloo. His wife Theresa and her first child Joseph age 1 are not with him.

During summer 1871, for the 16 days from June 27 to July 12, Private "Jos. Maffre" earned 50 cts/day in the Band of the 52nd Volunteer Militia for a total of $8.00. The Serjeant was Albert E. Mitchell. During the summer of 1872, for the 16 days from June 21 to July 6, Private "Jos. Maffre" once again earned 50 cts/day in the Band of the 52nd Volunteer Militia for a total of $8.00. The Serjeant was once again Albert E. Mitchell. After 1873, he is no longer listed in the Montreal City Directory. He would have been 56 years old.

In April 1875, "MM. Maffre (violiniste)" performed "Les Noces de Jeannette" with several other musicians at Mechanics' Hall in celebration of Mr. Labelle's 25th Anniversary as Notre Dame organist. Joseph, 57, and his son L. A., 31, both played violin.

The 1881 Census places musician "Joseph Maffie" age 64, wife "Terase" (ethnic origin: Indian) age 38, and his two young children ages 11 and 10 in St. Anne's Ward, Montreal. It has not been possible to learn more about son Joseph Maffre III but daughter Marie Lucy Maffre entered in the 1883 Kahnawake Agricultural Exposition and won "Penmanship — 1st, Mary L. Maffre" according to Blanchard's *Seven Generations: A History of the Kanienkehaka.* The Kanienkehaka are one of the Mohawk tribes, located in Quebec, Ontario, and New York. This was their first Exposition.

Joseph died August 2, 1881 of an aneurism a few days short of age 65. His final service was held at St. Stephen's Anglican church at St. Paul and Inspector Streets (now St. Edward's St.) and he was buried in Mount Royal cemetery with granddaughter Charlotte Fairbairn. Joseph's third wife is not buried in this plot. By 1883, she was living with the Kanienkehaka tribe.

According to the St. Stephen's Church burial record: Maffre; Buried; Joseph Maffre of the City of Montreal died August the Second A.D. Eighteen Hundred and Eighty-one and was Buried the Fourth day of the same month and Year Aged Sixty Four Years; By me: Ernest [*unreadable*]; Witnesses: *L. A. Maffre; F. A. Maffre.*

4. Charlotte Maffre McDonnell

Charlotte Maffre was born January 8, 1820 in Leicester, and was baptized February 1, 1820 in Leicester's Holy Cross Roman Catholic Church. The baptismal entry reads, "Die 13a Februarii 1820. Baptisair Carolettam filiam Josephi et Lucia Maffré conjugum, natam die 8a ejusdem mensis. Susceperunt Joannem Smith et Sara Thomlinson. Bentus Caestryck. Ord FF Praed Messius Apticus." This translates to: "The 13th of February. Baptized Charlotte child of Joseph and Lucy Maffré who are married, born the 8th this month. Godparents were John Smith and Sarah Thomlinson. Priest Caestryck, ordained Missionary Apostle." Godfather John Smith was an early member of this congregation and baptized many children before the priest arrived to care for the flock.

Charlotte must have accompanied her family to Montreal in summer 1838 since her father claimed to have eight children living at home in April 1842 when he wrote his letter to Colonel Cathcart about releasing Joseph Jr. from the Army. A few months later, in August 1842, she was not enumerated with her family in the Canadian Census. Unlike her older sister Ann, however, she did not disappear from the records.

In July 1843, Charlotte, at age 23, and her sisters may have learned to dance from Anne Fairbrother Hill, aka Mrs. Charles Hill, who had just opened a Ladies Dancing Academy and who sought clients through Joseph Maffre Sr. In exchange, Maffre may have asked Mrs. Hill to teach his daughters.

On February 27, 1845, Charlotte Maffre witnessed her sister Maria's marriage to William Tate.

In July 1845, at age 25, the Maffre sisters may have learned to dance the polka from Miss St. Clair, who was in town for only a few weeks. Miss Clair sought clients through Joseph Maffre Sr.

In November 1847, "Miss Maffre" opened a Dancing Academy and gave her residence as 77 Rousseau, near Dalhousie Square. The *Transcript* editor must have made a transcription error because 77 Rousseau didn't exist. In January 1848, Miss Maffre's address was listed as No. 11, the same as her father's. Alas, there is no evidence to indicate which sister (Ann, Charlotte, Maria, or Mary Anne) was "Miss Maffre" of Dancing Academy fame. We have chosen Charlotte because she was almost 28 years old and it fits her life's trajectory the best.

Montreal Transcript
November 2, 1847
DANCING ACADEMY.

———

A Card.

MISS MAFFRE respectfully announces to the Montreal Public, that she has opened a DANCING ACADEMY, for the Instruction of Young Ladies and Gentleman.

Seminaries and Private Families punctually attended too. Terms moderate.

For particulars apply at her Residence, 77, Rousseau Street, near Dalhousie Square.

On February 1 and March 17 in 1848, "Miss Maffre" held two balls. The first ball featured, "Mr. Crerar the confectioner." The second ball featured, "Maffre's full Quadrille Band."

Miss Maffre's Dancing School ceased to exist at the about the same time as Joseph and Lucy's deaths in late July 1849.

Charlotte Maffre, age approximately 29, married George McDonnell, age unknown, between March 1848 and July 1850. In the Montreal Directories from 1842 to 1846, George was a pawnbroker at 26 St. Mary Street, near Campeau Street. After 1847, he was no longer listed as a pawnbroker. From 1847 to 1852, his house was at 4 Rousseau Street, just a few doors away from the Maffres, providing him with plenty of opportunity to cross paths with Charlotte. The death of her parents in late July 1849 may have left Charlotte in a poor financial position so that she had to marry to support herself.

On July 31, 1850, Charlotte McDonnald [*sic*] was one of the sponsors to the baptism of Lucy Jane Tate in Christ Church Anglican Cathedral. Lucy Jane Tate was the second child of William and Maria Tate. Charlotte's sponsorship was a proxy, indicating she was not present.

On July 13, 1853, Charlotte died in Toronto, age 33. She was buried on July 15 in Montreal's New Burying Ground with a service at Memorial Trinity Anglican Church. The interment entry reads "Charlotte McDonnell by maiden name Maffre wife of George McDonnell aged thirty three years and six months died on the thirteenth and was Buried on the fifteenth of July Eighteen hundred and fifty three. By me Alex Digby Campbell. In the Presence of *Geo McDonnell* [*his signature*]."

In the 1853 and 1854 Montreal Directories, George McDonnell is living on Champ de Mars, near Campeau Street. On October 4, 1854, widower George McDonnell married spinster Esther Waldron, age 19, in Christ Church Anglican Cathedral. The witnesses were A. Handsby, and her brother Charles Waldron. Esther was born about 1835 in Quebec. In 1856, Esther gave birth to their daughter Emilie Ann [*also known as Amelia*], who was baptized February 6, 1856 in Notre Dame Cathedral and whose godmother was Mary Ann Lavery. From 1858 to 1867, George McDonnell's directory entry indicates he lived at 6 Rousseau.

On November 20, 1867, George McDonnell died in Montreal and was buried on the 23rd with a service from St. John the Evangelist Anglican Church. The witnesses were A. Handsby and his brother-in-law C. Waldron. Beginning in 1869, McDonnell's second widow has an entry in the City Directory as "McDonnell, Mrs. Esther, wid George, 20 Rousseau." She soon moved to 16 and then 18 Rousseau. In the 1871 Census, widow Esther McDonnell, 36, is living at 16 Rousseau with her daughter Amelia McDonnell 15, who is going to school. Esther, widow of George McDonnell, died July 6, 1912 in the St. Patrice parish of Montreal.

5. Maria Maffre Tate

Maria Maffre was born October 12, 1821 in Leicester, and was baptized November 1, 1821 in Leicester's Holy Cross Roman Catholic Church. The baptismal entry reads, "Die 1a Novbris 1821. Baptisair Mariam filiam Josephi et Lucia Maffré conjugum, natam 12a Octobris proximé praeter iti. Susceperunt Jacobus Smith et Lucia Wilkins. Bent Caestryck. Ord FF Praed Messius Apticus," which translates to "The 1st of November. Baptized Marie child of Joseph and Lucy Maffré who are married, born the 12th October prior. The godparents were Jacob Smith and Lucy Wilkins. Priest Caestryck, ordained Missionary Apostle." Jacob Smith was an early member of this congregation and had many of his own children baptized in this church.

Maria must have accompanied her family to Montreal in summer 1838 because her father claimed to have eight children living at home in April 1842 when he wrote his letter to Colonel George Cathcart about releasing Joseph Jr. from the Army. A few months later, in August 1842, she was not enumerated with her family in the Canadian Census. At age 21, she was probably earning her keep by working as a servant in someone's home.

Maria Maffre, age 24, married February 27, 1845 to William Tate, age 41, in Montreal's Trinity Anglican Church. The witnesses were her siblings Joseph Maffre Jr. and Charlotte Maffre. It is not clear how William and Maria met. Perhaps William attended one of the many quadrilles parties at which Joseph Maffre performed and that Maria must have attended.

If William and Maria's photos (Figure 10.5) were taken in 1845, the year of their marriage, they would have been early Daguerreotypes. However, her photo is embossed "Martin Photographist, corner of Craig and Bleury." George Martin was a Daguerreotypist at the corner of St. Peter & Craig from 1854 until 1858. His house was located on Bleury Street. After 1859, he was a photographic artist at the same location. Maria may have had her old daguerreotype copied at his photograph shop.

William Tate was born September 16, 1804 in Wigginton, Yorkshire. He immigrated in 1824 at age 20 to Montreal with his parents and eight siblings. Most of the Tate family settled in Ormstown, just south of Montreal while three sons settled in Montreal, notably William, Charles, and George.

Figure 10.5: Photos of William Tate and Maria Maffre Tate, possibly taken in 1845. The authors' personal collection.

In 1841, William and his brothers Charles and George started the first regular steamship line between Montreal and Quebec City (Figure 10.6). William and Charles ran the office and kept the books while George captained one of the ships. An early contract was to convey the Royal Mail service between the two growing cities. Their steamship *Lord Sydenham* is reported to have been the first vessel to run the Lachine Rapids. That ship was named after Lord Sydenham, Governor General from 1838 to 1841. Their other steamship, *Lady Colborne*, was named after a British Army General's wife. According to an advertisement they placed in *The Transcript*, Captain George Tate left on the *Lord Sydenham* from the port of Montreal at 5 pm every Monday, Wednesday, and Friday. It arrived in Quebec City the following morning at 8 am. Likewise, Captain W. H. Haycock left on the *Lady Colborne* from the port of Quebec City at 6 pm every Tuesday, Thursday, and Saturday and arrived in Montreal the following morning at 10 am.

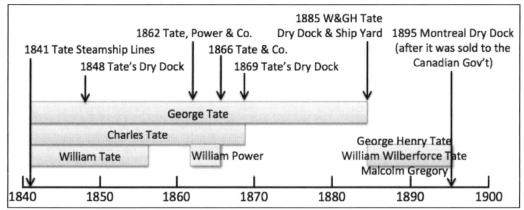

Figure 10.6: Tate Brothers Business Timeline. William Tate was married to Maria Maffre and their sons were George Henry Tate and William Wilberforce Tate. Malcolm Gregory was their son-in-law. Illustration by Mark Griep.

The 1842-3 Montreal Directory entry reads, "Tate, W. & G., Royal mail steamboats, office Commissioner street." The 1843-4 Directory clarifies "66 and 67 Commissioner street", but there is no entry in the next three Directories.

Maria and William had four children, all born in Montreal: William Wilberforce Tate born December 21, 1845; Lucy Jane Tate born May 23, 1850; John Tate born 1853 and died January 1854; and George Henry Tate born May 7, 1856. William Wilberforce Tate never married, had a long career in business including with Tate's Dry Dock, and died March 7, 1923 in Montreal at age 77. Lucy Jane Tate married Malcolm Gregory either before or after he started working at Tate's Dry Dock. They did not have any children. George Henry Tate married Harriett C. Ricard in Montreal and their descendants live in Montreal today. Their only child to survive to adulthood was daughter Winnifred who was the main heir to the funds from selling Tate's Dry Dock to the Canadian Government.

Tate's Dry Dock was founded in about 1848 when William and Captain George purchased 4.5 acres near the Lachine Rapids to begin building steamships. The land housed a sawmill and nail factory. Charles helped run the dry dock, ship repair, and ship building company. After a ship would enter the enclosed dock, it would be locked into place, and the water drained from the dock so the ship could be repaired. They used a hydraulic energy pump system to empty the dock. All three worked at the company until their deaths, William at age 52 in 1857, Charles at age 69 in 1876, and George at age 76 in 1885.

In April 1848, there was a fire in the Tate's blacksmith shop. It consumed a steamship they were building along with nine houses. George's hands and face were "severely burnt" according to the news report. The Montreal Directories of 1848, 1849, and 1850 have entries for "Tate, Captain George" who is living on Hochelaga Street.

In the Montreal Directories from 1853 to 1862, there was an entry for "Tate, Brothers, dry docks and shipyard, south side of the Canal." These same Directories have separate entries for Captain George and Charles, indicating they lived on Bonsecours Street near St. Paul Street. Charles is not listed in the 1861 or 1862 Directories.

In 1856, the Tate Brother's sister, Jane Tate, used money and land she appears to have inherited from her mother to pay her brothers to construct two adjacent buildings for retail and residential use on Bonsecours Street (Number 16 in 1856 but Number 430 in 2002). Jane was the owner/manufacturer and may have paid her brothers from rents received from tenants. These buildings were still standing in 2002. After 1865, the Montreal Directories list "Tate, Miss Jane, 16 Bonsecours." She died in 1874.

Maria Maffre Tate's husband William died August 26, 1857 of cholera after 8 years of marriage. He was buried on the 28th from Ormstown's United Church of England and Ireland. The witnesses were his brothers John, Henry, and Charles Tate. He is buried in St. James Churchyard, Ormstown, with other Tates. Upon her husband's death, Maria inherited half of Tate's Dry Dock partnership. It is not clear how much of a role she played in running the business.

The 1861 Census enumerates "Maria Tate" 40 as living with brother-in-law "Geo Tate" 50 "Ship Builder" along with her children W. W. 16, Lucy 11, George 5, and two servants 20 and 21. George Tate has $12,000 invested in "Dry Docks." They are living on 5 acres of land in a two-story frame house, have a horse and cow worth $175, and two carriages worth $100.

In the 1863, 1864, and 1865 Montreal Directories, the business is called "Tate, Power, & Co." It was run by Captain George Tate and a fellow named William Power. George was living at 2 Wellington in Point St. Charles, next to the shipyard. His brother Charles was still living on

Bonsecours. William Power was listed as a shipbuilder living on Grand Trunk Street. It was during this time, in 1865 and 1869, that Maria Tate had her photograph taken at Notman Studios.

In the 1866 and 1867 Montreal Directories, the business is called "Tate & Co.", indicating that William Power was no longer part of the business. After 1869, the business is listed as "Tate's Dry Docks" in the Montreal Directories. For the four years from 1877 to 1880, Maria Tate's son, William Wilberforce Tate, ran a wholesale and retail tea business at 14 Bonsecours Street. In 1885, after the death of their uncle Captain George, Maria's two sons, William Wilberforce Tate and George Henry Tate formed "W. & G. H. Tate" to run Tate's Dry Dock and shipyard. George Henry Tate lived at 12 Bayle Street and William Wilberforce Tate lived at 14 Fort Street.

The 1881 Census lists widow "Marie Taite", age 59, as the head of the household. She is living with her children William age 35, Lucey age 30, and George age 24. Marie's brother-in-law "George Taite" age 73 is also living with her and she has a 19-year-old Welsh maid. The occupation of the two Georges is listed as "Ship Builder."

Maria's daughter Lucy married June 25, 1889 in St. James The Apostle Anglican Church to Malcolm Gregory. The witnesses were Lucy's cousin, L. A. Maffre, and V. E. Sadler. Malcolm was born in Scotland in 1858, immigrated to Canada in 1862 with his family, and became the bookkeeper at Tate's Dry Dock, which must be how he met Lucy Tate. Maria lived with Lucy and Malcolm Gregory for the rest of her life. The 1891 Census lists widow "Mrs. W. Tate", age 69, as living in the house headed by Malcolm Gregory 32 "Book keeper for Ship Yard & Dry Dock" and his wife Lucy 40. In separate entries of the 1891 Census, Maria's sons George and William are listed as "Ship Builders" (Figure 10.7).

TATE W. & G. H.,
Dry Dock and Ship Yard.
TATE'S DRY DOCK,
127 Mill st
South Side Lachine Canal,
Point St Charles

Figure 10.7: "Tate's Dry Dock" advertisement from the 1890 Montreal Directory.

In 1895-1896, Tate's Dry Dock was purchased by the Canadian Government and renamed the Montreal Dry Docks. In the early 1900s, the Lachine Canal was broadened to handle the 15,000 ships using it every year. The Montreal Dry Dock continued to repair vessels until the canal was closed in 1970. In the early 2000s, recreational trails were built along the old Lachine Canal, bringing life back to the area.

The 1901 Census enumerates widowed mother "Marie Tait", age 79, living in a house in the St. Antoine Ward headed by Contractor Malcolm Gregory 42 and his wife Lucy 40 [*she didn't age a single year since the 1891 census*]. Maria was born in England and immigrated to Canada in 1837. Also living with them is their niece Winnifred Tait 15, nephew Louis Tait 13, and servant Annie McFarlane 19.

Maria Maffre Tate died February 2, 1907, in Montreal at age 86. Her last residence was 14 Fort Street. She's buried in Mount Royal Cemetery section B-34 with the Tates and Mitchells.

6. Henry Maffre

Henry Maffre was baptized January 26, 1823 in St. Nicholas Church, Leicester. He must have accompanied his family to Montreal in summer 1838 since his father claimed to have eight children living at home in April 1842 when he wrote his letter to Colonel Cathcart about releasing Joseph Jr. from the Army. A few months later, in August 1842, Henry was enumerated in the Canadian Census with his family as one of three males age 18-20.

On June 28, 1843, Henry was a witness to his brother Joseph Jr.'s marriage to Julie Perrault at Montreal's Trinity Church. On November 4, 1843, at age 20, Henry was one of the musicians who signed his father's petition to Lieutenant-General Sir Richard Jackson, requesting that military bands stop playing quadrille parties.

The signature of "H[enry] Maffre Esquire, Montreal" is on some sheet music in the McGill University Music Library titled "Collection de tous les Duos concerta pour deux Violons." It was composed by Giovanni Battista Viotti.

Henry died January 1, 1848 in Montreal, age 24, of consumption. The Christ Church burial entry reads: 1848 "Maffree; Buried" "Henry Maffree of Montreal Musician, died on the first day of January, One thousand eight hundred and forty eight aged twenty four years, and was buried on the fifth following by me; W. Agee Adamson, Assistant Minister. Witnesses Present: J. Folsom; A. F. M[unreadable]lby"

7. Frederick Maffre

Frederick Maffre was born in about 1824 in Leicester if he was 18-20 in the 1842 Census. We have been unable to find his baptismal record. Frederick must have accompanied his family to Montreal in summer 1838 since his father claimed to have eight children living at home in April 1842 when he wrote his letter to Colonel Cathcart about releasing Joseph Jr. from the Army. A few months later, in August 1842, he was enumerated in the Canadian Census with his family as one of three males age 18-20.

Frederick became a carpenter and married Mary Mullen in about 1848. In 1830, "Mary Mullin" was baptized in the Christ Anglican Church. She may have been the daughter of Mr. F. Mullin who leased buildings in downtown Montreal. Soon, Frederick and Mary had one child, Frederick Maffre Jr., whose baptismal record provides the primary source describing Frederick's life. The Christ Church baptismal entry reads: "Frederick son of Frederick Maffry of Montreal Carpenter and of Mary Mullen his wife was born on the thirteenth day of June 1849 and was privately baptized on the 15th day of March 1850 by me; John Bethany, Rector."

There is no further information about Frederick.

8. Mary Anne Maffre Buckley

Mary Anne Maffre was baptized August 6, 1826 in Leicester's St. Nicholas Church. She must have accompanied her family to Montreal in summer 1838 since her father claimed to have eight children living at home in April 1842 when he wrote his letter to Colonel Cathcart about releasing Joseph Jr. from the Army. A few months later, in August 1842, she was the only daughter enumerated in the Canadian Census with her family.

Mary Anne, age 21, married February 26, 1847 to Thomas Buckley, age 36, in St. Thomas Anglican Church, Montreal. The witnesses were E. F. Caid [*spelling?*] and E. Pillar. Note that Joseph Maffre Jr. married Jeanne Carruthers eleven years later and that her sister was Mrs. Pillar. Thomas may be the "T. William Buckley" who was a schoolmaster in the 1842 Canadian Census for Chambly, southeast of Montreal.

Thomas Buckley died September 30, 1847 in New Orleans at age 36, after only 7 months marriage. The death notice said he was "late of Montreal"

In the 1850-51 Toronto City Directory, Mrs. Mary Buckley is living at 62 Victoria Street. As mentioned earlier, her sister Charlotte died in Toronto in 1853. It is possible that Charlotte was visiting Mary Anne when she died. There is no further information about Mary Anne.

9. Alfred Maffre

Alfred Maffre was baptized January 16, 1830 in Leicester's St. George Church. In August 1842, he was enumerated in the Canadian Census with his family as a male age 14-17. He studied at Le Collège de Montréal in 1857 and 1858 and became a "Professeur de musique." One of the only other records for him is a note in volume 1, issue 3 (November 1, 1866), of *Le Canada Musical Revue Artistique et Littéraire* that indicates "Alfred Maffré" of Malone, N.Y. paid his subscription.

In the 1871 Montreal Directory, Alfred is a "Professor" living in Waterloo, Quebec. However, it is difficult to differentiate the records for Alfred Maffre, son of Joseph Maffre, Sr., and Leopold Alfred Maffre, son of Joseph Maffre Jr., especially since both of them appear to have moved from Montreal to the Waterloo area at about the same time.

10. Francis Maffre

Francis Maffre was born within a month of 8th March 1830 in Leicester; this month and year are consistent with his Discharge papers from the 100th Regiment of Foot on October 8, 1861 when he was 30 ½ years. In the 1842 Canadian Census, he would have been 11 years old living with his family in August 1842.

As an adult, Francis was a cabinetmaker. He may have joined in partnership with his brother Frederick, whom we know was a carpenter in 1849.

On March 26, 1858, Francis, a "Cabinet Maker," born in "Leicester" and the age of "27 years" joined the 100th Regiment of Foot in Montreal to become "No. 203 Private Francis Maffre." The British Army created the 100th Prince of Wales Regiment in 1858 to be composed of Canadian troops as a way to enhance the ties between England and Canada. On June 18, 1858, the 100th Foot left for their term of duty in Gibraltar. The date is based on the report of 84 days in Montreal (5 days March + 30 days April + 31 days May + 18 days June).

On September 2, 1860, Francis was imprisoned for two days for an unknown reason.

On September 3, 1861, Francis was imprisoned again for two days. Apparently, he was inebriated when he returned to camp, tried to run from the duty guard, twisted his leg in a hole or ditch, and tore the ligament in his knee. He suffered pain for a considerable time afterward. On September 19, 1861, the disability discharge proceedings began. On September 30, 1861, he sailed to Chatham, England, where he was honorably discharged on October 8, 1861 after a total of three years and 188 days in service. His service was deemed "good" despite his two incarcerations. He was age 30 ½, was 5 foot 8 ½ inches, had a sallow complexion, dark brown eyes, dark hair, and his trade was Cabinet Maker. There is no further information about Francis, suggesting he may have remained in England after his discharge.

11

MUSIC BY JOSEPH MAFFRE

This chapter contains reproductions of the six published works by Joseph Maffre that are known to exist. There are no known copies of opuses 3 or 7, or of his instruction manual.

Opus 1. *A New Set of Quadrilles*
Leicester, March 1827, 3 shillings [*36 pence*], cover and five pages.
This copy is signed "J Maffre" in the lower right corner.
Reproduced from the authors' personal collection.

Opus 2. *A New Military March, Concertant*
Leicester, November 1828, 2 shillings [*24 pence*], cover and four pages.
This copy is signed "JM" in the lower right corner.
Reproduced by kind permission of the Syndics of Cambridge University Library.

Opus 3. *For a Military Band Beethoven's Grand Quintetto No 1 of String Instruments*
Leicester, about 1829
No copies of this piece have been found.

Opus 4. *A Set of Quadrilles*
Dublin, circa 1837, 3 shillings [*36 pence*], cover and five pages
Reproduced courtesy of the National Library of Ireland.

Opus 5. *Quadrille*
Montreal, *Literary Garland* May 1840, two pages
Reproduced from Archive.org.

Opus 6. *Quadrille, No. II*
Montreal, *Literary Garland* October 1840, two pages
Reproduced from Archive.org.

Opus 7. *Notes of the Forest; or, Eastern Township Melodies*
Montreal, 1845, 5 shillings [*60 pence*], two sets quadrilles, six waltzes, and five marches
No copies of this piece have been found.

Opus 8. *The Original Canadian Quadrilles*
Montreal, 1847, 38 cents, cover and five pages
Reproduced from the authors' personal collection.

Instruction Manual.
Method of Teaching Psalmody (or possibly *Parochial Psalmody*)
Leicester, early 1829, 15 shillings [*180 pence*]
No copies of this book have been found.

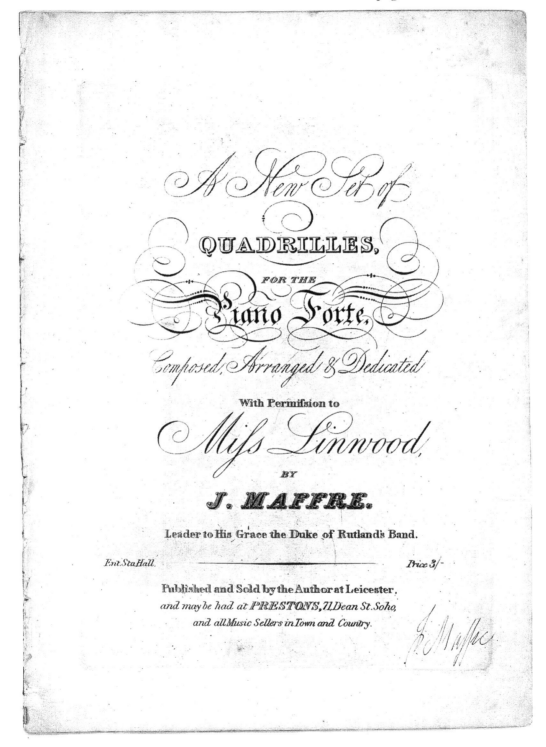

LA VIOTTI

N° 1.

FIGURE *Le Pantalon.*

LA BEETHOVEN

FIGURE   L'Ete.

4

LA PIELTIN.

FIGURE   *La Poule*

FIGURE   La Trenise

LA MAFFRE

FIGURE La Finale

LEICESTER WALTZ

Opus 2. *A New Military March, Concertant.*
Leicester, November 1828, cover and four pages
For the Sheet Music Cover, see Figure 6.1

MARCH.

MARCH.

MARCH.

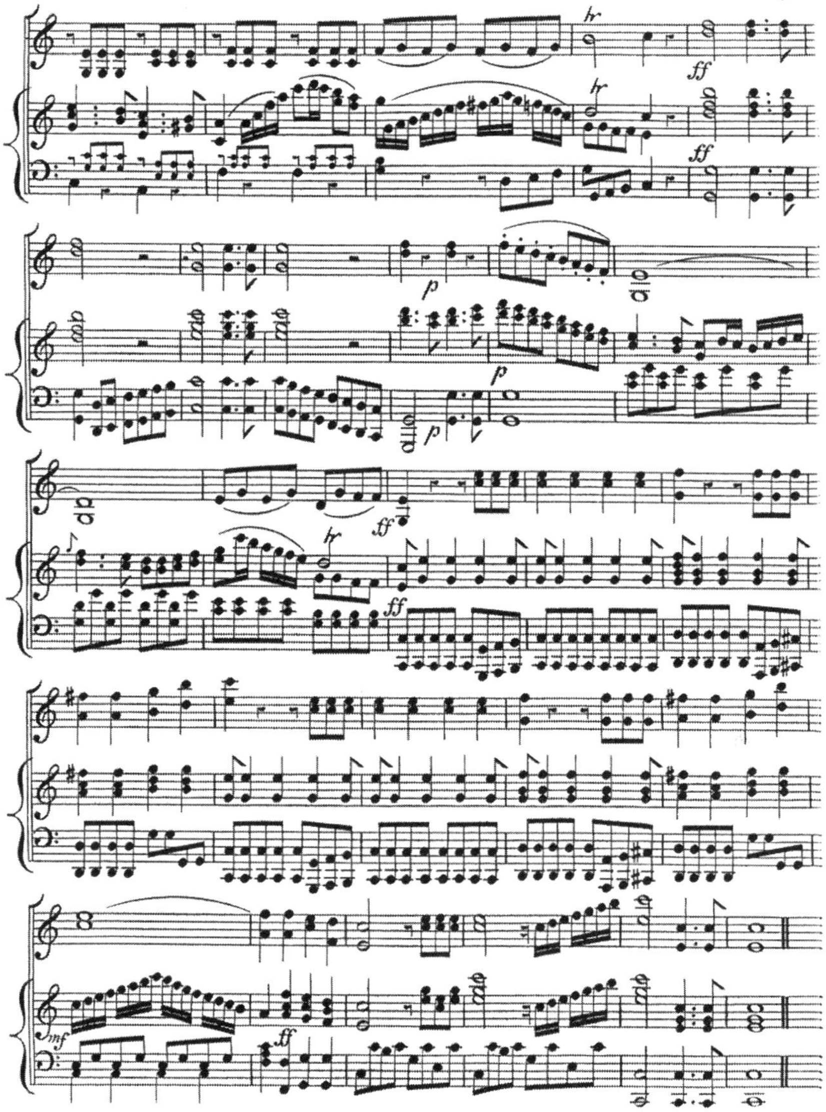

CAMBRIDGE
14 DEC 1984
MUS#
UNIV. LIBR.

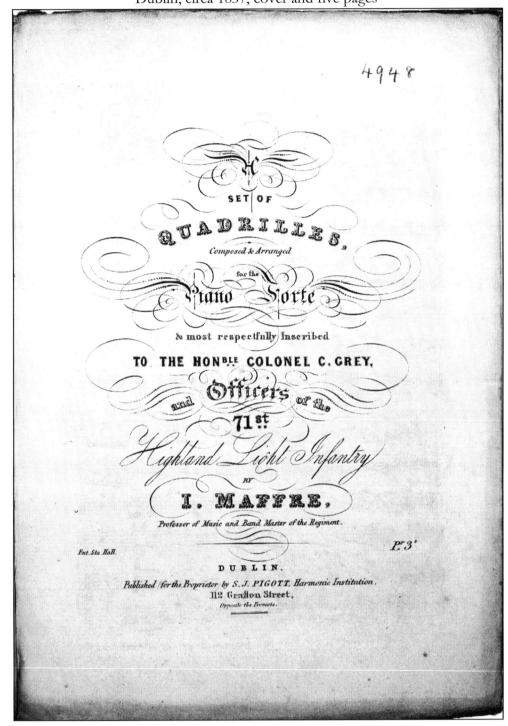

Solo Cornetto.

D.C.

Da Capo

La Pantalon.

(163)

L E'te.
(163)

La Poule.

(163)

La Trenise.

(163)

La Finale.
(163)

(ORIGINAL.)

ON THE DEPARTURE OF A FRIEND.

————Came winter then,
With his rugged brow and aspect stern,
And his rough winds swept over all, the young
Nor aged sparing : and some grew bold,
As if their youthful thoughts found kindred joy
In the frosty crackling sound which followed
Their light footsteps. Some had seen him come
And go, and come again, adding wrinkles
To their now deeply furrowed brows, till time
'Gainst nature would prevail, and sweep them off,
Each after each, to be remembered never.
Then came the blithesome spring in her gay robe
Attired, and with her came a whispering dark,
Forboding tidings ill : it told that friends,
Dear friends, must part ! Alas, too true, for once

Was rumour with her hundred tongues—she said,
A friend indeed, who had in need proved such,
Whose ready hand was e'er outstretched to soothe
The fever'd head, who toilsome watched o'er the sick
And restless, wishing for light to drive away
The deathlike image of the night ; whose aid,
Unasked for, was bestowed e'en on the DEAD ;
Fearful, that on the solitude of grief
There might intrude a thought of disrespect,
To those whom God had called to live with him ;
Would go with all he held most dear, and leave
Behind a friendless blank.

B*****.

Montreal, 25th April, 1840.

D.C.$

(ORIGINAL.)

ON THE LATE DECEASE OF A VALUED FRIEND.

BY "MUSOPHILUS."

—

"Who comes to the chamber?
It is Azrael the Angel of Death?"
(Southey's Thalaba.)

The sound of the death-bell was heard o'er the plain,
And mournfully boomed its monotonous strain;
The voice of the tomb seemed to speak in its toll,
And Sorrow's dark Mantle enshrouded the soul.

The decree has gone forth!—the flower in its bloom
Is plucked but to fade o'er the lone, ivied tomb;—
'Tis gone from the spot where its beauty had grown,
And death leaves us sorrowful,—silent—alone!

In my spring-time of life, a dear friend I found thee,
With beauty and innocence shining around thee;
Thy smile of true friendship delighted us all—
It is lost!—and we weep o'er thy sad, sable pall!

Mourn not, beloved friends, though cold marble rest
On the lips that affection full often has prest;
True friends, in this world, may be severed in twain,
But in Heaven they will soon be united again.

CONSUMPTION.

There is a sweetness in woman's decay,
When the light of beauty is fading away;
When the bright enchantment of youth has gone,
And the tint that glow'd, and the eye that shone
And darted around its glance of power,
And the lip that vied with the sweetest flower
That ever in Pæstum's garden blew,
Or ever was steeped in fragrant dew;
When all that was bright and fair is fled,
But the loveliness lingering around the dead.

O, there is a sweetness in beauty's close,
Like the perfume scenting the withered rose;
For a nameless charm around her plays,
And her eyes are kindled with hallow'd rays,
And a veil of spotless purity
Has mantled her cheek with its heavenly dye,
Like a land wherein the Queen of Night
Has pour'd her softest tint of light;
And there is a blending of white and blue,
Where the purple blood is melting through
The snow of her pale and tender cheek;
And there are tones that sweetly speak
Of a spirit that longs for a purer day,
And is ready to wing its flight away.

THE ORIGINAL
CANADIAN QUADRILLES,

G. & W. ENDICOTT LITH. N. YORK.

ARRANGED FOR THE
PIANO FORTE,
AND RESPECTFULLY DEDICATED TO
The Countess of Elgin,
BY
J. MAFFRE.
New York,
38 cts. nett

PUBLISHED BY FIRTH & HALL Nº 1 FRANKLIN SQ. AND FIRTH HALL & POND Nº 239 BROADWAY.
J. W. HERBERT & Cº MONTREAL.

Entered according to act of Congress in the year 1847, by Firth & Hall, in the Clerks Office of the district court of the Southern district of New York.

CANADIEN QUADRILLES

4

No. 4.

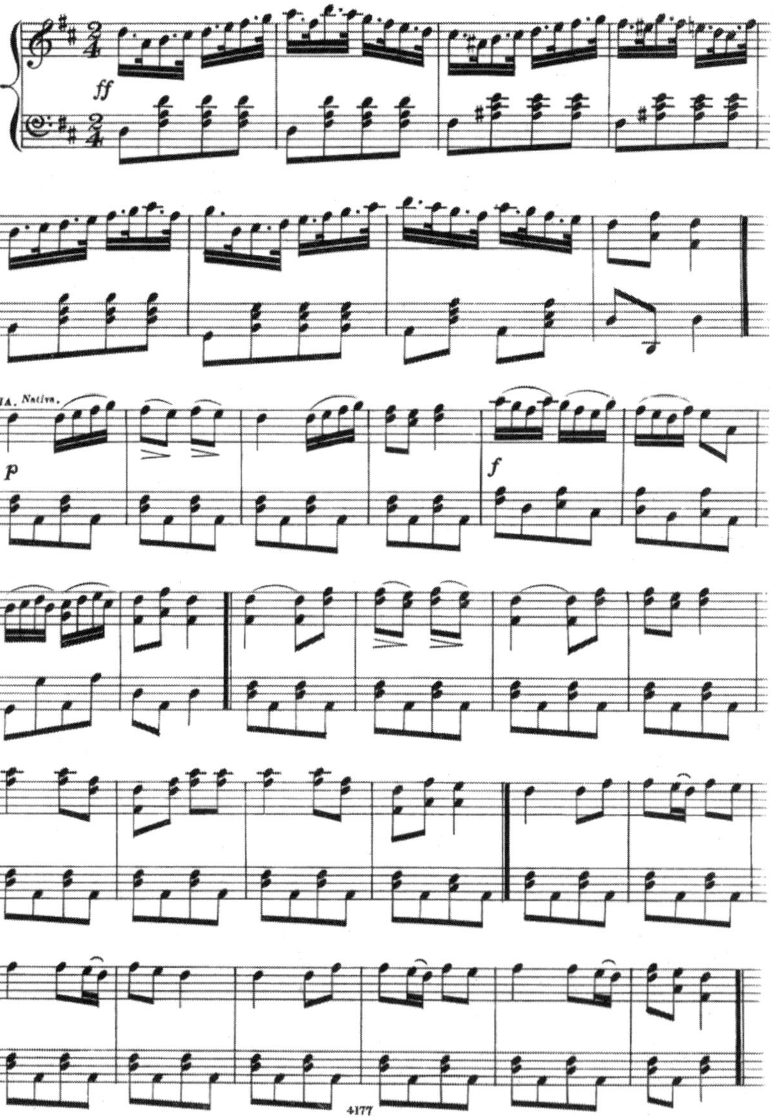

4177

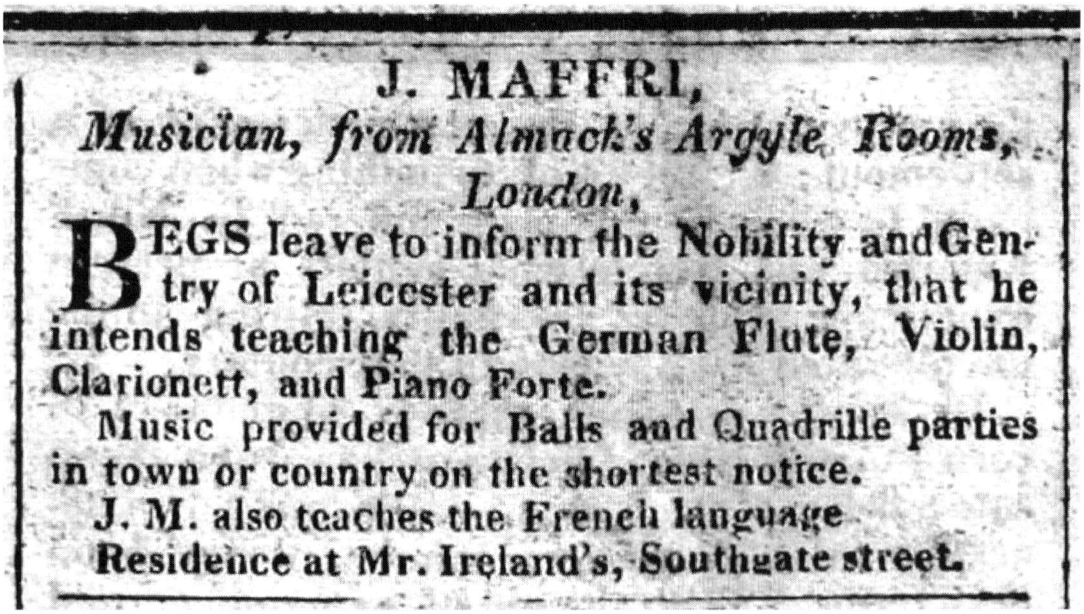

J. MAFFRI,

Musician, from Almach's Argyle Rooms,
London,

BEGS leave to inform the Nobility and Gentry of Leicester and its vicinity, that he intends teaching the German Flute, Violin, Clarionett, and Piano Forte.

Music provided for Balls and Quadrille parties in town or country on the shortest notice.

J. M. also teaches the French language

Residence at Mr. Ireland's, Southgate street.

Figure 12.1: Joseph Maffre's first newspaper advertisement. Leicester Journal, Friday, August 6, 1819, p. 3, c. 3, top item.

12

A PERFECT KNOWLEDGE

Joseph Maffre was mentioned in scores of newspaper entries in the form of advertisements, playbills, and reviews. The following excerpts are for as many events as we have been able to discover. The most productive source was the *Montreal Transcript* with over 100 entries. The other Montreal newspapers (*La Minerve*, the *Montreal Gazette*, and the *Montreal Witness*) were consulted when there was known missing material in the *Transcript*. Maffre was in the news much less frequently during his time in the United Kingdom and Ireland but the most frequent sources are the *Leicester Journal* and *Leicester Chronicle*. This chapter also contains excerpts from city directories and other printed sources.

Leicester Journal
Friday, August 6, 1819, p. 3, c. 3, top item

J. MAFFRI,

Musician, from Almack's Argyle Rooms, London,

BEGS leave to inform the Nobility and Gentry of Leicester and its vicinity, that he intends teaching the German Flute, Violin, Clarionett, and Piano Forte.

Music provided for Balls and Quadrille parties in town or country on the shortest notice.

J. M. also teaches the French language.

Residence at Mr. Ireland's, Southgate street.

[German flute is the archaic name for the flute and is used to distinguish it from the English flute, or recorder. In the 1826 Poll Book, Robert Ireland is a brewer residing on Southgate Street.]

Jackson's Oxford Journal
Saturday, June 3, 1820

Oxford has during the last week presented quite a military appearance; in addition to our County Militia, which has been nearly three weeks with us, Major Stratton's Troops of Yeomanry Cavalry marched in on Saturday last, for eight days' training and exercise, accompanied with an excellent band of music. The conduct of both classes of the military has been extremely good.

[George Frederick Stratton became sheriff of Oxford in 1806. Yeomanry Cavalry were extrajudicial military forces that were precursors to the modern police force.]

[This news article was adjacent to the advertisement that follows. The implication is that Maffre led the band of the Bloxham and Banbury Yeomanry in 1820.]

Jackson's Oxford Journal
Saturday, June 3, 1820

Advertisements & Notices
Under the patronage of Major Stratton, and officers of the Bloxham and Banbury Squadron of Yeomanry
Mr. MAFFRE will on WEDNESDAY NEXT, the 7th of June, 1820, give a CONCERT and BALL, at the White Lion Assembly Room, Banbury, where a variety of Vocal and Instrumental Music will be performed.

Tickets, 10s. 6d. each; Tea included—Concert to begin at 8 o'clock.

[The White Lion was a coaching inn.]

Leicester Journal
Friday, October 12, 1821, p. 3, c. 2

Catholic Chapel, Leicester.

THE Reverend Mr. Caestryck informs his friends and the public, that the
OPENING OF HIS CHAPEL
will take place
On Wednesday Morning, the 24th of October,
BY A SOLEMN SERVICE.

THE First Mass of Haydn will be performed by the Organ and the Choir; and a Discourse will be delivered by the Rev. Mr. ABBOT, from St. Mary's College, Oscott; after which a Collection will be made for the benefit of the Chapel, the erection of which has entailed a heavy debt on the Rev. Mr. Caestryck. Considering the smallness of the place, to consult the convenience of the public, the same service will be repeated the following day. Free Tickets of admission may be had of the Rev. Mr. Caestryck, and places will be reserved for those Ladies and Gentlemen who mean to favour him with their attendance. Doors to open at half-past ten, and service to begin precisely at eleven.

N. B. The same will be performed several successive Sundays, that those who could not be present at the opening, may have the opportunity of contributing to the support of this religious establishment.

[Although Maffre is not mentioned, he was likely involved.]

1822-1823 Leicester Directory

Deacon, Samuel, music seller Gallowtree
[This is the only music-related entry in the 1822-1823 Directory.]

Leicester Chronicle
Saturday, August 17, 1822, p. 3, c. 1

Theatre, Leicester.

THE Public are respectfully informed that a
CONCERT
OF
SACRED MUSIC
IN THREE ACTS,
Will be performed on Thursday evening, the 22d, inst.,
FOR THE
BENEFIT
OF THE
WIDOW AND NINE CHILDREN
OF THE
LATE Mr. C. JARVIS,
[*much omitted*]
Part II.
Clarionet Concerto—Mr. MAFFRE.

Leicester Journal
Friday, August 23, 1822, p. 3

The Concert at the Theatre on Thursday evening the 22d instant, for the benefit of the widow of the late C. Jarvis, and her infantine family, was most respectably attended, and in justice to the exertion of the musical talent assembled upon this charitable occasion, we cannot refrain from observing that it gave great and general satisfaction: Miss Hewitt's Concerto upon the Piano Forte was most delightfully and brilliantly executed, and drew from the audience the most decided applause, as did also her performance upon the Organ, the receipts, we understand amounted to about 50 pounds, the expence [*sic*] of the Theatre &c. which were unavoidable being deducted, leave a remainder for Mrs. Jarvis of nearly 45 pounds.

Leicester Journal
Friday, October 18, 1822, p. 3, c. 3

To the Nobility, Gentry &c. of Leicester and its vicinity

J. MAFFRE Professor of Music, returns his grateful thanks for the distinguished support he met with amongst those Families who did him the honour to sanction him the last Winter Season. And begs most respectfully to assure them he has provided himself with a complete collection of *quadrilles* and fashionable *dances*.

J. M. has the means of providing a large or small Band for Public or private Parties, and can inform them nothing shall be wanting on his part to ensure their approbation.

N. B. The Flute, Clarionette and Violin taught.
St. Nicholas Street, October 17th, 1822

Leicester Journal
Friday, March 14, 1823, p. 3, c. 5

LEICESTER MUSICAL SOCIETY.

A CONCERT of VOCAL and INSTRUMENTAL Music will be performed, in Three Parts, on Monday the 17th inst.

AT THE THEATRE.
PART 1st.
Overture.— *Clemenza di Tito.*
Here in Cool Grot.— *Glee.*
The Manly Heart.— *Duet.*
To all you Ladies.— *Glee.*
PART 2d.
Overture.— *Zauberflote.*
Thine Eye Jove Lightning seems.— *Glee.*
The Red Cross Knights.— *Glee.*
One Morning very early.— *Song.*
Piano Forte, Concerto.— MISS HEWITT.
O sleep my Baby Boy.— *Song.*
When Winds breathe soft.— *Glee.*
PART 3d.
Overture.— *Prometheus.*
It was the Nightingale.— *Glee.*
Bassoon, Concerto.— MR. WALDRON.
Auld Robin Gray.— *Song.*
Givonerto.— *Don Giovanni.*
Bid me Discourse.— *Song.*
Vive Enrico.— *Chorus.*
GOD SAVE THE KING.
Leader of the Band,
Mr. MAFFRE.
Boxes, 3s., *Pit*, 2s., *Gallery*, 1s.

Doors to be opened at 6, and the Performance to begin precisely at 7 o'clock.

Tickets and Places in the Boxes to be taken at MRS. ELLA's. Where Books of the performance may be had.

Leicester Journal
Friday, March 21, 1823, p. 3, c. 6

The Concert at the Theatre on Monday Evening was well attended. Miss Hewitt's performance on the Piano Forte, and Miss Jarvis's singing produced considerable effect. Mr. Waldron's Bassoon Concerto excited much admiration. The whole thing passed off with great éclat.

Leicester Journal
Saturday, May 24, 1823

An individual named Whittingham, met with a melancholy death near Narborough, on Thursday evening. It appears, that the deceased and five other persons belonging to the Leicestershire Militia band, were returning home from a country wake, in a light cart, when the horse taking fright, ran off at full speed, and the deceased, with four others, were thrown from the cart; and one of the wheels passing over his body killed him on the spot. The others escaped without any serious injury; though one of them (Waldrom) was very perilously situated for some moments. Being seated on the front of the cart when the affrighted animal set off, he fell forward, and remained suspended upon its hind legs for a considerable time. Had the horse began to kick, the consequences must have been most serious to him.

[*Henry Nicholson, a flautist, was the leader of the Militia band and may have been one of the other unnamed musicians. John Waldrom, a bassoonist, was a member of Nicholson's quadrille band as early as 1820, performed with Maffre as early as 1822, and opened a music shop in 1823. The earliest evidence that Maffre was in the Militia band dates to 1828.*]

Leicester Journal
Friday, February 27, 1824, p. 3, c. 4
[*This ad also appeared on March 5 and 12.*]

LEICESTER MUSICAL SOCIETY.

THE ANNUAL CONCERT of this Society will take place at the THEATRE, on MONDAY, the 15th of MARCH next. In the course of the performance, the following Vocal Pieces will be introduced: —

Leader of the Band, MR. MAFFRE.

GLEE.—"You gave me your heart." (*Webbe.*)
SONG.—Miss Sharpe. "In that dread hour."
DUETTO.—Lady of the Lake. (*Rossini.*)
　　　　　"Think not you unexpected come."
SONG.—Miss Russell. "Sweet Home."
TRIO.—"Cough and Crow." Miss Jarvis and Mr. Handscomb.
CONCERTO.—Miss Hewitt, on a New Patent Grand Piano-Forte.
SONG.—Miss Russell. "Auld Robin Gray."
GLEE.—"Oh share my cottage."
COMIC DUETTO.—(*Mazziughi.*)
SONG & CHORUS.—"Viva Enrico."
SONG.—Miss Russell. "Bid me discourse."
"God save the King."—Full Orchestra.

Books of the performance to be had of MRS. ELLA, 3d each; where places for the Boxes may be taken.

Doors to be opened at Six and begin precisely at Seven o'Clock.

　Boxes, 3s.—Pit, 2s.—Gallery, 1s.

Northampton Mercury
Friday, November 6, 1824
[*The November 13 review says Maffre replaced the leader Mr. Muston as Principal Violinist at the last minute.*]

MOULTON
GRAND MUSICAL FESTIVAL
Under the Patronage of

Hon. & Rev. R. Carlton	Rev. R. H. Knight, Sen.
Rev. L. Rokeby	Rev. R. H. Knight, Jun.
Rev. J. Dean, D. D.	Rev. Wm. Stanton
Rev. J. Wright, D. D.	Rev. J. Stanton
Clarke Hillyard, Esq.	Rev. H. Isham
Rev. William Stockdale	Rev. C. C. Wright
R. N. Stanton, M. D.	Rev. J. Greville

ON TUESDAY Morning, November 9, 1824,

WILL be PERFORMED, in the Church, at MOULTON, Northamptonshire,

A GRAND SELECTION OF
SACRED MUSIC,
From the Works of Handel, Haydn, Mozart, Pargoteni, and other eminent Composers

———

And on the Evening of the same Day will be performed,
A GRAND
MISCELLANEOUS CONCERT,
Of vocal and instrumental Music in which will be introduced, the celebrated HUNTING CHORUS, from the New Opera Freiseburge, by Weber, which has been performed with such unprecedented Applause at the English Opera.

The Profits arising from the Festival will be applied in charitable Purposes.

The Morning's Performance will consist of a Selection from Handel's Dettengen TE DEUM, the MESSIAH, Haydn's CREATION, Beethoven's MOUNT OF OLIVES, &c. &c.

The Evening's Performance will consist of Songs, Duets, Glees, Overtures, &c. &c.

Principal Vocal Performers
Mrs. Muston, of Drury Lane Theatre,
And Miss Melville of the Oratorium at Covent Garden and Drury Lane
PRINCIPAL INSTRUMENTAL PERFORMERS
Leader of the Band,
Mr. Muston, of Drury Lane Theatre.
Grand Pianoforte, Master McKorkell (by Permission of Mr. Barrett),
Principal Second Violin, Mr. Dubney;
Principal Viola, Mr. Tomson;

Principal Violoncello, Mr. J. MARSHALL, of Warwick; Double Basses, Messrs. Jarman and Patrick;
Principal Clarionet, Mr. Maffre;
Flute, Mr. Gibson;
Bassoon, Mr. Dalby;
First Horn, Mr. Hewitt;
First Trumpet, Mr. Crisp;
Trombone, Mr. Nicholson, of Leicester;
Double Drums, Mr. J. Edens.
Violins, Messrs. Muston, Dobney, McKorkell, Gardiner, Mr. Reichenbach.
The Whole under the Direction of Mr. C. MORRIE.

The Choruses will be full and complete in every Department, as none but the most efficient Performers are engaged.

A spacious Orchestra for the Occasion will be erected in front of the Gallery in the Church.

The Concert will be performed in the Evening in a large and commodious Building belonging to the Rev. W. STANTON, which is kindly offered for the Occasion, and which will be lighted up with upwards of 400 registered Lamps.

The Performance in the Church will commence precisely at a Quarter before Eleven, and the Concert in the Evening presently at Six. [*Many details omitted*]

Northampton Mercury
Saturday, November 13, 1824

Moulton Musical Feast, on Tuesday last.—A correspondent says,—"As a disinterested admirer of the Moulton musical performance, I hope you will allow me to express an opinion, that in the compass necessarily assigned to such undertakings, there has not been anything altogether equal to it in this town or its vicinity. The choruses were sung with admirable precision; and, except the trebles, which wanted nothing in the merit, only in the number of the voices, the parts were excellently sustained, and accurately balanced. There certainly appeared to me a most conspicuous improvement in the manner of pronouncing the words so as to be more intelligible than I have observed on former occasions. The reputation of Miss Melville, Mr. Cunningham, and Mr. Morris is too well established to require commendation from me; I must however take the liberty to say, that since the last time I had the pleasure of listening to them, they are all manifestly improved, and would certainly take a higher rank in the gradations of musical talent. Miss Melville's song "Rejoice greatly," from the Oratorio of the Messiah, was finely articulated, and had an air of animation, the want of which has sometimes proved fatal to the effect of that beautiful composition. Gratins agimus, by the same performer, was excellently accompanied on the clarionette by Mr. Maffre, who, in consequence of Mr.

Muston's unavoidable absence, was kindly induced to take the principal violin, and he acquitted himself up both instruments (notwithstanding the difficulty of such a transition) to the entire satisfaction of the orchestra and the audience. It is scarcely necessary to state, that the whole performance was closely kept together by the able assistance of Mr. Marshall, of Warwick, whose violoncello accompaniments are far above my praise.

A.B.

Leicester Chronicle
November 27, 1824, p. 3, c. 4

CONCERT.

MISS HEWITT

MOST respectfully informs the Nobility, Gentry, and Public in general of the town and county of Leicester it is her intention to give

A CONCERT AT THE THEATRE,

On TUESDAY Evening, the 7th of December, which is honoured by the patronage of
[*39 names including Earl and Lady Howe*]

MISS MELVILLE,
(Pupil of Rossini), of the late Oratorios, Covent-garden and Drury-lane,
MISS JARVIS, MISS RUSSELL, MISS SHARPE, MR. MORRIS, AND MR. HANSCOMB.
HARP—Master C. MCKORKELL, Pupil of Barrett.
GRAND PIANO FORTE—Miss and Miss M. HEWITT.
LEADER—Mr. ELLA
Member of the Philharmonic, King's Ancient, and Italian Opera Orchestra.

ACT I.
Occasional Overture—Handel.
Glee—"Great Apollo Strike the Lyre"—Webbe.
Duett—"Together let us range the Fields"— MISS SHARPE and MR. MORRIS.
Duett—"Te mi Credi, Amato bene"—Rossini—MISS MELVILLE and MISS JARVIS.
Duett—Harp and Piano Forte—MISS M. HEWITT and Master MCKORKELL.
Song—"Should be Upbraid"—Bishop—MISS JARVIS.
Solo—Clarionet—MR. MAFFRE.
Song—"Di Placer"—Rossini—MISS MELVILLE.

ACT II.
Overture—"La Clemenza Di Tito"—Mozart.
Duett—"As it fell upon a day"—Bishop—MISS

MELVILLE and Miss JARVIS
Concerto—Grand Piano Forte—Miss HEWITT.
Song—"Dried be that Tear"— Miss MELVILLE.
Duett—"Think not you unexpected come"—Rossini—
Miss JARVIS and Miss RUSSELL.
Song—"The Death of Nelson"—Dr. Clarke—Mr.
MORRIS.
Glee—"The Chough and Crow"—Bishop.

————

ACT III.
Overture—"Il Tancredi"—Rossini.
Song—"County Guy"—Knapton—Miss JARVIS.
Duett—"Tell me, gentle Stranger"—Parry—Miss
MELVILLE and Miss RUSSELL.
Duett—Harp—Master MᶜKORKELL.
Song—"Tu che accendi"—Rossini—Miss MELVILLE.
Glee—"Viva Enrico, vivo il forte"
"God save the King."

————

Boxes, 5s.—Pit, 3s.—Gallery, 1s, 6d.
Doors to be opened at six, and the Performance to commence precisely at seven o'clock.
Tickets and Places in the Boxes to be taken at Miss HEWITT's, Southgate-street, and Mrs. ELLA's, Market-place.

Coventry Herald
Friday, May 13, 1825

CONCERTS,
UNDER THE PATRONAGE OF
The Right Hon. the EARL & COUNTESS of WARWICK,
The Right Honourable LORD MONSON,
CHANDOS LEIGH, Esq. High Sherriff,
The Worshipful the MAYOR of WARWICK,
The Reverend Dr. WOOLL, of Rugby.

————

MESSRS. MARSHALL
Have the honour to announce to the Nobility, Clergy, and Gentry, of the County and Borough of Warwick, their intention to have

TWO GRAND
Miscellaneous Concerts,
THE FIRST AT THE
NEW ASSEMBLY ROOMS, RUGBY
On Tuesday, May the 17ᵗʰ, and
THE SECOND AT THE
COURT HOUSE, WARWICK
On Friday, May the 20ᵗʰ,
To which their attention and patronage is most respectfully solicited

————

Principal Vocal Performers

MISS MELVILLE,
(A Pupil of Signor Rossini)
INSTRUMENTAL PERFORMERS ALREADY ENGAGED
Leader of the Band,
MR. MARSHALL, OF OXFORD:
Principal Second Violin—Mr. SHARP.
Viola—Mr. JACKSON.
Violoncello—Mr. J. MARSHALL.
Flute—Mr. HEWITT.
Clarionet—Mr. MAFFRE.
Bassoon—Mr. FRANCOMB.
Drum—Mr. SHEPPERD.
Harp—MASTER C. MᶜKORKELL.
Trumpet—Mr. NORTON.
Grand Piano Forte—Mr. F. MARSHALL.
The BAND will be full and complete, as Performers are engaged from London, Oxford, Northampton, and Leamington

————

After each Concert will be a BALL
**TICKETS, *Seven Shillings* each, and at *One Guinea* (admitting four persons of the same family) may be obtained at Warwick, of Mr. Marshall, Church-street; Mr. Sharp Advertiser Office, and Messrs. Merridew, Heathcote, [unreadable] and Forlen, Booksellers;—at Leamington, of Mr. F. Marshall, Ely Cottage, Charlotte-street; Elliston's L[unreadable]; Merridew's Establishment; and of Mr. Rose, Bookseller, Clemen's-street; at Rugby, of Messrs. Rowell, Bookseller and at the Spread Eagle Inn.

Coventry Herald
Friday, May 20, 1825

GRAND CONCERT AT RUGBY.—The first of two miscellaneous Concerts announced in our paper, to take place at Rugby and Warwick, was held at the new Assembly Room, Rugby, on Tuesday evening last, and we have pleasure in saying was exceedingly well attended. The Messrs. Marshalls' exertions in catering for the public, were crowned with flattering success.

Miss Melville, a pupil of Rossini, was the principal Singer, and her performance elicited great applause. The new song, *"Fly away Dove,"* from the Hebrew Family, and the glee, *"We three merry Gypsies,"* were sung in a very playful manner, and, as is usually the case with such compositions, pleased generally. *"Softly Sweet,"* with Mr. Marshall's celebrated obligato violoncello accompaniment; and *"Gratias assimus [agimus] tibi,"* accompanied by Mr. Maffre, on the Clarionet, were fine specimens of both vocal and instrumental music. The overtures and concertos of Handel, and the fine old music of Corelli, were admirably performed. Mr. Wm.

Marshall, of Oxford, led the band; Mr. F. Marshall, who presided at the Piano Forte, played a difficult Fantasia of his own composition, on that instrument. The Rev. Dr. Wooll, Head Master of Rugby School, patronized the Concert, and attended with a numerous party. Messrs. Marshalls' second Concert takes place at the Court House, Warwick, this evening, and we have every reason to calculate on there being a crowded audience.

Coventry Herald
Friday, May 27, 1825

MESSRS. MARSHALL'S CONCERTS.

On Friday night, upwards of 300 persons of the highest respectability in Warwick and its neighborhood, assembled at the Court-house to hear Messrs. Marshall's second grand Miscellaneous Concert.—The First Act opened with Haydn's *Surprise Overture*. The Song, "*A dove in terror flying*," from the new and popular play of the *Hebrew Family*, and set to music by Whittaker, was charmingly sung by Miss Melville. Bishop's beautiful Glee, "*Yes 'tis the Indian Drum*," was tastefully sung by Miss Melville, and Messrs. H. Marshall and Shepherd. [*much of the review has been omitted*] and the *Clarionet Obligato*, by Mr. Maffre was scientifically executed.

Leicester Journal
Friday, July 22, 1825

Mr. Green to make his 26th Aerial Voyage in a Balloon....The Duke of Rutland's Band will perform during the inflation.

Leicester Journal
Friday, September 2, 1825

Fireworks at New Cricket Ground, Humberstone Gate...prepared by Mr. Read...to celebrate the Races...The Duke of Rutland's Band will attend at Seven o'clock.

Leicester Journal
Friday, October 7, 1825

Grand Gala Fireworks

...to coincide with the County Fair...The Duke of Rutland's Band will attend at 7.

Leicester Journal
Friday, November 26, 1825, p. 3

MISS HEWITT most respectfully announces to the Nobility, Gentry, and Public in general of the Town and Country, that she has engaged that highly celebrated and favorite Singer

MISS TRAVIS,

To perform at her Concert, which will take place
At the Theatre,

On TUESDAY Evening, the 20th of December next, honored by the Patronage of
[*39 names including Earl and Lady Howe*]
The full particulars of what will be performed will appear in next week's paper.

The Scheme of the Theatre will be opened on Wednesday the 7th, when places may be taken at MRS. ELLA'S, Market Place, where tickets and books of the performance may be had. Tickets may also be had of MISS HEWITT, South Gate-street.

PRICE OF TICKETS – 5s—3s—1s. 6d.

Leicester Journal
Friday, December 3, 1825, p. 3, c. 3
[Repeated December 17 in the Leicester Chronicle]

MISS HEWITT'S
GRAND MISCELLANEOUS CONCERT OF
Vocal and Instrumental Music.

MISS HEWITT most respectfully announces to the Nobility, Gentry, and Public in general of the Town and Country, that she has engaged that highly celebrated and favorite Singer

MISS TRAVIS,

To perform at her Concert, which will take place
At the Theatre,

On TUESDAY Evening, the 20th of December next, honored by the Patronage of
[*39 names including Earl and Lady Howe*]
PRINCIPAL VOCAL PERFORMERS,
MISS TRAVIS,
MISS JARVIS, MISS SHARPE, AND
MR. HANSCOMB.
GRAND PIANO FORTE,
MISS AND MISS M. HEWITT.
Principal Violoncello,
MR. MARSHALL, OF WARWICK.
LEADER, MR. MAFFRE.
An excellent BAND is engaged.
Act 1st.

Overture—Men of Prometheus	Beethoven.
Glee—Glorious Apollo	Webbe.
Song—Miss Jarvis—By the simplicity of Venus' doves	Bishop.
Concerto—Mr. Marshall	Corelli.
Song—Miss Travis—Tranquillo	Guglielma.
Glee—Chough and Crow	Bishop.

Act 2d.

Symphony—Surprise ....Haydn.
Glee—Oh! Stranger, lend thy gentle
    Barque ....Stevenson.
Duett—Miss Travis and Miss Jarvis
    —As it fell upon a day..............................Bishop.
Cavatina—Miss Jarvis—Vittima ....Pucitta.
Duett—Grand Piano Forte—Miss
    and Miss M. Hewitt.
Song—Miss Travis—Auld Robin Gray.
Huntsman's Chorus..Weber.

Act 3d.

Overture—Der Freischutz ....Weber.
Song—Miss Travis—Jock o' Hazledean,
    (words by Sir Walter Scott)
Concerto—Grand Piano Forte—Miss Hewitt.
Glee—When winds breathe soft ....Webbe.
Song—Miss Travis—The Lark......................Bishop.
GOD SAVE THE KING.

Boxes 5s—Pit 3s—Gallery 1s. 6d.

Doors to be opened at Six, and the Performance to begin precisely at Seven.

Tickets and Places in the Boxes to be taken at Mrs. Ella's, Market Place — Tickets may also be had of Miss Hewitt's, South Gate Street.

Leicester Chronicle
Monday, December 24, 1825, p. 3, c. 3

MISS HEWITT'S CONCERT.— A week of awful alarm — of extensive impending peril to the monied and trading interests, has been happily followed by a night of delightful and unmingled enchantment, to those who relish "*the concord of sweet sounds.*" The pieces selected for this musical treat, evince equal taste and judgment in the choice. There was a judicious union of the more complex, elaborate, terrific, and almost superhuman compositions of HAYDN, BEETHOVEN, and WEBER— from a school, which has carried intricate harmonical combinations to the highest conceivable point of subtilization, with the truly simple, pleasing, and national harmonics of WEBBE, BISHOP, STEVENSON, &c. [*polysyllabic digression about harmonious music omitted*] To return more specifically to the subject, it is a high compliment to our native and resident musical talent, that a CONCERT of such magnitude can be accomplished in so satisfactory a style, with so little exotic aid. The sole novel attraction of the evening, was MISS TRAVIS, the exercise of whose abilities in this instance, amply justified her exalted fame. Her voice possesses at least three essential attributes—strength, compass, and sweetness; and her songs were all given with that powerfully impressive effect which called down most rapturous plaudits. "*Auld Robin Gray*" was a delicious specimen of the pathetic, which touched every heart, and thrilled every nerve of the audience. Not less impressive, but with more variety in manner, was the "*Jock o'Hazledean.*" In short, it would be a difficult task for the soundest judgment to decide, in which song her talents shone most conspicuously. The striking characteristics of her execution, are power and versatility, chastened with delicacy, governed, nay, subdued with uncommon discretion. Under such judicious management, her transitions, however sudden or unexpected, all produced a magical effect. The remaining vocal pieces, particularly the glees, were all achieved in that excellent style, which will always deserve unqualified praise. It would be almost invidious not to mention the merits of MISSES JARVIS and SHARPE, and MESSRS. HANDSCOMB and T. JARVIS, whose concordant tones in the GLEES and CHORUS, formed so material a portion of the evening's regale. HANDSCOMB's bass is remarkable for its depth and smoothness, and when mingled with the mellow alto of T. JARVIS, and the sweet tribles of the MISSES JARVIS and SHARPE, form altogether what may justly be denominated a bowl of musical punch; a beverage palatable and exhilarating, when every ingredient, as in the present instance, is genuine in quality, and exactly proportioned. The overtures of BEETHOVEN and WEBER, & the Huntsman's Chorus of the latter, are extraordinary, almost extravagant productions; the orchestra however, proved themselves fully equal to their execution, a eulogy of no ordinary weight and value. Every other piece was given with equal skill. The duet on the grand piano, by the Misses Hewitt, with the slight occasional accompaniment of Mr. Maffre, attracted particular attention, such was the correctness, that the three pair of hands seemed to be moved by only one volition. The house was well filled, the boxes were graced with the rank and fashion of the town and county, and such was the satisfaction, that there is no doubt Miss Hewitt will find it her duty and interest to make this festival annual. A criticism on a Concert ought to be written during its performance, there would then be a strong probability of receiving and imparting that kind of inspiration, which the vivid impressions of the moment never fail to excite, but which from their evanescent nature, are dissipated or but faintly recollected in a few hours.

Leicester Journal
Friday, December 28, 1825, p. 3, c. 5

Miss Hewitt's Concert at the Theatre, on Tuesday evening was well attended, and the company present appeared highly gratified. — Miss Travis is a delightful singer, and drew loud and repeated applause from the audience. Mr. Maffre as Leader, gave great satisfaction. The Overtures were well performed, and the Band was extremely good. The Concert altogether went off with great éclat.

The Poll for the Election of Two Representatives in Parliament for the Borough of Leicester
published 1826 by Thomas Combe & Son

Commenced June 13 and closed June 23, 1826

Candidates
Sir C. Abney Hastings, Bart. [*baronet*]
Robert Otway Cave, Esq.
William Evans, Esq.
Thomas Denman, Esq.

[*Hastings and Cave were elected because they were strongly favored throughout the County and moderately favored by the Town.*]

p. 13: Dobney, Frederick
p. 27: Maffre, Joseph, St. Peter's lane, musician
p. 26: Mavius, Charles
p. 38: Sternberg, Thomas
[*The musicians and music sellers listed above voted for the two winners. The following did not vote: Deacon, Hewitt, Jones, Nicholson, and Waldrom.*]

Leicester Chronicle
September 16, 1826, p. 3, c. 3

MARKET HARBOROUGH
GRAND MUSICAL FESTIVAL,
For the BENEFIT of
MASTER BARKER.

———

UNDER THE IMMEDIATE PATRONAGE OF
The Right Hon. the Viscountess Howe
The Rt. Hon. the Viscountess of Denbigh
The Hon. Lady Palmer
The Hon. Mrs. Cockayne Medlicott
[*19 female names omitted*]
The Right Hon. the Earl Howe
The Rt. Hon. the Earl of Denbigh
[*Over 120 male names omitted*]
On MONDAY MORNING, Sept. 18th, 1826
WILL BE PERFORMED,
In the CHURCH at MARKET HARBOROUGH
THE MESSIAH,
With the additional ACCOMPANIMENTS by MOZART

———

On MONDAY EVENING will be given, in the

TOWN HALL, a
GRAND MISCELLANEOUS CONCERT.
Part 1st.
Overture to Der Freischütz.
Glee–"Blow, gentle Gales"–(Bishop).
Song, Mr. Braham–"Nelson"–(Braham).
Song, Master Barker–"The little Kiss"–(Watson).
Song, Mr. Tinney–"Soldier, rest"–(Watson).
Song, a young Lady–"My Lodging is on the cold Ground–(Drovett).
Concerto–Clarionet–Mr. Maffre.
Duet, Miss Travis and Master Barker–"As it fell upon a Day"–(Bishop).
Song, Mr. Robinson–"Orynthia"–(Bishop).
Song, Miss Travis–"Bid me discourse"–(Bishop).
Duet, Mr. Braham and Master Barker–"All's well."
Song, a young Lady–"There's a Grief"–(Rossini).
Song, Mr. Braham–"Scots wha ha'e."
Song, Miss Travis–"Cupid, one day"–(Parry).
Glee, Masters Barker and Watsons, and Mr. Tinney–"The three Crows"–(Phillips).
Between the First and Second Parts, a Concerto on the Grand Piano Forte, by Miss Hewitt.
Part 2nd.
Overture–(Mozart).
Duet, Masters J. and H. Watson–"Lo, when Showers"–(Horn).
Glee–"Come on the Brook"–(Bishop).
Song, Master Barker–"The Gipsy Boy"–(Rooke).
Song, Mr. Braham–"Kelvin Grove"–(Braham).
Capriccio on the Horn, Mr. Tully
Duet, a young Lady and Master Barker–"My pretty Page"–(Bishop).
Song, Miss Travis–"Bonny brave Scotland"–(Watson).
Duet, Mr. Robinson and Mr. Tinney–"George and Victory"–(Williams).
Song, a young Lady–"The Soldier tir'd"–(Dr. Arne).
Song, Mr. Braham–"The blue Bonnets"–(A. Lee).
Finale–"God save the King."

———

On TUESDAY MORNING, Sept. 19, will be performed in the CHURCH,
A GRAND SELECTION of
SACRED MUSIC,
[*Omitted because Maffre is not mentioned*]

———

On TUESDAY EVENING, Sept. 19th, at the TOWN HALL,
A Grand Miscellaneous Concert.
[*Omitted because Maffre is not mentioned*]
PRINCIPAL VOCAL PERFORMERS.

MISS TRAVIS
(From the Ancient Concerts);
MASTER BARKER
(From the Theatre Royal, Covent-garden, and Vauxhall
and Pupil of Mr. Watson);
Mr. ROBINSON
(From the Theatre Royal, Covent-garden);
A YOUNG LADY, Pupil of Mr. Watson (her first
appearance);
MASTERS J. & H. WATSON
(From the Theatre Royal, Covent-garden);
Mr. TINNEY
(From the Oratorios of the Theatres Royal, Covent-
garden and Drury lane);
Mr. CUNNINGTON, Mr. MORRISS, and
Mr. Braham.
The Instrument Department will be sustained by a
concentration of the first talent.
Leader, Mr. ROOKE (From the Theatre Royal, Drury-
lane).
Principal Second Violin, Mr. HICKSON.
First Violoncello, Mr. HATTON (from the Theatre
Royal, Covent-garden).
First Clarionet, Mr. MAFFRE.
Principal Bassoon, Mr. WALDRUM.
Principal Trumpet, Mr. NORTON (from the King's
Theatre), who will also perform a Concerto.
Principal Horn, Mr. TULLY (of the Antient Concerts),
who will perform a Capriccio on the Horn.
Double Basses, Messrs. HICKSON and PATRICK.
Trombones, Messrs. NICHOLSON and ADCOCK.
Double Drums, Mr. GOODWIN (from the Theatre
Royal, Covent-garden).
Miss HEWITT has kindly consented to perform a
Concerto on the Piano Forte.
The Choruses will be supported by a powerful and
choice selection of Performers from London,
Birmingham, Leicester, Northampton, Melton Mowbray,
Kettering, Hinckley, and Clipson, under the direction of
Mr. JARMAN.
The whole under the superintendance [sic] of Mr.
WATSON, Composer to the Theatre Royal, Covent-
garden, who has kindly consented to preside at the
Organ and Piano Forte.
The mornings' performance to commence at eleven
o'clock, the evenings' precisely at seven.
The Performers are particularly requested to attend a
rehearsal of the Sacred Music, at five o'clock on Sunday
evening, the 17th inst., at the Town Hall.
Tickets of admission to the Middle Aisle and Chancel
of the Church, 10s., Side Aisles, 7s., Gallery, 3s. 6d.; to
the Concerts in the Town-Hall, 10s. 6d. To be had of
Mr. Abbott, Stationer, &c., at the principal Inns, and at
the Post Office, Harborough.

1827 Leicester Directory
[*Entries related to dance and music*]

Bland, Mr., dancing master, New-street
Deacon, Samuel, music warehouse, Gallowtree-gate
Dobney, Frederick, musician and broker, Belgrave-gate
Ella, Kitty, confectioner, Market-place
Freake, Joseph Frederick, dancing master, Granby-place
Hewitt, John, teacher of music, Southgate-street
Hewitt, Messdms., organists, teachers of music, &c,
    High-street
Jarvis, Miss, teacher of music, York-street, London-road
Jones, Ebenezer Tristram, musician, Oxford-street
Linwood, Miss, seminary for young ladies, Belgrave-gate
Maffre, Joseph, musician, St-Peters lane
Mavius, Charles, professor of music, and music
    warehouse, Gallowtree-gate
Nicholson, Henry, musician, New-walk
Partington, George, dancing master, Rutland-street
Sternberg, Thomas, pianoforte tuner and repairer, New-
    walk
Valentine, Miss, Organist, Belgrave-gate
Waldrom, John, musician and music seller, Market-street

[page xxi]
ALDERMAN NEWTON'S SCHOOL.
[*The one and a quarter page summary of this School includes the
following paragraph.*]

The School is regularly subjected to a vigilant
inspection, examination and superintendance by a
Committee selected from the body with a most
beneficial effect.—The master is Mr. Appleby, and the
singing master, Mr. Maffre.

Leicester Chronicle
January 27, 1827

The concert and ball, which took place last Tuesday
evening, at the Queen's Head Inn, Ashby-de-la-Zouch,
was extremely well attended, there being upwards of one
hundred ladies and gentlemen present, among whom
were noticed W. Shirley and R. Beaumont, Esqrs., the
Revds. J. Piddocke, Tunnecliffe, Pratt, and Merewether,
Valentine Green, L. Fosbrooke, and R. Cresswell,
Esqrs., and most of the neighbouring gentry and their
families. The pieces, both vocal and instrumental,
selected for the concert, did credit to the taste and
judgment of the caterers for the amusement of the
audience, and we must add, they were executed by the
performers with a truth and feeling seldom witnessed.
Messrs. Nicholson, Maffre, and Waldrom, sustained
their parts with their wonted excellence. Miss Sharpe

sang "The War has Ceased," "The Soldier Tired," and "Cherry Ripe," in monst beautiful style. The musical talents of this young vocalist promise to rival some of our first rate concert singers. Mr. E. Mammatt presided at the piano forte. His performance of the celebrated concerto of Kalkbrenner was rapturously received. The amateur proved himself indeed a lover of his art, and he was encored in that beautiful amatory song, "Oh, no! we never mention her." After the concert the ball was opened by L. Piddocke, Esq. and Miss Piddocke, and kept up with great spirit until four o'clock in the morning. The patronage afforded upon this occasion augurs well of what may be expected to take place, when the spacious and elegant concert room at the baths is finished. We ought in justice to add, that the arrangements made by the stewards, L. Piddocke and E. Fisher, Esqrs., gave the highest satisfaction to the company.

Leicester Chronicle
March 9, 1827

In a few days will be published, price 4s.

A New Set of QUADRILLES, for the Piano Forte, composed and arranged by J. Maffre, Musician to his Grace the Duke of Rutland, and dedicated (with permission) to Miss Linwood.

Sold by the Author, St. Peter's lane, and may be had at the different Musical Warehouses, in Leicester.

Leicester Chronicle
Wednesday, June 2, 1827

CHORAL SOCIETY.—On Monday last this society had a private rehearsal of the pieces to be performed at St. Margaret's church, on Wednesday next. Judging from the style and ability, as well as the care and attention with which the whole performance was gone through, the society may be truly said to have earned the patronage and support which it claims at the hands of the public, on the forthcoming occasion. We, therefore, sincerely trust, that its efforts will be crowned with success.—*See advertisement.*

Leicester Chronicle
Wednesday, June 2, 1827

LEICESTER CHORAL SOCIETY.

————

THIS Society is instituted for the purpose of cultivating SACRED MUSIC, and has received the patronage and support of the following Noblemen and

Gentlemen:—

His Grace the Duke of RUTLAND
The Right Hon. the Earl HOWE
W. Arnold, M. D.
J. Hill, M. D.
J. B. Freer, M. D.
John Mansfield, Esq.
Rev. Thomas Burnaby
Rev. R. Burnaby
[*and 35 others including*]
W. Gardiner
C. Mavius

The Nobility and Gentry of town and country are respectfully informed, that the Society, consisting of upwards of 100 Performers, intend having a PERFORMANCE on WEDNESDAY, June 6th, for the purpose of raising a Fund for purchasing Music, &c. and with the permission of the Rev. Thomas Burnaby and the Churchwardens,…[*remainder of details omitted*]

Leicester Chronicle
Wednesday, June 2, 1827

A GRAND SELECTION OF SACRED MUSIC,
WILL BE PERFORMED
At St. Margaret's Church,
In the Morning.

————

PRINCIPAL VOCAL PERFORMERS,
MISS JARVIS,
MISS SHARP, (Pupil of Signor Begrez),
Mr. HANDSCOMB, Mr. CRADOCK
MISS HEWITT will preside at the Organ.

FIRST PART.

Overture—Messiah	Handel
Recitation and Air—Comfort ye my people— Miss JARVIS	Ditto
Chorus—And the glory of the Lord	Ditto
Recitation and Air—For behold darkness shall cover the earth—Mr. CRADOCK	Ditto
Chorus—For unto us a child is born	Ditto
Air—Rejoice greatly—Miss SHARP	Ditto
Chorus—All we like sheep	Ditto
Solo and Chorus—Adestes Fideles	Ditto
Chorus—Hallelujah	Ditto

PART SECOND.

Overture—Iphigenia	Gluck
Song—The marvellous work—Miss SHARP	Haydn
Chorus—To the etherial vaults	Ditto
Song—With verdure clad—Miss JARVIS	Ditto
Chorus—The heavens are telling	Ditto
Song—Shall I in Manner's fertile plain—Mr. HANDS-	

COMB ....Handel
Chorus—Sing to Jehovah.....................................Graun
Song—Gratias Agimus—Miss SHARP, accompanied on
the Clarionet by Mr. MAFFRE ....Gullielmi
Chorus—Great and glorious............................ Melodies
Song—He that ruleth Israel ....Judah
Chorus—The King shall rejoice.................... Melodies

Leader of the Band, Mr. MAFFRE

The doors will open at Ten, and the performance to commence precisely at Eleven.

At the request of a considerable number of Subscribers, the following ALTERATIONS IN THE PRICE OF ADMISSION has been made, viz.:—For the body of the Church, and Chancel, 2s. 6d.; Side Aisles and Seats, 1s.

—The 2s. 6. Tickets to be admitted at the south door; the 1s. Tickets at the west door. Children to be admitted at half-price.

N.B. Tickets and books of the performance to be had at Mr. DEACON's and Mr. MAVIUS's Music Warehouse, as no money will be taken at the doors.

The Subscribers to the Choral Musical Meetings, are respectfully informed that the next Rehearsal will take place on the 18th of June inst.

Leicester Chronicle
Tuesday, June 8, 1827

The performance of sacred music at St. Margaret's church Wednesday last, by the Choral Society, was most respectably attended, & gave very general satisfaction, particularly the choruses, which were executed with great precision and effect, considering the comparatively short period which the society has been formed. The choir consisted of more than 100 performers. The amount received for tickets of admission was, we understand, about £45.

Leicester Chronicle
June 27, 1827, p. 3, c. 1

KIBWORTH
GRAND CONCERT.

MR. W. P. CUNNINGTON, PROFESSOR OF MUSIC, *Harborough*, most respectfully announces to the Nobility and Gentry of KIBWORTH and its vicinity, that
A GRAND CONCERT
OF VOCAL AND INSTRUMENTAL MUSIC,
Will be Performed
IN THE LARGE SCHOOL ROOM OF KIBWORTH,
(*By permission of the Rev. J. Goodman,*)

On MONDAY EVENING, July 2nd, 1827
PRINCIPAL VOCAL PERFORMERS.
MISS HUGHES,
(The Young Lady who was so rapturously received at the late Grand Musical Festival at Market Harborough.)
MISS SHARPE,
(Pupil of Signor Berger, of the Italian Opera.)
MASTER WATSON,
(Of the Theatre Royal, Covent Garden.)
MR. MORRIS, and MR. CUNNINGTON.—Mr. WATSON, Composer and Director of the Music at the Theatre Royal, Covent Garden, will conduct the Performance and preside at the PIANO-FORTE.

FIRST PART.
Overture, Calipha di Bagdat–*Boieldieu.*
Glee–(by particular desire)–"The Wreath"—*Mazzinghi.*
Song–Miss Sharpe–"In that dread hour"–Horn Obligato–Mr. S. Cunnington–*Drouett.*
Duett–Miss Hughes and Master Watson–"As it fell upon a day"–*Bishop.*
Song–Mr. Morris–"Last words of Marmion"–*Dr. Clarke.*
Song–Miss Hughes–"There's a Grief"–*Rossini.*
Overture, (by desire) Zauberflote—*Mozart.*
Song–Master Watson–"One Winter's Morn a Robin"–*Watson.*
Glee–"Blow gentle gales"–*Bishop.*
Song–Miss Sharpe and Mr. Morris–"I love thee"–Ditto.
Song–Miss Sharpe–"My lodging is on the cold ground" with variations–*Drouett.*
Glee with Chorus–"Viva Enrico" with full Accompaniments.–*Pucitta.*

PART SECOND.
Grand Overture to the Opera of Der Freischutz–*Weber.*
Song–Mr. Cunnington–"The Battle of Hohenlinden"–*C. Smith.*
Concerto Clarionet–Mr. Maffre–*Maffre.*
Song–Miss Hughes–"Comin' thro' the Rye"–*Parry.*
Song–Master Watson–"Oh! no; we never mention her"–*Bishop.*
Sinfonia (by desire)–*Haydn.*
Glee–"Faithless Emma."
Song–Miss Sharpe–"The Soldier tir'd"–*Arne.*
Song–Miss Hughes–"Last Rose of Summer"–*Irish Melodies.*
Glee–"The Bells of St. Michael's Tower"–*Knyvett.*
Duett–Miss Hughes and Master Watson–"Yes, Yes, I read it"–*Bishop.*
Finale–"God Save the King" (verse and chorus).

The Band will be numerous and efficient, consisting of Violins, Violas, Violoncellos, Double Bass, Flutes, Clarionets, Trumpets, French Horns, Trombone,

---

182

Bassoons, Double Drums, &c., by the most approved professional Performers, the whole forming a very powerful and effective orchestra.

The Door will be open at Six o'clock, and the Concert will commence at Seven precisely.

Admittance–Front Seats, 6s.; Back Seats, 3 s.

Tickets may be had of Mr. CUNNINGTON, and Mr. ABBOTT, Bookseller, &c., Harborough; and at the ROSE and CROWN INN, Kibworth.

Leicester Music Festival Programs
September 4, 5, 6, 1827

[There are five half-day programs, each of which begins with a cover page. The three morning performances were sacred music and the two evening performances were Grand Concerts. Each cover page is followed by a common list of patrons, different Principal Vocal Performers, and a common list of Instrumental and Vocal Performers. Each program ends with a playbill.]

[*Summary of the five programs.*]

September 4, Tuesday Morning
Cathedral Service
Beethoven's Grand Chorus from Mount of Olives
Handel's Air
Haydn's Chorus from a Mass
September 4, Tuesday Evening
First Grand Concert
September 5, Wednesday Morning
Selection of Sacred Music
September 5, Wednesday Evening
Second Grand Concert
September 6, Thursday Morning
Haydn's The Messiah, with Mozart's Accompaniments

[First Program Cover Page]
Leicester Musical Festival,
1827,

———

On TUESDAY MORNING, SEPTEMBER 4,
AT
ST. MARGARET'S CHURCH,
Full
CATHEDRAL SERVICE,
CHANTED BY THE
REV. H. W. SALMON, A.M.
AND A
Selection of Sacred Music
BY THE FULL ORCHESTRA,

———

BY PERMISSION OF THE
Rev. T. Burnsby, Vicar, and the Rev. G. O. Fenwick,
Lessee of the Chancel.

———

SOLD FOR THE BENEFIT OF THE INFIRMARY, LUNATIC ASYLUM, AND FRYER HOUSE OF RECOVERY.

———

Price Sixpence.

———

LEICESTER:
PRINTED BY A. COCKSHAW, HIGH-STREET

[*List of Principal Performers in the First Program.*]
Principal Instrumental Performers

MESSRS. CRAMER, KIESEWETTER, AND OURY,
Leaders
MR. MORALT, *Principal Second*
MR. R. ASHLEY *Principal Viola*
MR. DANIELS, *Principal Second*
MR. LINDLEY, *Principal Violoncello*
SIGNOR DRAGONETTI, *Principal Double Bass*
Violins.—Messrs. Guynemer, Ella, Nix, Gledhill, Griesbach, Watkins, Anderson, Nadaud, Litoff, Adams, & Jackson, London; Mavius, W. Marshall, Marshall, jun. Fritch, Ware, Salmon, Owencroft, Fritch, Maffre, McEwan, Hickson, Graham, Gill, J. Owencroft, McKorkell, and twenty-three others.

Leicester Chronicle
March 15, 1828

Miss Sharpe's Concert, at the Theatre, on Wednesday evening, went off with an *éclat* which, in our opinion, deserved a much better audience. Signor Begrez, the grand attraction of the evening, delighted every one by the elegant style in which he gave three of four English ballads, particularly "Oh! no, we never mention her." He certainly surpasses every singer of the present day. Miss Sharpe is much improved since we last heard her, and sang several pieces with Begrez, which drew from the audience a loud *encore*. She has naturally a very good voice, but it requires to be more polished in its execution. Neither of these requisites, however, are sufficient to constitute true excellence in a singer; there must be the assistance of the mind superadded to both; and we would recommend Miss S. in aspiring to greatness, to encourage somewhat of that feeling and expression which her tutor, Signor Begrez, so pre-eminently possesses. Mr. Charles Bland, of Covent-garden Theatre (son of the celebrated Mrs. Bland), made his first appearance here, and sang three or four songs with considerable spirit and ability. He exhibited a clear and melodious voice, and was warmly *encored*. The orchestra, which was led by Mr. Maffre, executed the instrumental part with a precision highly creditable. The first horn, clarionet, and bassoon distinguished themselves by a purity of tone, and cleverness of execution, seldom heard in the country. In noticing this performance, we cannot omit pointing out the necessity of some steps being taken to erect a concert-room in this town. The Theatre is such an inconvenient place for sound that the feeble tones of stringed instruments scarcely travel across the pit; they are, as it were, swallowed up by the caverns at the back of the stage, or escape through the roof into empty air. Could we see a little more public spirit displayed in our town for supporting the arts, and not so exclusively leaving the march of intellect to one particular class, we might hope for the erection of a concert room, in which our friends and families might occasionally assemble for the enjoyment of a little music.—The receipts, on Wednesday evening, we are sorry to learn, did not cover the expenses; but it is hoped Miss Sharpe will not be suffered to be a loser on the occasion.

Leicester Journal
Friday, May 23, 1828, p. 3, c. 1

THE ANNUAL CONCERT
OF THE
Melton-Mowbray Harmonic Society,

Assisted by Professional Performers from Birmingham and Leicester, the Gentlemen Amateurs of Oakham, &c.

WILL BE HELD
IN THE NATIONAL SCHOOL ROOM,
ON WEDNESDAY EVENING NEXT,
Under the Patronage of
George Pachin, Esq. *High Sheriff*
Sir F. G. Fowke, Bart.
[*List of 21 other patrons omitted*]

Principal Vocal Performers,
MISS HEATON & MR. MACHIN,
(From the Private Concerts, Birmingham)
MR. NICHOLSON,
And several Amateurs,

Instrumental Performers,
Harp, MISS E. WOOLLEY, Nottingham
Principal Clarinet—MR. MAFFRE, who will play a
Concerto on that Instrument.

LEADER,—MR. T. HICKSON

Tickets 3s each, to be had of Mr. R. Tyler, and Mr. Day, Bookseller.—Performance to commence at 8 o'clock precisely.
N.B. No Money taken at the doors.

Leicester Journal
Friday, November 21, 1828
[*There was a similar ad in the Leicester Chronicle on this day.*]

MUSIC.
———

JUST PUBLISHED,
FOR THE PIANO FORTE,
With Violin and Flute Accompaniment,
A New Military March,
Composed and Respectfully Inscribed to the
RIGHT HON. COUNTESS HOWE,
BY J. MAFFRE
———

J. MAFFRE having continued his practice on the Piano Forte, and studied under the best Masters, respectfully informs the Nobility and Gentry of Leicester and its Vicinity, that he will immediately commence his instruction on that instrument. He begs to state also, that he has availed himself of the skill of the celebrated Monsieur Femy, and now teaches the Violin according to the method adopted by the Conservatory of Music in Paris.

J. M. is sincerely grateful for the liberal patronage with which he has been hitherto honoured; and hopes, by unremitting attention to his duties, both to merit and insure continued support.

Terms moderate.

N.B. Shortly will be published, by J. Maffre, a Parochial Psalmody for the use of the Church of England, Price 15s.

This work is already highly patronized.
Leicester, November 20, 1828

1828-1829 & 1830 Leicester Directories
[*Maffre and most other musicians are not listed.*]

1831 Leicester Directory
[*Only four Musicians are listed.*]

Deacon, Samuel, music warehouse, Gallowtree-gate
Dobney, Frederick, musician and broker, Belgrave-gate
Mavius, Charles, professor of music, and music warehouse, Gallowtree-gate
Nicholson, Henry, musician, Granby-street

Leicester Chronicle
January 3, 1829
[*Did Maffre lead this variant of the Leicester Militia band? In the next entry, he is listed as "formerly of the Leicester Militia."*]

Belvoir.—The Duke of Rutland, the Duchess Isabella, the Marquis of Granby, and the Lords and Ladies Manners, are at present at Belvoir. It is expected that the Castle will be crowded with distinguished visitants for the Duke's birth day, which is always celebrated on the 24th of January. Mr. Sanders, the artist, is now actively employed at Belvoir, in completing two whole length portraits of the Duke and late Duchess, intended to occupy vacant compartments in the grand drawing room, which will be opened for the first time on this occasion. The furniture is all completing in the florid style of Louis XIV. The Leicestershire militia band is engaged for a fortnight at the Castle.

Leicester Chronicle
February 19, 1830

West Indies.—A concert was given at the Theatre Royal, Bridgetown, in the island of Barbardoes [*sic*], on the 11th of December, in aid of the funds for erecting a House of Industry [*poor house*]. It was conducted by Mr. Maffre, of the 18th [*19th?*] Foot, (formerly of the Leicestershire Militia). In noticing the performance, *The Barbadian* newspaper says—"Mr. Maffre, leader of the band, availed himself most happily of the resources of his orchestra in furnishing as delightful a selection of overtures, concertos, &c., as we have for a long time met with, which we conceive must have kindled and allured a stronger desire of further acquaintance with musical entertainments, than has hitherto excited in this community. It would be tedious to attempt panegyric [*public praise*] on all the overtures, &c. (more especially as our knowledge on that interminable subject, music, is very imperfect) which were varied, most judiciously selected, and executed in charming modulation and scientific management, and, to the lovers of harmony, could not fail in attraction."

Stamford Mercury
November 18, 1831

The Depot of the 19th Regiment of Foot, consisting of four companies under the command of Major Campbell, with an excellent brass band are now quartered at Grantham. If they continue the good behavior which has distinguished them since they have been there, they will deserve a high compliment on their departure, for it is remarked at almost every inn that they hardly know that a soldier is in the house, and the wives and children of the men are particularly cleanly and remarkable for good behavior.—The majority of the men and their wives are from the sister kingdom.

St. Vincent Gazette
March 1832

At a meeting of the House of Assembly on Tuesday the 6th March, Mr. Munro moved and it was resolved— 'That the thanks of this House be given to Lieutenant-Colonel Hardy, the officers, non-commissioned officers and soldiers of the 19th Regiment for their meritorious, peaceful and excellent conduct during their residence in this colony. That the inhabitants of Kingstown will ever remember with the deepest gratitude the prompt and ample protection afforded to themselves and their property by the detachment of that gallant regiment sent by Colonel Hardy, when the town was almost devastated and all the shipping wrecked by the hurricane on the 11th August last. Nor will the poor forget to offer their prayers and thanks for the prosperity and happiness of their benefactors who generously contributed to their relief when bereft of their homes and means of subsistence by the furious elements.'

Caledonian Mercury, Edinburgh
Thursday, February 14, 1833

ARMY IN SCOTLAND—Drafts from the under-mentioned depots are assembling in Edinburgh, preparatory for their embarking for Chatham, whence they will re-embark to join their respective regiments in the colonies:—
[*Among the listings are the following two regiments*]
19th Foot, 2 officers and 55 rank and file—West Indies
71st Highland Light Infantry, 3 officers and 50 rank and file, Bermuda

Caledonian Mercury, Edinburgh
Thursday, February 21, 1833

THE ARMY
EMBARKATION OF TROOPS—…Detachments for the 19th foot, at Trinidad; 25th ditto, at Demerara; 71st Highland light infantry, at Bermuda; and 72d Highlanders at the Cape of Good Hope, embarked on Tuesday on board the Royal William steamship, at Leith.

Poll year: 1833   Name: Joseph Maffree
Parish or Rectory: Westgate   Address: William Street

Newcastle Journal
Saturday, August 2, 1834

HIGHWAY ROBBERY.—An atrocious and daring act, accompanied by violence, was perpetrated near this town on Tuesday evening by three privates of the 19th regiment of foot, at present stationed in Newcastle barracks. It appears that Thomas Thompson, a tinker in one of the neighboring collieries, was on his road homewards about nine o'clock, and when he had reached the hollow, about half way between the Cowgate and Kenton, he was suddenly attacked by three men wearing the uniform of the 19th regiment, one of whom struck him a violent blow on the eye, from the effects of which he was completely stunned; he was then dragged to the ground by all three of the assailants, who rifled through his pockets of 10s. and his watch.—He struggled hard to preserve that latter, but the chain broke in his hand, and the watch-pocket with part of his trowsers, was torn away. The villains then decamped, but have since been apprehended, and will take their trials in the Moot-Hall, this (Saturday) morning, before Mr. Baron Gurney. A report of the trial will be given in our second edition, along with the important case against William Willis, charged with willful murder.

Newcastle Journal
May 16, 1835

The half-yearly inspection of the Garrison her took place in the Barrack-yard on Thursday morning. The force now here, consisting of three troops of the Carabineers commanded by Brevet Lieut.-Colonel Jackson, three companies of the 19th infantry, and one troop of the Royal Artillery, with two guns, &c., were inspected by General Bouverie and his Aide-de-Camp.

Newcastle Courant
June 13, 1835

NEWCASTLE POLICE.—On Wednesday last, George Watson, late of Fawdon Square, pitman, was convicted of the mutiny act, of having unlawfully received the regimentals and appointments of a soldier belonging to the 19th Regiment of Foot, stationed at the Newcastle Barracks, and was adjudged to pay a penalty of 20l., and 6l. 13s. 6d., being treble the value of the regimentals and

appointments received; and in default of payment was committed to gaol [*jail*] for one month.

Yorkshire Gazette
September 12, 1835

1835 YORKSHIRE MUSICAL FESTIVAL
[*long summary omitted*]
THE BAND.
VIOLINS. — *Leaders.* — Mr. Cramer, Mr. Mori — *Principal 2d Violin* — Mr. Wagstaff — [*many others listed alphabetically including "Maffre, Newcastle"*]
OBOES. — *Principal 1st.* — G. Cooke, London — *Principal 2d Violin* — Florke, London. — [*among ten others is "Maffre, jun., Newcastle"*]

Caledonian Mercury, Edinburgh
Monday, May 9, 1836

The 7th, or Royal English fusiliers, from Portsmouth, are to replace the 71st or Highland light infantry, at Edinburgh, the latter having got the route for Dublin.

Drogheda Journal, or Meath & Louth Advertiser
Saturday, June 18, 1836

THE ARMY.
(From a Dublin Paper.)
KING'S BIRTH DAY—REVIEW IN THE PHOENIX PARK.—This day being appointed for the celebration of his Majesty's Birthday, a review of the troops composing the garrison of Dublin will take place in the Phoenix Park. The following corps—the Royal Artillery, 1st (or Royal) Dragoons, 8th (or the King's Royal Irish) Hussars, 15th (or King's) Hussars, 1st Battalion Grenadier Guards, 12th, 33d, 71st, and 93d Regiments will assemble on the Fifteen Acres, at noon, under the orders of Major-General the Right Hon. Sir Edward Blakency, K.C.B., Commanding the Forces in Ireland, and will commence at one o'clock.

Drogheda Journal, or Meath & Louth Advertiser
Saturday, June 25, 1836

REVIEW IN THE PHOENIX PARK.
Saturday being the anniversary of the glorious 18th of June, the customary inspection of the troops by the Lord Lieutenant took place in the Phoenix Park, and was followed by a sham battle. The splendid spectacle attracted, as usual, immense numbers from the metropolis. The troops arrived on the ground at about half-past twelve, when a line was drawn by the cavalry round the Fifteen Acres, in order to prevent the encroachments of the crowd. There were eight

regiments present, consisting of the following:—the Royal Artillery, 1st Royal Dragoons, 8th Hussars, 15th Hussars, Grenadier Guards, 12th Regiment, 71st Regiment, and 93d Highlanders. Their Excellencies the Lord Lieutenant and Countess of Mulgrave, arrived about two o'clock. On his Excellency's appearance, the troops who had been drawn up in the line lowered their flags, the guns fired a salute, and the bands of several regiments struck up "God save the King." They were then put through the different military maneuvers, and certainly nothing could be finer than the general appearance and discipline of the men. The charges of the cavalry, the formation of hollow squares by the infantry, and the movements of the artillery, excited the utmost astonishment and admiration by their extreme rapidity and yet perfect regularity and precision—*Dublin Paper.*

Dublin Evening Packet and Correspondent
Saturday, December 10, 1836
[*Maffre's Dublin Quadrilles were published when Pigott was located at 112 Grafton Street.*]

HARMONIC INSTITUTION,
13, WESTMORLAND-STREET.
S. J. PIGOTT

RESPECTFULLY begs to inform his Friends and the Public, that on Monday next, 12th December, the Business of his Establishment will be Removed to

112, GRAFTON STREET

(Immediately opposite the Provost's)
the spacious Premises recently occupied by Mr. Jackson, China Merchant.

S. J. Pigott solicits an inspection of his extensive Stock which has been considerably increased, of Piano Fortes, Harps, Seraphines, Guitars, &c., &c., carefully selected from the Manufactories of Broadwood, Collard, Erard, Tomkinson, Wornum, Kirkman, Lacote, Panormo, &c., &c., the whole of which are for sale at the lowest London prices.

Just received, a Case of Roman Harp, Violin, and Guitar Strings, of a very superior description. A further supply of genuine Steel Violin and Violincello Bows, direct from Paris.

Piano-fortes, Harps—double and single action—for Hire in Town and Country.

A large assortment of Accordions.

The New Foreign and English Publication received Weekly.

Experienced Turners always in attendance—Musical Instruments repaired—a Covered Caravan for the removal of Instruments in Town or Country—Country orders punctually attended to.

S. J. Pigott respectfully solicits a continuance of the kind patronage he has already experienced.

N.B.—The House and Concerns, No. 13, Westmorland-street, to be let either with or without lease.

Caledonian Mercury, Edinburgh
Thursday, December 15, 1836

71st—On Friday, the 25th ultimo [*November 25*], Colour-Serjeants Brown and Caldwell, of this regiment, were entertained to a ball and supper in Dublin, by their brother Serjeants. Dancing commensed at seven o'clock P.M.; at eleven o'clock Colonel the Hon. Charles Grey, and a number of the officers of the regiment, honoured the party with their presence; when the whole company, including adjutants' wives, seventy in number, sat down to a sumptuous supper, consisting of every delicacy of the season. The President, Quartermaster-Serjeant Harkness, in an appropriate speech, proposed the health of Colonel Grey and the officers of the regiment who had honoured the company with their presence; it was drunk with three times three with the most unanimous applause, which continued several minutes. When the cheering had subsided, Colonel Grey returned thanks, and in the most eloquent terms proposed the toast of the evening, "The healths of Colour-Serjeants Brown and Caldwell;" he said he never had more pleasure in drinking a health in his life—they were met to pay a parting tribute of respect to two old companions ere they had left a corps in its present high character—they were now about to retire with the approbation of their officers, the esteem and friendship of their brother Serjeants, and the respect of the regiment generally; their country was about to provide for them with as good pensions as its laws would allow. The Colonel was most enthusiastically cheered upon leaving the room. The companies of the respective Serjeants (Brown and Caldwell) presented them—Brown with a silver cup, and Caldwell with a silver-mounted pipe, as a testimony to mark their esteem of their characters for integrity and honour.

Dublin Morning Register
Tuesday, January 10, 1837

ANNIVERSARY BALL.

The grand anniversary ball for the purpose of aiding the funds raising [*sic*] for roofing and finishing the parish chapel of Ballybohill, county of Dublin, was given last night in the Rotundo. The object for which this ball was given is as novel as it is laudable; and we are happy to say that the rooms were crowded with all the beauty and fashion of our metropolis. The dancing commenced at about ten o'clock, and the sets were well arranged. Everything relating to their department was beautifully regulated by Messrs. Barnet and Williams. Refreshments were plentifully provided. The tables were splendidly laid out with all the secondary delicacies, under the direction of Mr. Shields, of Stephen's-green. The rooms were decorated in an exceedingly elegant manner; in fact, no expense seems to have been spared to render everything connected with the ball attractive and splendid. We should think that there were upwards of four hundred persons in attendance; and in this vast concourse we could not see one discontented countenance. The dancing was continued to a late hour, or rather a very early hour in the morning. The band of the 71st regiment was in attendance, and consequently the music was as good as could be desired. Much praise is due to Mr. Effie, who was the chief manager of the affair, for the style in which it was got up. He has often before deserved the public praise for his skill in the management of other similar fetes; but never, whether we take the object or the style of last night's entertainment into consideration, was he more deserving of the need for public approbation. We trust that the funds raised on the occasion will be sufficient to accomplish the laudable design for which the ball was given, and that the reverend gentleman who originated the experiment will be as fully satisfied with the charity and liberality of the citizens of Dublin as all claimants upon their generosity have hitherto been.

Freeman's Journal and Daily Commercial Advertiser, Dublin
Saturday, January 28, 1837
[*This was preceded by a Thursday matinee performance, also featuring the "elegant Band of that distinguished Regiment."*]

BATTY'S CIRCUS ROYAL
ABBEY STREET, DUBLIN.

Another Change — More Novelty

By desire and under the immediate Patronage of the Lieutenant-Colonel the Honourable C. GREY, M.P., and the Officers of the 71st Royal Highland Light Infantry; on which occasion the elegant Band of that distinguished Regiment will attend and perform several select Pieces of Music.

ON THIS EVENING, January 28, the performances will commence, at Half past Seven precisely, with an act of horsemanship by Mr. Young, as:

THE INDIAN HUNTER

A peculiar entertainment, invented and arranged entirely for this Establishment, embracing the whole troop of Veltigeurs Somersaultists, wherein by the strength of the Muscle, the elasticity of the spring, and

the height of the leap, the Spectator is convinced he is gazing upon a party of

FLYING MEN.

Mrs. Mackintosh, in a graceful scene of Equestrianism, as

THE MAID OF SARAGOSSA.

MR. GRAHAM,

The modern Aleides, will perform his wonderful Poses and Equilibrium of light and heavy substances, and will actually raise and support on his chin an immense Beam of Timber, being a greater weight than can be lifted any other person.

ENGLAND, IRELAND, and SCOTLAND,
By Mr. Mosely

Mr. PADDINGTON,
In his wonderful evolutions of Corde Crescent.

After which,

A SPLENDID ENTREE and CAVALCADE,
called

THE TRIUMPH OF THE ALHAMBRA

After which,

THE HIBERNIAN HERO,
Principal character by Mr. Powell.

MR. HULSE

Will appear with his highly trained horse, Prince George.

MR. BATTY

Will appear in his wonderful act called

THE COURIER OF ST. PETERSBURGH

A Ballet Scene for two on the Double Tight Rope as

THE TWO GREEK LOVERS,
By Miss Lee and Miss Smith.

THE GRAND PONEY RACES,

In this Scene a Match for Twenty Sovereigns will be rode by Jocko and Springtrap, the only two trained monkeys in the Kingdom.

DRESS BOXES 2s 6d. Side Boxes 1s 6. Pit 1s. Gallery 6d.

The Champion and Weekly Herald, London
Sunday, February 5, 1837

A very alarming riot took place on Saturday night last [*January 28*], at Batty's Circus, Dublin. The entertainments were under the patronage of Col. McGregor and the officers of the 71st regiment. It commenced by the shouting of the rabble in the gallery crying out the name of "O'Connell;" this was resented by the "Conservative fire," and a *melée* took place. The O'Connellites went into the streets, armed themselves with stones, and on returning to the house, discharged them in volleys. The soldiers interfered, and a very alarming riot ensued, in which serious injury was sustained by several of the auditory. One gentleman had his arm broken, others their heads cut.

Freeman's Journal and Daily Commercial Advertiser, Dublin
Thursday, February 2, 1837

THEATRE ROYAL,
DUBLIN.

THIS EVENING, THURSDAY, there will be no Performance.
Books of the different Operas, with English translations, may be had at the Box Office, price 1s.
Tenth night of
THE ITALIAN OPERA.

ON TO-MORROW, (Friday), February 3, the Performance will commence with the Comic Piece
MY NEIGHBOUR'S WIFE
[The singers are listed]
After which, Rossini's Grand Melodramatic Opera of
LA DONNA DEL LAGO
[The Lady of the Lake, by Sir Walter Scott]
[The singers are listed]
By the kind permission of the Lieut.-Colonel Grey, the Band of the 71st Highlanders will assist in the Opera to give greater effect to the Martial Music.
[The performance included a dance and more music]

Freeman's Journal and Daily Commercial Advertiser, Dublin
Friday, February 17, 1837

THEATRE ROYAL,
DUBLIN.

———

LAST NIGHT BUT TWO OF THE ITALIAN OPERA.
THIS PRESENT FRIDAY, February 17, 1837, the performance will commence with the comic piece of
THE FOUR LOVERS
[The singers are listed]
After which, Rossini's Grand Melodramatic Opera of
LA DONNA DEL LAGO
[The singers are listed]
By the kind permission of the Hon. Lieutenant-Colonel Grey, the Band of the 71st Highlanders will assist in the Opera to give greater effect to the Martial Music.
[The performance included a dance and more music]

Waterford Chronicle
Saturday, May 27, 1837

PRESENTATION OF COLOURS TO THE 71st HIGHLANDERS.

————

The ceremony of presenting a new stand of colours to the gallant 71st regiment of Highland Light Infantry having been announced to take place in the Phoenix Park on Friday (the anniversary of the battle of Almarez,) crowds of our good citizens, as well as the more fashionable sight-seekers, proceeded to the Park at an early hour, to witness the animating spectacle. The weather was remarkably favourable, the day being on of the very few genial summer days we have yet had. Shortly after two o'clock the 71st regiment proceeded from the Royal Barracks to the Phoenix Park, and drew out in line on the beautiful level in front of the Chief Secretary's Lodge. The excellent band of the Regiment was placed at a short distance, playing several enlivening marches, while dragoons [*cavalry*] were stationed in every direction to prevent the crowd intruding upon the ground upon which it was intended that the troops should manoeuvre.—About half past two the Commander of the Forces, Sir Edward Blakeny, and his staff, rode into the field.—The crowd of spectators was at this time considerable, and it is impossible to imagine a more varied and animating sight than the scene presented. In the centre of the line the old colours of the regiment were elevated, crowned with wreaths of laurel, which insignia of victory was also plentifully bestowed upon all the instruments and arms of the band.

The Commander of the Forces and his aides-de-camp, accompanied by Town Major White, rode several times along the lines, and afterwards witnessed the soldiers going through several military evolutions. About half past three o'clock the band played Lord Cromarty's march, while the soldiers presented arms, and immediately afterwards formed into a hollow square. The new colours were then unfurled in the centre of the square.—One of the banners was formed in a St. George's cross of blue, white and scarlet, in the centre of which was a circle of shamrocks, roses, and thistles, the whole surmounted by a crown. In the circle were the letters "W.R.," and round it, in letters of gold, "The Seventy-first Regiment of Highland Light Infantry."—Immediately below that was another circle, bearing the motto, "*Nemo me impune lacescit*," with a thistle in the centre. The other banner was of buff and blue, and had a similar circle, crown, and inscription as the first; but instead of the lower circle there was a branch of laurel, on each leaf of which was the name of the battle in which they had been victorious, or a country in which they had fought. On one side were "Corunna," "Almarez," "Waterloo," Ciudad Rodrigo," on the other, "Hindostan," "Peninsula," "Pyrenees," "America." The inscriptions on the colours were of the most beautiful workmanship, and excited general admiration.

The regiment was again directed to present arms.

Sir E. Blakeny then rode to the front of the line, while the regiment presented arms. The gallant officer took one of the colours in his hand, and said—Officers and soldiers of the 71st regiment, I have the honour this day, a day glorious in your recollections, to present to you the King's colour. I deliver it to you with no ordinary confidence, assured as I am, from the high discipline of the regiment that it will ever be maintained by distinguished gallant conduct; in the field, as well as by regularity and strict discipline in quarters.—It is usual on those occasions to refer to former services of a regiment, Yours, gallant 71st, are well recorded in history; but I cannot resist referring to two battles in which you most largely partook, and most gallantly performed your duty. The one, Fuentes d'Honor, under the immediate eye of the great captain, the Duke of Wellington, the hero of a hundred victories; the other under the command of our excellent and able Commander-in-Chief, Lord Hill. In both of these actions, 71st, you greatly distinguished yourselves. In the latter the historian describes you as bounding over the hills to the attack of Almarez on the 19th of May 1812, the anniversary of that day we are now commemorating. Soldiers, I have every confidence in your emulating these deeds should an opportunity offer; but to be prepared for this you must maintain the reputation you enjoy and persevere in the discipline you now possess. You have always been commanded by most distinguished officers; and I have only to refer you to their names to remind you of their gallant exploits. Pack, Cadogan, Reynell, and Arbuthnot, are of the first military order. To these names I will add my gallant friend, your present commander, Lieut. Colonel Grey, who possesses my fullest confidence; and who will, I feel assured, whenever an opportunity offers, equally distinguish himself with those who have gone before him. Lieutenant Colonel Grey, you are well supported by an excellent corps of officers; and I have great satisfaction on this most interesting occasion in paying this public testimony to their merits, while I gladly add an equal tribute of my approbation to the non-commissioned officers and corps at large. May you, therefore, 71st, long enjoy that high reputation you deservedly have attained; and when your services may be required be assured that my warmest wishes for your prosperity and success will always attend you.

When Sir Edward Blakeney had concluded, the strand of colours were carried to the Honourable Mrs. Grey, the lady of the Colonel commanding the gallant 71st. She then stood up in her carriage, and gently leaning forward, with a deeply impressive and dignified air, she said—

Soldiers!—I am most flattered at having been requested to present the regimental colour to the 71st; and the more gratified, because my husband has the honour to command it. I need not tell you that you have my most anxious and cordial good wishes; and I feel confident that the new colour is entrusted to those by whom the honour and credit of the regiment will be ever upheld, and in whose care, should an opportunity offer, it will become entitled to an addition to the badges it already bears.

The colours were then handed to the ensigns, while the men gave a joyful and triumphant cheer at the honour which had been conferred upon them. The old colours—

> The flags that braved a thousand years
> The battle with the foe—

were then removed to the Lord Morpeth's lodge, from whence it is intended that they shall be conveyed to Kilkenny, there to have them buried with the remains of the late brave commander of the 71st, the gallant Sir Denis Pack.

[*Colonel Grey thanked Lord Hill, the troops formed another hollow square, Lord Hill addressed them again, and then 300 guests enjoyed a meal at the Lodge of the Chief Secretary at which*] the refreshements consisted of the richest and rarest viands that could be procured, and were laid out with great taste.

Caledonian Mercury, Edinburgh
Thursday, July 27, 1837

71ST HIGHLAND LIGHT INFANTRY.—On Friday the 4th inst, the serjeants of the Highland light infantry, assembled in Kilkenny barracks, to do honour to their late Serjeant-Major John Aiton, on his promotion to an Ensigncy in the regiment, and to present him with a silver cup, made by Mr. Bennett, Dame Street, Dublin, as a testimony of their esteem for him, as their serjeant-major, for a period of ten years. On the one side of the cup was engraved—"71st Highland Light Infantry — Presented at Kilkenny, to Serjeant-Major John Aiton, by his comrade serjeants, as a mark of their esteem." On the reverse side was displayed a bugle, inside of which was engraved "Peninsula, Waterloo", where he had been engaged with the regiment. At 7 o'clock P.M., the whole sat down to an excellent supper—Quartermaster Serjeant Robert Harkness, presiding (who will succeed him as serjeant-major).

Freeman's Journal and Daily Commercial Advertiser, Dublin
Saturday, March 3, 1838

GRAND FANCY BALL

OF THE 71ST REGIMENT (HONORARY MEMBERS OF THE
KILKENNY HUNT) AT KILKENNY

This ball, which for some weeks past has formed the all-absorbing topic of conversation throughout this county, took place at the barracks last night (Tuesday). The very splendid entertainments given by this regiment when in Edinburgh, and their more recent magnificent *fete* in Dublin, caused the public to look forward to this ball with an unusual degree of pleasurable curiosity, and most fully were the sanguine anticipations realized. The rooms were arranged with the most chaste simplicity with draperies of muslin, edged with blue, and chandeliers festooned with the most delicate artificial flowers, while around the walls were hung the portraits of the many distinguished colonels who have severally commanded the regiment at different periods. At the head of the main ball-room was hung the portrait of our gracious Queen.

The supper-room was not less remarkable for its decorations than the ball-room, being draped with fawn-coloured moreen, and as for the tables they were quite dazzling, from the quantity of regimental plate displayed thereon, and set off with the most handsome and tasteful of spun-sugar and other ornaments, having all more or less allusion to the regiment and the Kilkenny Hunt; the latter, indeed, being in one piece alone represented by a numerous hunting-field of men and horses, and dogs in full cry.

Kentish Gazette
Tuesday, April 3, 1838

His high mightiness the mock king of Canada, *alias* the Durham small coal man is, we hear, giving himself some very royal airs on the subject of his outfit. First he could not sail, and would not be hurried, until Rundell and Bridge had finished (at the nation's expense, of course) a new splendid service of plate. We should like to know what has become of his Russian service. Then he must have a band to accompany him on board of ship,—covers for twenty every day. The guards' band could not be spared, Lord Durham would not sail without one; so the ministers have sent for the band of the 71st, who are to be taken on board at Portsmouth. We suppose that his next request will be for half the corps of gentlemen at arms to attend upon his levees, and thirty of the yeomen of the guard to line his presence chamber—and this is the gentleman who takes no salary! Faugh! the humbug is too gross to deceive any one.

It is said that the outfit of plate and china for Lord Durham's mission alone amounts to £15,000. We take it for granted that this must be chiefly paid for out of his own pocket; and yet, even so, the ministers, we suspect will have to ask a reformed parliament to sanction a monstrous charge which an unreformed parliament would have scouted with indignations. We would ask Lord Durham, if we thought there was any chance for penetrating his vanity-crusted intellect, for what purpose he seeks all this parade? He is going to inquire into the grievances and allay the heats of a distracted colony; he is not going to assist at the coronation of M. Papineau, or at the inauguration of an indivisible republic under the presidency of Dr. McKenzie. Why then does he go forth with a train of liveried lackies, with a shipload of costly furniture, and crates of porcelain enough to stock a china-shop? What an idea he must have of the duties of a political functionary sent to tranquilise or subdue a disturbed country? But how greatly do those ministers pervert their office who have the shameless and unprincipled audacity to indulge him at the nation's charge with these expensive follies. To please his ear they call the poor deputy a Dictator—to tickle his pride they dazzle him with glittering gewgaws. Verily, Lord Durham has much of the Roman dictator about him. The resemblance to Cincinnatus and Camillus must strike even a schoolboy in his noviciate.—

The Torch [a Protestant Periodical], London
Edited by Felix Fax [a pseudonym]
Saturday, April 14, 1838, p. 277

Meanwhile there is another pleasant incident that must in some shape come before our readers. Lord Durham, with characteristic affection for the Protestant Church, has dismissed the chaplain of the man-of-war that takes him to Canada, by another conveyance, and taken on board in its stead the band of the 71st regiment, maintained at the sole expense of the officers of that regiment, *who do not sail in the same vessel!* This is, to say the least, a specimen of Durham arrogance, from the noble Earl, to whom Theodore Hook has given two excellent titles, by way of rider to the Grand Cross of St. Andrew. We will throw them into a couple of stanzas.

I.

As he draws his estate from the bowels of the earth,
And tho' major by age is a *miner* by birth,
I think 'twould be not very wrong, on my soul,
To dub this new Canada Viceroy KING COAL!

II.

But if this offend you, as being too wholesale,
There's another name yet may be drawn from the coal-

sale;
And as type of what coalheaver bear on their backs,
You may call the great gentleman plain Marshal SACKS!

Well, King Coal, or Marshal Sacks, has dispensed with the chaplain, not only to his grandeeship, but to the whole of the retinue, officers and crew, of a fine seventy-four gun ship, who may go to Canada, or to Davy Jones, without a spiritual comforters. In other words—

However Marshal Sacks may value coal,
He little care has for the cure of souls.

In a moral point of view the action is an atrocious one; in a ludicrous point—the only one in which it is likely to sting the Earl of Durham—it is so absurdly frivolous, that we almost wonder he ran the hazard of ridicule with which that, and the buying of his Field Marshal's uniform—an uniform for Marshal *Sacks*—must fix on him. A military band instead of a clergyman ! Beautiful !

Whene'er, my Lord, the sea gets *you* sick,
Instead of parson you'll make music;
In lieu of priest's more pious prayers,
Prefer your band's refreshing airs;
Or reading (Heav'n forgive the libel),
Take up Mozart before your Bible.
Hunt from you soul its thoughts of sin
With tabour, pipe, and violin;
Or, 'fore your mind should Satan come,
Pat him to flight with beat of drum;
Content to know, as on you skip,
God's worshipped in the other ship.

Devizes Wiltshire Gazette
Thursday, April 12, 1838

LORD DURHAM.—Upon the triumphant majority of two, of Mr. Hedworth Lambton, Lord Durham's brother, and Mr. Charles Buller, the President of Lord Durham's Council, Ministers resolve to send forth their Dictator, invested with military command; an armed steamer under his orders, a-line-of-battle-ship fitted up for his *seventy* followers, two batallions of Foot Guards as his body guard, and two squadrons of Life Guards for his guard of honour, together with plate, furniture, linen, &c., and a *batterie de cuisine*, occupying of itself four tons—and in addition to this, in order that his High Mightiness may be indulged in the harmony of sweet sounds, the band of the 71st Regiment, one of the best bands in the service, has been ordered away from that corps, and a steamer has been actually sent to Ireland to bring it to Portsmouth, that it may accompany his High

Mightiness to Barrataria.

There never yet has been attempted anything in the way of job upon so enormous a scale as this. The country is deeply obliged to Lord Chandos for having brought the matter before the House of Commons, the more especially as Ministers have thought proper to state that these arrangements are all made under the special command of the Queen. This is too gross and too flagrant an evasion to be borne. Certain we are that *if* the Queen *had*, upon the suggestion of anybody else, personally interfered in the arrangements, her Majesty would have given way to the feeling expressed upon the subject in the House of Commons, when her Majesty's intentions were only supported by a majority composed of Lord Durham's brother and one of Lord Durham's *attaché.—Bull.*

The Morning Chronicle, London
Monday, April 16, 1838

PORTSMOUTH—SATURDAY.
The Hastings, 74 [*guns*], Captain Loeb, arrived yesterday, to take on board the Earl of Durham, her Majesty's high commissioner for the settlement of the Canadian disputes. His lordship's stock was embarked to-day, with the exception of the live portion of it, which will be sent off on the eve of his embarkation, which is expected to be about Tuesday next. The fine band of the 71st Regiment was landed here on Wednesday, by an Irish steamer, from Cork, to embark on board the Hastings for the use of the Earl of Durham. It is understood that the chaste, elegant, and inexpensive fittings in the Hastings for the reception of his lordship's family and suite, reflect the highest credit on John Fineham, Esq., master shipwright of her Majesty's deck-yard, Sheerness; permission to view these fittings, however, is refused by the orders of Lord Durham.

Newcastle Journal
Saturday, April 21, 1838

At verse 58 we read—
"Behind the throttle triumphant musle shed
Its loudest notes around the monarch's head;
The shrill tongu'd trumpet and the deep bassoon,
And cymbal, emblem of the pale-faced moon."
Here we have described the duties of the band of her Majesty's 71st Regiment, which, although supported by the subscriptions of the officers of the corps, has been taken from it, and attached to the Court of the Dictator, for his Mightiness's personal amusement.

—*John Bull*

The Ipswich Journal
Saturday, April 28, 1838

DEPARTURE OF LORD DURHAM—A letter from Portsmouth dated April 24th, says—"The Earl of Durham, with his family and suite, arrived at the George Hotel yesterday to dinner. This day, at one p.m., the *Lightning* steam vessel, with Sir Philip Durham's band on board, took his lordship, the countess, and three daughters, with a number of his attachés, on board the *Hastings*, 74 [guns]. On his arrival on board, the Hastings immediately got under weigh, was taken in tow by the *Lightning*, and towed round St. Helen's, from whence she made sail with a fair wind for Quebec. His lordship was attended at his embarkation by the Earls Radnor and Dundonald., Admirals Sir F. Durham, Flemming, Sir T. Briggs and Bouverie; Captains the Hon. F. Grey and A. Ellice; and the Lieut.-Governor Sir Thomas McMahon, &c &c.

Quebec Gazette
May 15, 1838
On Thursday evening about half-past seven
[as reprinted in the Montreal Transcript]

ARRIVAL OF THE 71st REGIMENT.

There were 500 men of the 71st on board the *Molabar* [*Malabar*]; 120 more are expected in the *Barossa* transport; and 32 men (the Band) with Lord Durham and suite on board the *Hastings*, 74 [*guns*].

The following is a list of the officers of the 71st who came by the *Malubar* [*Malabar*]:—

Lieut. Col. Com. Hon. C. Grey (son of Earl Grey, and brother-in-law of Lord Durham.) Captains—A.R. L'Estrange, W. Denny, John Impett, Lord A. Lennox (son of the late and brother of the present Duke of Richmond), Edw. Troy, W. Spier. Lieutenants—Sir H. Dalrymple, Bart.; J. H. C. Robertson, Adit.; R.I. Brickenden, W. Wilkieson, A.P.G. Dumming, J. Colville.

Ensigns, B. Blennerhasset, W. Fairholm, G. Dame, G.A. Bayley, S.G. Lord Aberdour.

Paymaster F. Dutton; Surgeon, T. Bulkley, M.D.

Colonel Guy is accompanied by his lady.

Of the 500 men of the 71st Regiment, 19 are Volunteers from the 79th which left Quebec so much regretted.

———

The *Malabar* had on board in all, 1120 persons; she made the passage from Cork to Quebec in three weeks less one day, having left the 24th April and arrived the 14th May. She was equipped and fitted out for sea in the short space of one month.—Thirty days before her departure, there was not a piece of cording on board.

The Montreal Transcript
Friday, May 19, 1838

ARRIVAL OF THE 71st REGIMENT.

On Thursday evening about half-past seven o'clock the *British America* arrived from Quebec, having on board the 71st Highlanders. As soon as she had stemmed the current, the beautiful bugles of the regiment struck up and played with the happiest effect [*This is the 71st bugle band and not Maffre's*]. When fairly alongside the Quebec Suburbs, the march they had been playing was changed for *Voulez vous danser Mademoiselle;* this air was continued and they were abreast of the Water Works, when it was changed for *A la Claire Fontaine,* [*a popular French Canadian song*] and, having passed the New Market, they approached the port with *Auld Lang Syne.* There was a great assemblage of the citizens on the wharf, who cheered on the arrival of the British America, and which was heartily returned by the gallant soldiers on board. Batteaux immediately came alongside and commenced the conveyance of the women and baggage to Saint Helens, where this beautiful regiment is to be stationed.

———

Lieut. Col. the Honble. C. Grey, who commands the 71st regiment, is a son of Earl Grey, brother of Lord Hardwick, the Secretary of War, and brother-in-law to Earl Durham, the Governor in Chief of this Colony.

———

This day, at ten o'clock, Major General Clitheroe will inspect the 71st Regiment, in marching order, on the Island of St. Helens.

Quebec Mercury
Tuesday, May 29, 1838
This article was reproduced in:
Caledonian Mercury, Thursday, July 5, 1838
Newcastle Courant, Friday, July 6, 1838

LOWER CANADA, QUEBEC.

On Sunday forenoon [*May 27*] the telegraph displayed the signal for the line of battle within site of the lower station, and about noon her lofty canvas was seen towering above Point Levy with signals flying from the mast head, from which it was speedily ascertained that the noble vessel was her Majesty's ship Hastings, having on board the Right Honourable, the Earl of Durham, Governor-General, Vice-Admiral, Captain-General of all her Majesty's Provinces within and adjacent to the continent of North America, with his family and suite. The wind blew fresh from the east, and the Hastings stood on, under easy sail, till she arrived nearly opposite the Queen's Wharf, where she let go her anchor. The fine band of the 71st Light Infantry was on the quarter deck, and, as the ship passed the town, played the air of "Rule Britannia" with powerful effect. The glacis [*the gentle slope leading down from a fort*] of the citadel, garden walk, and grand battery, were crowded with spectators, expecting that the noble earl would immediately disembark. It was, however, soon made public that his lordship would not come on shore till Monday at two o'clock, and orders were issued to receive the Governor-General with all honours due to his rank. The appearance of the weather yesterday, about noon, indicated an afternoon of heavy rain, and the disembarkation was postponed till this day at the same hour.

[*The other ships Malabar, Inconstant, Pique, and Racehorse were flying their colors and were aligned to complement the Hastings; Sir James MacDonald, commander of the local forces, rowed out to meet Durham; all military personnel simultaneously saluted Durham as he stepped on land; and Durham and his Generals mounted horses to make their way to the Castle where they received a proclamation from the town.*]

Lord Durham and family were in excellent health and spirits during the whole of its continuance. The total number of his Lordship's family, suite, and servants on board the Hastings is sixty-one.

There are on board the Hastings, ten fine English sheep and two milch cows; the latter supplied milk and fresh butter for the Earl of Durham's table during the whole voyage.

The Montreal Transcript
Tuesday, June 19, 1838
reprinted from Quebec Mercury of June 12

On Tuesday evening [*12th*], about eight o'clock, Her Majesty's steamship Medea arrived in harbor, having on board a detachment of the 24th Regiment. At the moment of the arrival of the Medea, the harbor presented an imposing scene. The lofty ships of the line, with the splendid frigates, six sail of men of war, at anchor in the basin, are themselves objects of deep interest to all who love the recollection of the glorious deeds achieved by England's floating castles; whilst, as if by appointment, just as the first steam vessel of war anchored in our waters, the sounds of music were heard proceeding from the band of Her Majesty's ship Hastings, on board the Eagle, which was returning from a trip to Chaudiere, which the Countess of Durham had enjoyed, with her family and a party, in the barge of the Hastings, which for greater certainty was towed by the Eagle.

The Belfast News-Letter
Tuesday, June 26, 1838

CANADA—THE UNITED STATES.

ARRIVAL OF LORD DURHAM—QUEBEC, May 28.— Her Majesty's ship Hastings in thirty three days from Portsmouth, arrived here yesterday afternoon, having on board his Excellency the Right Honourable the Earl of Durham, Governor General of British North America, the Countess of Durham, family and suite. The streets and wharfs were crowded with the inhabitants in the expectation of his Excellency's landing. Finally, it was understood that he would not land till this day at two o'clock. At one o'clock the whole of the city and suburbs seemed to be collecting in the Lower Town, but on learning that to-morrow at two o'clock was fixed for the landing of his Excellency, the crowd dispersed. The following, we believe, is a correct list of passengers in the Hastings:—Earl and Countess of Durham, and family; Mr. and Mrs. Elliott; Miss Balfour; Mr. Charles Buller, Chief Secretary; Mr. Turton, Legal Adviser; the Honourable E. P. Bouverie, Mr. Arthur Buller, Mr. Bushy, attaches; Hon. Frederick Villiers, Capt. Ponsonby, C.A. Dillon, Esq., Fred Cavendish, Esq., Sir John Doratt, Aides-de-Camp;

Her Majesty's ship Pique, Captain Boxer, arrived this morning from Halifax, in twenty-seven days, with detachments for the 15th, 34th, 66th, and 85th Regiments, now stationed in Canada. We understand she brings for the Commissariat £125,000 in specie. The troops have been put on board the British America steamer, which starts for Montreal at eleven to-night. The Stakesby transport, which left Portsmout on the 20th, arrived today. She brings out twenty-one horses, eleven of which belong to Lord Durham, and the remainder to the officers of the guards; together with carriages and other articles belonging to his Lordship.

Newcastle Courant
Friday, September 21, 1838
[*Governor-General Lord Durham steamed up and down the St. Lawrence the entire summer. This is an example of his arrival in Montreal after one of these excursions. Maffre is not mentioned.*]

CANADA.

Montreal, August 21, 1838—Yesterday about mid-day a salute from the Island announced the arrival of his Excellency the Governor-General. A vast concourse of persons of all classes were assembled to witness the disembarkation, which was attended with as much ceremony as on the previous arrivals. The Governor-General was accompanied by their Excellencies Sir Colin Campbell and Sir C. A. Fitzroy, Vice Admiral Sir C.

Paget, Sir John Colborne, and the staff and family of his lordship. They shortly afterwards proceeded to the race course.

After the middle of the day, Montreal presented the appearance of a deserted town, all persons, high and low, having left their usual avocations to be present at the race ground. The fact of his excellency the Governor-General being a spectator added considerably to the attraction. We regret to hear, that from the folly of some few individuals in thrusting themselves forward on the course, two or three accidents of a serious nature occurred, but we have not been able to ascertain whether any has proved fatal.

The Montreal Transcript
March 6, 1841; March 11, 1841

MUSICAL TUITION.

MR. MAFFRE, PROFESSOR of MUSIC and late Master of the Band of the 71st Highland Light Infantry, most respectfully begs leave to announce to the Public, that by the request of several families he has been induced to settle on Montreal, for the purpose of following his profession, and trusts that his terms as well as his abilities will meet their approbation. Mr. M. has had the advantage for a series of years to study the Art under the most eminent masters, and has a perfect knowledge of the following Instruments:—Pianoforte, Organ, Violin, Viola, Violoncello, Clarionet, Flute, Oboe, and all WIND INSTRUMENTS—also teaches the ELEMENTS OF SINGING, and thorough BASS, with the art of SCOREING MUSIC for ORCÆ STRA or MILITARY BAND. Mr. M. will attend any Ladies or Gentlemen as accompanying master, with the Violin, thereby inculcating a perfect knowledge of time and Musical expression. Seminaries and Schools punctually attended to. For terms, &c. apply at Mr. M.'s Residence in Sanguinet Street, near the Champs de Mars.

Mr. M. has for disposal, a choice collection of the most recent ITALIAN OPERA MUSIC, arranged for a MILITARY BAND, the list of which may be perused at MEAD'S and HERBERT'S MUSIC STORES, where may be had, A NEW SET OF QUADRILLES, for the PIANOFORTE, lately composed by J. M., and also his METHOD of TEACHING PSALMODY to the children of Free and Parochial Schools, as adapted by him for the use of National Schools in England.

Montreal, March 6, 1841

The Montreal Transcript
Thursday, April 29, 1841

PROSPECTUS OF THE
Montreal Musical & Choral Society.

MR. MAFFRE, Professor of Music, viewing with regret the failure of several attempts to establish, in Montreal, a Permanent, and at the same time, an efficient SCHOOL of MUSIC, has determined to take upon himself the arduous task of forming a Society, which he hopes will supply the desideration, and in order to enable him to carry his intentions into effect he appeals to the public spirit of the inhabitants of Montreal and its vicinity, to support him in this undertaking. Independently of the Musical Society, Mr. M. also proposes to establish (in conjunction) a CHORAL SOCIETY for the practice of SACRET [*sic*] MUSIC; and as those societies have proved, in other countries, beneficial to the Public Charities, as well as to the science of Music, which humanizes and softens the feelings of men more than any other Art, it is hoped that the community will lend their aid to promote the desired object.

It is also proposed that the Societies, besides their private practice, will, for the development of Amateur Talent, give an ANNUAL SERIES OF PERFOR-MANCES, three Grand CONCERTS of VOCAL, and INSTRUMENTAL MUSIC, and three Miscellaneous PERFORMANCES of SACRED MUSIC, in some Sacred edifice: the receipts of the performances to be for the benefit of the Public Charities.

Terms of Subscription to be one pound per annum, which will entitle the Subscriber to two TRANSFER-ABLE TICKETS. And to accommodate friends from the country, &c., a limited number of single Admission Tickets will be issued previously to each performance.

The Society will be conducted on similar rules with those of the Musical Societies of Birmingham, Manchester, Leicester, Sheffield, and York, in England.

For further particulars due notice will be given.

Lists for Subscribers will be left at the Music Stores of Messrs. Mead, & Co. and Messrs. J. W. Herbert & Co.

Montreal, April 23, 1841   156

[*Image of sidewheel steamboat emitting steam*]
THE STEAM PACKETS
Lord Sydenham & Lady Colborne,
CONVEYING HER MAJESTY'S MAILS,
BETWEEN MONTREAL AND QUEBEC,

WILL FORM A DAILY LINE between the above
PORTS, and until further notice, will leave as follows:—

STEAMER LORD SYDENHAM,
CAPTAIN GEORGE TAIT [*sic*].

MONTREAL ON	QUEBEC ON
MONDAY,	TUESDAY,
WEDNESDAY and	THURSDAY and
FRIDAY, at 6	SATURDAY, at 5
o'clock in the afternoon	o'clock in the afternoon.

STEAMER LADY COLBORNE,
CAPTAIN W. H. HAYCOCK.

MONTREAL ON	QUEBEC ON
TUESDAY,	MONDAY,
THURSDAY and	WEDNESDAY and
SATURDAY, at 6	FRIDAY, at 5
o'clock in the afternoon	o'clock in the afternoon.

The above Steamers, will generally arrive at their Port of destination, Quebec—at about 8 o'clock the following morning and Montreal about 10 o'clock the next morning after their departure from Quebec.

W & G TATE,
PROPRIETORS.

Montreal, May 18, 1841   164

GRAND MUSICAL FESTIVAL.

MR. MAFFRE has the honour to announce to the Nobility, Gentry and Public in general, of Montreal and its vicinity, that by the kind permission of the Rev. Dr. BETHUNE, a GRAND MUSICAL FESTIVAL will take place in CHRIST CHURCH for which occasion the Celebrated Vocalists MRS. SEGUIN, MISS MANVERS, MR. MANVERS, and MR. SEGUIN are expressly engaged. The Choral Department will also be very effective, and the Orchestra will be complete in all its parts.

Principal Violinist and Leader,	MR. MARKS.
Second do	MR. MAFFRE, JR.
Principal Double Basso,	MR. JACOBY

Mr. W. H. WARREN will preside at the Organ.

The whole will be under the direction of Mr. MAFFRE, Professor of Music.

The first parts will consist of selections from Handel's Oratorio of the "Messiah," and from Hayden's Oratorio of the "Creation," and various other Sacred Musical Works.

All vocal and instrumental Professors and Amateurs, who may be desirous to assist on this laudable occasion, are requested to send in their names without delay to Mr. MAFFRE, No. 11, Sanguinet Street.

As this will be the first time that an Oratorio, on a liberal scale, has ever been attempted in British North America and being for the purpose of laying a foundation to assist the Public Charities of the City, Mr. MAFFRE confidently hopes that this novel and great undertaking will be appreciated and supported by a generous public.

Reserved seats will be had at one dollar each, general seats at half a dollar each. Tickets may be procured at the Music Store of Mr. Herbert and Mr. Mead, and also at the Book Stores of Mr. Sharpley and Mr. Graham.

All further particulars of the Programme of the Performance, and of the date when it will take place, will be announced in a future advertisement without delay.

Montreal, July 27, 1841   24

[*There are no further advertisements for this event. On July 15, the Transcript carried an ad for a performance at the Theatre Royal for Bellini's Grand Opera 'La Somnambula!' that featured vocalists Mr. & Mrs. Seguin and Mr. & Miss Manvers. On August 5, they were performing a Farewell Benefit of the Musical Drama 'Rob Roy' and Donizetti's Opera 'L'Elixir D'Amour' prior to their departure to Europe.*]

L'aurore des Canadas
Tuesday, December 7, 1841 [Translation]

THE AMATEURS OF 71 Regt.
of
S T . J E A N

Offer a Singular Soiree.

Theatre Royal.

FOR PROFIT OF
"The Infant of Avon"

An Event to Benefit the Representatives
of the Emigrants Hospital

DECEMBER 8, 1841.
Will offer a performance of the popular
R O B   R O Y !

Rob Roy Macgregor, Bailie Nicol Jarvis, Rashling Osbaldiston, Dougal Creature, Helen Macgregor, Piper	by the Amateurs of the 7st Regt.

(WITH SINGERS)

Francis Osbaldiston	By a Montreal Gentlemen
Sir Frederick Vernon	By a Quebec Gentlemen
Major Galbraith	By a Montreal Amateur
Saundery Willis	By Mr. Jones
Capt. Thornton	Mr. William
Mr. Owen	Mr. Andrews
Mr. Stuart	Mr. Thomson
Jobson	Mr. Sloman
Laurie	Mr. Smith
Host	Mr. Bank
Andrew	Mr. Holmes
Sergeant	Mr. Williamson
Corporal	Mr. Brown

Soldiers, peasants, mountaineers, &c. &c.
Piano solo (with singing) by Miss Philip
With an interlude of dancing
THE HIGHLAND FLING
Matrile Miss Rose Jean McAlpine &c. &c.
Mr. Maffré to perform a Solo on the Violin.

———

The Montreal Transcript
Tuesday, June 7, 1842
[Maffre is not listed in this announcement but he is listed in the
next one and in the review that followed.]

SOIREE MUSICALE.

MISS JANE SLOMAN, PIANIST, has the honor to
announce that she will give her
PIANO FORTE RECITALS,
consisting of the greatest compositions of the most
eminent composers.—A Fantasia, by Doehler; a
Concerto, by Kalkbrenner; Variations on the Prayer
from "Mose in Egitto;" "Kalberg" and "Otello," by
Hertz, with Orchestrial accompaniments; with VOCAL
PERFORMANCES, which will be duly announced.

The CONCERT will take place at RASCO'S HOTEL,
on THURSDAY EVENING next, at half-past EIGHT
precisely. Tickets, $1.
June 7, 1842   3

———

The Montreal Transcript
Thursday, June 9, 1842

THE GOVERNOR GENERAL, having
signified his intention of visiting the Theatre This
Evening, MISS JANE SLOMAN respectfully announces
that her CONCERT is unavoidably POSTPONED til
MONDAY next, the 13th instant.

———

SOIREE MUSICALE.

MISS JANE SLOMAN, PIANIST, has the honor to
announce that she will give her
PIANO FORTE RECITALS,
consisting of the greatest compositions of THALBERG,
DOEHLER, KALKBRENNER, HERTZ, and other eminent
Composers.

The CONCERT will take place at RASCO'S HOTEL,
on MONDAY EVENING, June 13.

———

PROGRAMME.
PART I.
1. Introduction—Band.
2. Grand Fantasia and Variation on Airs from Rossini's
   Opera of "Guillaume Tell"—Piano Forte—Miss Jane
   Sloman,   *Doehler*
3. Song Comique—"Muscial Traveller"—Mr. Sloman,
                                                            Dibdin
4. Concerto and Brilliant Variations on the Air "My
   Lodging is on the cold ground"—Piano Forte—Miss
   Jane Sloman,   *Kalkbrenner*

———

An intermission of Fifteen Minutes will take place
between the first and second parts.

———

PART II.
5. Sinfonia—Band
6. Fantasia and Celebrated Variations on the Prayer in
   Rossini's Opera of "Mose in Egitto"—Piano Forte—

Miss Jane Sloman,   *Thalberg*
7. Song—Mr. Sloman.
8. Grand Concerto and Brilliant Variations on the March
   of Rossini's Opera of "Otello," (with Orchestrial
   accompaniments)—Piano Forte—Miss Jane Sloman,
                                                        Hertz

   ———

Concert to commence at half-past EIGHT precisely.
Tickets One Dollar each; may be obtained at Mead's
Music Saloon, Herbert's Music Store, Mr. Maffre,
Professor of Music, of Miss Jane Sloman, at Rasco's
Hotel, and at the Room on the evening of the Concert.
   June 9, 1842   4
*[Maffre's band performed an "Introduction" and a "Sinfonia",
both of which were probably a pastiche of the other featured music.]*

———

The Montreal Transcript
Thursday, June 9, 1842

Miss Jane Sloman's Concert, advertised for this
evening, is postponed till Monday next, in consequence
of the performance at the Theatre being by special
request. The play-going public may expect a rich treat,
which they will do well to avail themselves of. Mrs.
Sloman's performance on Tuesday, in the character of
Isabella, in the tragedy of "The Fatal Marriage," was of
this highest excellence, equaling the very exquisite acting
and singing of Mr. Sloman, in the afterpiece of "The
Wandering Minstrel."

———

The Montreal Transcript
Saturday, June 11, 1842

We are pleased to learn that tickets of admission to
Miss Sloman's Concert at Rasco's, on Monday next,
have been taken up by the *elite* of the city. We believe
His Excellency the Governor General patronizes the
accomplished Pianiste.

———

The Montreal Transcript
Thursday, June 16, 1842

The lovers of music will learn with pleasure that Miss
Jane Sloman has been prevailed upon to give another
Concert before leaving the city. The performance on
Monday last evinced most surprising power and
command over the instrument, (the Piano,) so much so
as to astonish the audience, who were evidently
unprepared for so admirable a display of musical ability.
In one who had spent a long time practicing, such
proficiency would shew [*sic*] great natural aptitude for
music; but in a young lady of seventeen, the wonder is
still more striking. Although Miss Sloman played without

notes, she seemed perfectly familiar with the most
intricate passages. The pieces were chiefly of the most
difficult kind; and, indeed, we suspect, rather too much
so to be fully appreciated by unpractised ears. It is to be
wished that simpler pieces better known, were selected,
at least in part; and if the voice occasionally
accompanied the instrument, so much the better. Mr.
Sloman sang some very common-place songs in good
style; and it is but justice to Mr. Maffree [*sic*] and the
other instrumental performers to add that they
performed their parts with spirit and effect.

It will be noticed that another Concert will be given
to-morrow evening, and for Miss Sloman we can wish
for no better wish than that the audience may be as
numerous and fashionable, and as highly gratified as on
the first evening.

———

The Montreal Transcript
Thursday, June 16, 1842
*[Maffre is not in this announcement but, his role in the previous
performance, suggests he was present.]*

CONCERT.
MISS JANE SLOMAN
Respectfully announces her Second and Last
CONCERT
ON FRIDAY EVENING, JUNE 17,
AT RASCO'S HOTEL

In addition to her Piano Forte Recitals, she will make
her First Appearance as a Vocalist, and sing "De Piacer,"
and a Song of her own composition, and perform on the
Piano Forte Hertz's "Le Petit Tambour," "Otello,"
Doehler's "Guillame Tell," Thalberg's Fantasia and
Variations on "God Save the Queen" and "Rule
Brittania," as performed before Her Majesty Queen
Victoria.

MR. SLOMAN will also appear.
Concert to commence at half-past EIGHT.
Tickets, One Dollar; Juvenile Tickets half price.
   June 16, 1842   7

———

The Montreal Transcript
Tuesday, June 21, 1842

The attendance at Miss Sloman's second concert on
Friday evening last, was quite as numerous and
fashionable, and the performance just as brilliant as on
the first evening—her appearance as a Vocalist gave
decided indications of future success.

———

The Montreal Transcript
Saturday, August 13, 1842

The Drawing Room of Lady Bagot, held on Thursday afternoon last, was pretty numerously attended. A guard of honor of the 71st was in attendance, as also the Band of the 71st and 43d Regiments. Both Ladies and Gentlemen were presented by Colonel Antrobus, the Aid de Camp in waiting. The Gazette of yesterday gives the following as a few of the names of the persons present:—

LADIES.—[*The list includes Mrs. Gore.*]

GENTLEMEN.—[*From the 71st Regt.: Sir Hew Dalrymple, Mr. Gore, Mr. Hamilton, and Mr. R. F. Hunter.*]

The Montreal Transcript
Thursday, August 18, 1842

On Friday evening, the 12th instant, the Serjeants of the 43d Light Infantry entertained their brother Serjeants of the 71st Light Infantry, with a Ball and Supper, which for elegance and good taste reflected the greatest credit on the gallant entertainers. The company began to arrive about eight o'clock, and at nine the large room in Pointe-a-Calliere Barracks, appropriated for the Ball room, was literally crowded with the *elite* of the rank of both Regiments, together with many fair ones whose hearts have been won by the gallant Brigade of Light Infantry. Nothing could exceed the fine and happy arrangement of the Ball room, which was tastefully festooned with oak leaves, and brilliantly lighted up; at the further end of the room, immediately to the right of the Orchestra, was a life-length representation of a Serjeant of each Corps in full dress, in the act of shaking hands, with the words "Monmouth and Highland Light Infantry" underneath. The dancing commenced a little after nine o'clock, and was kept up with the greatest spirit the whole evening, except the time occupied by supper, which was served in the room immediately above the Ball room, and where upwards of one hundred people sat down to partake of every delicacy the season could furnish. It is scarcely necessary to observe that the greatest harmony and good humour prevailed the whole evening; indeed every one seemed determined to please and be pleased, and the rosy god of day found the gallant company and their fair friends reluctant to leave so much happiness.

It is pleasing to reflect that the same good feeling which animated the old heroes of these splendid corps, has been transmitted to their successors; and we feel confident that with defenders ready for either ball room or battle field, Britain need fear no foe.

The Montreal Transcript
September 1, 1842
[*Maffre is only named in the third and truly final concert.*]

GRAND MUSICAL SOIREE,
BY SIGNOR NAGEL,
First Violin to the King of Sweden, and Pupil of
PAGANINI,
ASSISTED BY MR. AUG. NOURRIT,
The celebrated Tenor, and Professor of the Conservatoire of Paris
ON FRIDAY EVENING, SEPTEMBER 2d,
[*The rest is similar to the ad that follows*]

September 1, 1842   40

The Montreal Transcript
September 3, 1842

Second and Last Grand Concert
BY SIGNOR NAGEL,
First Violin to the King of Sweden, and Pupil of
PAGANINI,
ASSISTED BY MR. AUG. NOURRIT,
The celebrated Tenor, and Professor of the Conservatoire of Paris
ON TUESDAY EVENING, SEPTEMBER 6th,
AT RASCO'S HOTEL.

Several eminent Professors of this City have kindly volunteered their valuable service.

Tickets, One Dollar each; to be had at Mr. Fabre's and Messrs. Armour & Ramsay's Book Stores, and at Rasco's Hotel.

For Programme see Small Bills.

September 3, 1842   41

The Montreal Transcript
September 3, 1842

We had the pleasure of attending Signor Nagel's second Concert, given at Rasco's on Tuesday evening last. The attendance was large and fashionable, and bursts of applause shewed [*sic*] the impression made upon the listeners. The tones brought out of the violin by the wonderful skill of the performer, were occasionally flute-like, and so sweetly melting as to cause a general and involuntary movement among the audience. There was a surprising richness, fullness, and variety in his tones brought from a single string. Mr. Nouritt's singing excited universal applause. "*Colas vous ète si laid,*" was admirably sung.

It would be unjust to Mr. Brauneis and Mr. Eglauch to omit mentioning their able assistance afforded on the Piano during the evening. The latter gentleman performed a difficult and well known piece by Dochler, in a very masterly style, although a certain military man and a few ill-bred smaller fry were busily and so obtrusively loud in their genteel small talk, as to attract general notice and contempt. Those gentry who have seen and heard so much finer things should stay at home, and not by their chattering and laughter disturb others who prefer good music to insipid nonsense lisped even by the prettiest thing that ever wore uniform or sported a moustache.

The Montreal Transcript
Tuesday, September 13, 1842

[*Image of a windmill in which one rotor blade is replaced by a man waving two flags.*]

T H E A T R E   R O Y A L.

THE CELEBRATED ARTIST, surnamed "THE LION, THE MONSTER," has the honor to inform the public of Montreal and its vicinity, that he will make his first appearance at the THEATRE ROYAL of this City, on WEDNESDAY, THE 14TH SEPTEMBER, 1842

[*Omitted description of the six parts of the act.*]

By the kind permission of Major DENNY, the Band of the 71st Regiment, directed by Mr. MAFFRE, will execute Overtures and other pieces of Music during the evening.

Doors open at half-past Seven; Performance to commence at Eight o'clock.

Boxes may be secured on the day of performance, from 10 o'clock, a.m. till 5, p.m., at the Box Office at the Theatre, and at Messrs. Armour & Ramsay's, No. 126, St. Paul Street.

Boxes, 5s., Pit, 2s. 6d.; Gallery, 1s. 3d.
Montreal, September 13, 1842.   45

The Montreal Transcript
September 13, 1842

To the Editor of the MONTREAL TRANSCRIPT.

SIR,—After the last Concert given in Montreal, and since our arrival in Quebec, we have received several flattering letters from Gentlemen Amateurs, who delight in the "divine science," requesting us to give a third Soiree. It is a pleasing duty to express our gratitude for all the kindness we have experienced, and which these letters contain; and, to shew that we are not insensible to the flattering character of the request, we will, on our return to Montreal, give a Concert of Sacred Music, which will be in reality our Farewell Soiree.

Accept, Sir, the expression of our sincerest gratitude and consideration,   JEAN NAGEL
AUG. NOURRIT

Quebec, September 10, 1842

The Montreal Transcript
Thursday, September 15, 1842
[*This ad is similar to the one on the 13th except for its beginning and there is no image.*]

T H E A T R E   R O Y A L.

SECOND PERFORMANCE OF THE
CELEBRATED ARTIST, SURNAMED
T H E   L I O N ,   T H E   M O N S T E R
AND OF
M R .   A D R I E N T ,   T H E   M A G I C I A N
THIS EVENING, THURSDAY THE 15TH SEPT.
[*Same description as previous ad.*]
Montreal, September 15, 1842.   46

The Montreal Transcript
Saturday, September 17, 1842

The performance of the "Lion" at our Theatre on Wednesday evening were equal to promise and expectations. His conversion of himself into the carriage of cannon weighing 6 cwt., during time enough to allow it to be discharged, was a fine put perilous exploit. The momentary sway backwards and forwards communicated to the body by the explosion and recoil of the piece, combined with the haste evinced by his attendants to relieve him as instantaneously as possible of his enormous load, gave fearful interest to the scene. He mastered the strength of two horses, and drew them backwards after him. His joint exhibitor, the magician, made a ridiculous speech, performed *one trick*, and then abruptly quitted the stage altogether:—retired to bed, we presume, for the night.—*Times.*

La Minerve
Thursday, September 23, 1842

THEATRE ROYAL

Lundi prochain 26 Sept.
POUR SOIREE D'ADIEUX DEFINITIFS
Grand Concert
SACRE ET SPIRITUEL
DONNE PAR
S I G N O R   N A G E L,
*Premier violin de S. M. le Roi de
Suède, et élève de Paganini,*
ASSISTE PAR
M O N S .   N O U R R I T,
Célèbre tenor, et professeur du conservatoire de Paris.

MM. Brauneis et Eglauch

Pianistes distingues ont bien voulu preter le concours de leurs talents pour cette soirée,

PAR SPECIALE PERMISSION,

La Bande militaire sous la direction de M. MAFRE [sic], exceutera plusieurs morçeaux de choix.

Prix des places, Loges £1, deuxième loges 3s, parterre et galleries 2s 6d.

S'adresser pour les billets à l'avance, chez M. Fabre, libraire rue St. Vincent, et chez M. Armour et Ramsay rue St. Paul, et l'Hotel Rasco.

Les portes sefont ouvertes à 7 heures et demi, le spectacle commencera à 8 heures.

23 septembre, 1842.

The Montreal Transcript
Friday, September 24, 1842

THEATRE ROYAL.

FAREWELL OF MONTREAL.

GRAND SACRED AND MISCELLANEOUS
CONCERT,
ON MONDAY EVENING, SEPTEMBER 26 AT
THE THEATRE ROYAL,
BY
SIGNOR NAGEL,
First Violin to the King of Sweden, and Pupil of
Paganini,
ASSISTED BY
MONSIEUR NOURRIT,
The celebrated Vocalist Tenor, and Professor of the
Conservatoire , at Paris
MR. BRAUNEIS and MR. EGLAUCH,
The distinguished Professors of the Piano, have kindly volunteered their services on this occasion.

By special permission, the Band of the 71st Regt., under Mr. MAFFRE's direction, will attend the Concert.

Prices of Tickets, first tier of Boxes, $1; second tier, 3s; Pit and Gallery, 2s 6d.

Tickets to be had at Mr. FABRE's Bookstore, St. Vincent Street, at Messrs. ARMOUR & RAMSAY's, St. Paul Street, and at RASCO's Hotel.

Doors open at half-past seven o'clock; to commence at half past eight precisely.

Sept. 24.   50

The Montreal Transcript
Thursday, September 29, 1842

The Musical Soiree given by Messrs. Nagel and Nourrit, in the Theatre Royal, on Monday evening last [*September 26*], was fully and fashionably attended, and went off with as much éclat as on the previous two occasions at Rasco's. It was evident from a peep at the boxes that the great majority of the audience was composed of our French fellow citizens; and it is equally evident to those who have attended the musical treats which have been given in this city of late, that the French portion of the population are much more disposed to patronize the higher kinds of musical performances than the English—a fact which we attribute to their superior cultivation in the divine science of sounds and harmonies, and to the fact that both the Italian and German music approach nearer to the French than to the English style. We have noticed Concerts where scarcely three English speaking persons were present—while the French were in crowds, and in extacies—and with good reason too.

Major General Sir James Hope inspected the 1st and 2nd battalions of the 71st Regiment on the Champs de Mars, on Tuesday forenoon last. The brigade was under the command of Lieut. Col. England; and the precision with which the evolutions were performed attracted general admiration, as well from the spectators as from experienced judges. The 2d battalion is composed of recruits who have just joined, so that less could be expected from them.

The Montreal Transcript
Tuesday, November 1, 1842
[*This ad was repeated on Thursday, Nov. 3 except that tickets were only available at Mr. Herbert's Music Store.*]

CONCERT
Of Instrumental Music.

SINGORA DE GONDI, GUITARISTE and MONS. KNOOP, VIOLINCELLIST, have the honor of announcing to the Gentry and Inhabitants of Montreal, that they will give their

FIRST CONCERT
OF INSTRUMENTAL MUSIC
ON THURSDAY EVENING, 3d INSTANT
IN THE
SALOON OF THE ARCADE HOTEL
BONSECOURS STREET,
In the house formerly occupied by the Hon. L. J. Papineau.

SINGORA DE GONDI will perform some favorable Airs on the Guitar, and MONS. KNOOP on the violoncello, particulars of which will be given in a Programme.

The Performance to commence at Eight o'clock.

The apartments in the ARCADE HOTEL are particularly well adapted for private Concerts, but the accommodations being limited, not more than One Hundred Tickets can be issued. The Band of the 71st Regiment, by permission, will be in attendance, and, under the direction of Mr. MAFFRE, will perform music from the latest Opera of the most approved masters.

MR. COURTNEY, the proprietor of the Arcade will have Tea, Coffee, Ices, &c in readiness which will be furnished on most reasonable terms.

Tickets, 5s each, to be had at RASCO's Hotel, Messrs. Armour & Ramsay, Mr. Fabre, Mr. Mead and Mr. Herbert.

Doors open at half-past seven o'clock; to commence at half past eight precisely.

November 1, 1842   66

The Montreal Transcript
Thursday, November 10, 1842

NOTICE

MADAME DE GONI and M. KNOOP regret extremely that the very unpropitious state of the weather, together with other circumstances which were likely to prove unfavourable to their interest, obliged them most reluctantly to POSTPONE their intended CONCERT of Yesterday Evening.

They hope, however, to have the honour of the patronage of the Montreal Gentry and Citizens on SATURDAY EVENING, at RASCO's HOTEL, when an entirely new Programme will be offered.

Madame De Goni and Mr. Knoop regret to say that engagements at New York will compel them to leave Canada in the ensuing week, and previous to the close of the navigation on Lake Champlain.

Tickets for sale at Rasco's Hotel, Mead's and Herbert's Music Store, and at Messrs. Armour & Ramsay's and Mr. Fabre's Libraries.

Nov. 10, 1842   70

The Montreal Transcript
Saturday, November 12, 1842

THEATRE ROYAL.

MONDAY EVENING, NOVEMBER 14.

By the kind permission of Lieut. Col. England,
THE AMATEURS, 1st BATT., 71st HIGHLAND
LIGHT INFANTRY
Will appear in the favorite and popular Drama of
MASSARONI,
OR, THE BRIGAND CHIEF;
With the Original Music, &c, &c, &c

PRECEDED BY A
GRAND
CONCERT,
BY
MR. BRAHAM & MR. C. BRAHAM.

By the kind permission of the Commanding Officer, the band of the 43d Regiment will play several popular pieces, &c.

Doors open at Eight o'clock, Concert to commence at Half-Past EIGHT.

Boxes, 5s; Pit 2s 6d; Gallery, 1s 3d

Tickets to be had at the Theatre, where places can be secured; at Herbert's Music Store, and at Armour & Ramsay's Book

Box Office open from 10 to 4.

November 12.   71

The Montreal Transcript
Tuesday, November 29, 1842

THEATRE ROYAL.—On Friday evening last [*November 25*] this place of public entertainment was opened under new and most favourable auspices.—The new regime, the fresh and tasteful decorations, together with the unusual attractions of the evening, called forth a very large audience, some part of which, we are sorry to add, seemed wholly unable to appreciate the excellence of the first part of the evening's performance by Madame De Goni and Mons. Knoop, and were more inclined to hear themselves talk—to display their want of taste, as well as the first requisites of gentlemen, than listen to the sweet strains of these unrivaled performers, or allow those to enjoy them who were able to appreciate their excellence. Such persons should get up a bull fight or start a monkey show, or some other similar entertainments much more congenial to their taste and habits, as such a treat as was given on Friday evening is entirely lost on them—it is casting pearls before swine—and we hope arrangements will be made that hereafter such fellows may be kept in order, and prevented from displaying their ignorance and want of taste to the annoyance and disturbance of persons of a different character.

The amateurs of the 71st performed the play of "Rob

Roy" in a very creditable manner—and those in the character of *Rob Roy, The Dougal Creature*, and Mrs. Gibbs as *Diana Vernon*, especially deserve praise. Of the singing of the latter we need not speak; it was as usual—admirable; but we could not admire the taste of introducing the song "The days when we went a gipsying," into the middle of the play.

We have not room to give a full description of the changes made in the interior of the establishment; we can merely notice that the Pit is raised nearly on a level with the stage, furnished with comfortable seats supplied with backs, and having red merino coverings. It is entered through the boxes, two of which on either side of the stage are converted into private boxes, being separated from the rest of the boxes by scarlet curtains, and decorated in a very tasteful manner. The pannels [*sic*] of the boxes are beautifully painted, and adorned with the representations of wreaths and flowers, graceful figure, and chaste and elegant designs—and the whole establishment presents a neat and even splendid appearance, something resembling an Italian Opera House.

The Montreal Transcript
Tuesday, December 1, 1842

Yesterday, about 11 o'clock, the Members of the St. Andrew's Society walked in procession from Mack's Hotel to St. Andrew's Church, where an appropriate sermon was preached by the Rev. Dr. Mathieson, and a collection was made for the relief of the poor. In the evening, about eighty gentlemen sat down to an excellent Dinner, at Mack's Hotel—when the usual loyal and national toasts were given. The fine Band of the 71st Highland Light Infantry preceded the procession in the morning, and enlivened the company during the evening with the unrivaled airs of their native land.

Notes & Queries, published by G. Bell, 1913, p. 465

MONTREAL PLAYBILL ON SATIN, 1842.—
    I have a playbill, printed on pink satin, of a performance which took place in the Theatre Royal, Montreal, on 3 Dec., 1842. "The Garrison Gentlemen Amateurs" presented …band was under the direction of Mr. Maffre.

If there is any museum or dramatic club in Montreal to which it would be acceptable, I shall be happy to hand it over.

                                        W. E. WILSON
Riverview, Hawick, Roxburghshire.

Highland Light Infantry Chronicle, published by the Royal Highland Fusiliers, 1916, p. 77

The officers of the 1st Batt. recently obtained possession of rather an interesting old playbill, dating from the time that the 71st were in Canada in 1842. This playbill was secured by the Relic Fund, through Col. F. Lambton, from Mr. W. E. Wilson of Riverview, Hawick, in whose possession it was.

THEATRE ROYAL
———

FAREWELL CONCERT
For the benefit of
MME. DE GONI AND MR. KNOOP
On Saturday, 3rd December 1842
THE GARRISON GENTLEMEN AMATEURS
Will perform the favourite dramatic piece entitled
'THE SENTINEL'
Frederick, King of Prussia .... Major Denny
Prince Frederick ....Hon. A. Chichester
Baron.. Capt. Cuming
Schloppsen .... Doctor Whitelaw
            Corporal, Officers, etc.
Linda...Mrs. Gibb

———

Programme of Concert
1. Fantasia on Styrian Airs for Violoncello .. M. Knoop
2. Grand Solo for Guitar.........................Mme. de Goni
3. Fantasia for Guitar and Violoncello
....de Goni and M. Knoop
4. Set of Galop...Band
5. Pot-Pourri for Guitar ....Mme de Goni
6. Finale for Guitar and Violoncello
....Mme. de Goni and M. Knoop

After which the Amateurs, Highland Light Infantry, will perform the laughable farce of
'NO SONG, NO SUPPER'
Frederick.....................................H. Dogherty
Robin...Thos. Rose
Farmer Crop..J. Sutherland
Ernest (a lawyer)......................................John Whitelaw
William ....R. McQuarrie
Thomas ....L. Smith
Molly (the Cook) ....Mrs. Thompson
Dorothy ....Mrs. Donaldson

———

The Band, under the direction of Mr. Maffre, will play:—
Before the First Piece—Overture, 'Elligio E. Claudio,'
.... *Mercadante*
Before the Concert—Overture,....................... *Beethoven*
Before the Last Piece—Set of Waltz................ *Labitzky*
    Doors open at seven; the curtain will rise at half-past

seven o'clock. Boxes and Parterre, 5s; Upper Boxes, 2s 6d; Gallery closed. No smoking or noise
Montreal, 3rd December, 1842

The Montreal Transcript
Saturday, December 17, 1842
[The Amateurs performed a series of plays but this is the only ad that names the musicians and Mr. Maffre.]

THEATRE ROYAL.
THE RE-NAISSANCE

ON WEDNESDAY EVENING, DEC. 21,
HER MAJESTY'S SERVANTS,
THE GENTLEMEN GARRISON AMATEURS
Assisted by MRS. GIBBS, (with songs,)
Will perform
PERFECTION.
OR, THE MAID OF MUNSTER.
After which, the laughable interlude of
THE IRISHMAN IN LONDON.
To conclude with
MISCHIEF MAKING.
In which Mrs. Gibbs will perform in the favorite character of MADAME MANETTE, (with songs)

MR. BERLIN, Pianiste and MR. WALCOTT [*WOOLCOTT?*], Flautiste, have been engaged for the season, in order to give additional effect to the Orchestra.

The 71st Band, under the direction of MR. MAFFRE.

Boxes and seats can be secured by addressing the Manager, by note, the mornings of the performance.

Families and gentlemen wishing to subscribe for the season will meet with liberal encouragement, and a reduction of 20 per cent on fixed prices, (benefit nights excepted.)

Private Boxes or Stalls will be filled up for the accommodation of Subscribers.

Doors open at Seven, Curtain to rise at HALF-PAST SEVEN precisely.
Boxes and Parquets, 5s; Upper Boxes 2s 6d.
The Gallery closed to the public.
No Noise or Smoking tolerated.
Police in attendance.
VIVE LA REINE.
December 20, 1842.   87

The Montreal Transcript
December 20, 1842

LA RE-NAISSANCE—THEATRE ROYAL.—

The attractions of to-morrow evening are such as will ensure a crowded house. The amateurs will perform "Perfection," if not altogether to perfection at least in such a way as to furnish a very good substitute for it. "The Irishmen in London" and "Mischief Making" are both pieces of merit; and as the whole dramatic force of the Gentleman Amateurs will be combined in their representation, we expect a treat of a nature more than usually attractive.

The excellent management under which this place of public amusement is now found, has tendered it at once popular and fashionable; and we are pleased to learn that hereafter it will be open for the winter months, every Monday and Thursday, on which latter evening the Gentlemen Amateurs will always perform. The performances for Thursday, the 29th instant will be "A Cure for the Heartache," and "The Sentinel," on which occasion a lady from the Theatres of Edinburgh and Glasgow will make her first appearance in the Province.

The Montreal Transcript
Thursday, February 2, 1843

71st REGIMENT BALL.

On Friday evening last [*January 27*] the Serjeants of this gallant Regiment, (whose character for sobriety and perfection in discipline are probably unequalled by any Regiment in the service,) entertained their brother officers of the District in the most sumptuous and satisfactory manner. Every thing which could tend to please the eye, or gratify the more substantial calls of appetite, was by their profuse liberality supplied. On entering the room, we could have fancied *ourself* in Elysian fields; on either hand were tastily-arranged evergreen bowers, in which were to be found the veteran soldiers, who "for years have braved the battle and the breeze," some of them duly certified to have been the companions of the illustrious Wellington, all lost to the hardship of a soldier's life, deep in the mysteries of whist, and puffing the long smoked *dudeen.*—But hark! the loud peal of the stirring bugle's note calls on—we pass beneath the triumphal arch surmounted by transparent crowns, and wreathed with flowers of every hue. What a sight greets the silent spectator! all is life and merriment, the martial cadence of a march invites each hero the make choice from out that array of beauty, some fair damsel who will kindly listen to his tale of love, or gaze upon his manly face, proud that she is a soldier's bride. The busy hum of voices almost drowns the music—this measure is too slow! and all become impatient for the mazy [labyrinthine] dance. The bugles cease, and the more lively tones of violin [Maffre Jr.] and clarinet [Maffre Sr.], with deeper bass, resound along the hall.—All meet as men and soldiers, distinction leveled, and Lordship thrown aside; the Colonel, and those with him, "born to command," all mingle with the gay and cheerful crowd, their ladies do not fear the rough grasp of an honest soldier's hand as they thread the brisk quadrille. Not being of Terpsicore's disciples [Roman Muse of poetry and dancing], we will in the mean time view the decorations of the brilliantly illuminated apartment.

[The following was selected from the lengthy description.]

The orchestras on each side of the room were very neatly fitted up and decorated with appropriate musical devices.

Old Scotia's choicest melodies warm the blood of her assembled sons, and the excitement is at its height—they reel and waltz—then waltz and reel unwittingly—gallopades and cotillions, are all called into requisition. Dancing commenced at eight o'clock precisely, and was continued without intermission until midnight, when the "Kail brose of auld Scotland" invited the company to an excellent supper got up in Mr. Courtney's best style.

The number of "braw braw lads and bonny lasses" present was 460, as near we could ascertain.

Dancing was continued till grey morn warned the stars to sleep, and the hilarity of the night was concluded to the perfect gratification of all concerned, undisturbed by aught but the crowing cock, and the shouts of *ignoble carters*, eager for employment.

The Montreal Transcript
Saturday, February 4, 1843

CONCERT.

MR. ANDERSON begs to announce that he will give a CONCERT of SECULAR MUSIC in RASCO'S HOTEL, on TUESDAY EVENING, the 7th inst., for the BENEFITS OF THE LADIES BENEVOLENT SOCIETY, and the HOUSE OF INDUSTRY, on which occasion he will be assisted by Mrs. GIBBS, the City Amateur Glee Singers, and the Band of the 71st Regt. Mr. Brauneis will preside at the Piano Forte.

Tickets, 5s. each; Family Tickets, for 5 persons, 20s; may be had at Armour & Ramsay's, Herbert's Music Store, St. Gabriel Street, and Mr. Anderson, St. John Street.

Doors open at half-past Seven; Concert to commence at 8 o'clock.

The Montreal Transcript
February 16, 1843
[*"Mr. Brown" sings in this & other concerts. "Private Brown" witnessed Joseph Maffre Jr. and Julie Perrault's 1843 wedding.*]

GRAND CONCERT
OF
VOCAL & INSTRUMENTAL MUSIC,
FOR THE BENEFIT OF
THE MONTREAL GENERAL HOSPITAL,
UNDER DISTINGUISHED PATRONAGE.

The Ladies and Gentlemen of this city, and its environs, are respectfully informed that a CONCERT of VOCAL and INSTRUMENTAL MUSIC, under the direction of Mr. FAX, will be given at RASCO'S HOTEL, on FRIDAY EVENING, February 17th, 1843—on which occasion he will be assisted by Mrs. GIBBS, Vocalist; Mr. EGLAUCH, Pianist; Mr. MAFFRE, Leader of the 71st Band; and by Messrs. BROWN, S. and D. FAX, Glee Singers.

By the kind permission of Col. ENGLAND, the Band of the 71st Regiment will attend, and play several favorite Overtures. Mr. EGLAUCH will preside at the Pianoforte, and play some splendid and difficult pieces.

Tickets—Single, 5s.; do. to admit a Lady and Gentleman, 7s. 6d.; and a Family Ticket to admit four, 12s. 6d.—To be had at Mead's Music Saloon, Herbert's Music Store, and at Rasco's Hotel. Doors open at half-past Seven and Concert to commence at half past EIGHT precisely.

For particulars see hand bills.
February 11, 1843.   110

The Montreal Transcript
March 2, 1843
[*Marriage of a member of the 71st Band.*]

MARRIED

In this city, on the 27th ult., by the Rev. Mr. Roy, Methodist Minister, Private John Sutherland, 71st Regimental Band, to Miss May Frazier, eldest daughter of John Frazier, Pioneer of Her Majesty's Royal Sappers and Miners.

The Montreal Transcript
Saturday, March 18, 1843

Yesterday being St. Patrick's Day, was celebrated by the sons of Erin with the accustomed honour and ceremonies. The turn out on the part of the St. Patrick and Temperance Societies, notwithstanding a heavy fall of snow, which lasted almost without intermission, was very numerous. In the morning High Mass was performed in the French Church by the Superior of the Seminary, after which an eloquent and exceedingly appropriate sermon was delivered by the Very Rev. P. Phelan, on the advantages, both temporal and spiritual, of providing for the poor; and we are informed that the liberal collection which was made by Messrs. Holmes, Dunn, W. Workman, Conlan, O'Meara and Cassady, shewed the deep impression made by the speaker. Besides the united Choirs of the Recollet and Bonsecours Churches, the Band of the 71st Regiment was present, and contributed much to the harmony and effect of the services. After leaving the Church, which was crowded in all parts, the Societies, accompanied by a large concourse of citizens, marched in procession through some of the principal streets of the city.

At the Montreal Bank, the Societies halted, and gave several cheers for Benjamin Holmes, Esquire, the President of the St. Patrick's Society, who briefly returned thanks for the many honours conferred upon him by his countrymen; and after renewed cheers the Societies and the multitude shortly afterwards dispersed. The inclemency of the weather prevented the numerous and splendid Banners of the Societies from being seen to advantage.

Montreal Transcript
Thursday, May 18, 1843

The Concert à la Musard [*meaning a concert at which people could promenade, or walk about, was popularized by Phillipe Musard who was active during the 1830s and 1840s; the first promenade concert in London took place in 1838*], given by Mrs. Gibbs at Rasco's Hotel, on Monday evening, was, we are sorry to say, very thinly attended. We are compelled to say, the manner in which entertainments of like character and excellence are sustained in Montreal, reflects no great credit on the taste of our citizens, when we recollect the numbers which, in the worst of time, are called forth by any one who will dance Jim Crow or sing Jim-along-Josey in the most approved nigger style. Notwithstanding the unfavorable circumstances on Monday evening, Mrs. Gibbs went through the whole programme in a manner which called forth the warm applause of the audience.

Montreal Transcript
Saturday, May 20, 1843

MRS. GIBBS, FORMERLY MISS GRADDON.— Our readers will perceive, by reference to our advertising columns, that it is the intention of Mrs. Gibbs to give instruction in French, English and Italian Singing. We are sure that the opportunity thus afforded to the Ladies of Montreal of acquiring these fashionable accomplishments, under the tuition of this accomplished lady, will be duly appreciated. There are few communities that can boast of the possession of a late *Prima Donna* from London, to direct the musical studies of its ladies.

Montreal Transcript
Saturday, May 27, 1843

Mr. Wall, the celebrated Irish Harper, has arrived in town, and will give a Concert on Monday evening, when he will be assisted by several of our city amateurs. One of the bands will also be in attendance [*it was the 71st led by Maffre*]. The fame of Mr. Wall is well known to our citizens. In the upper province he has been quite the rage; and we hope that, notwithstanding the late failures in musical entertainments, the Irish Harper will meet with a support similar to that given in every other place he has visited.—*See Advertisement.*

Montreal Transcript
Saturday, May 27, 1843

CONCERT,
FOR ONE NIGHT ONLY, AT RASCO'S HOTEL
[*Image of Irish harp with slogan "Erin Go Bragh"*]

MR. WALL
THE BLIND HARPER,

RESPECTFULLY announces to the citizens of Montreal and its vicinity, that he will give a CONCERT of VOCAL and INSTRUMENTAL MUSIC, on MONDAY EVENING, the 29th instant, at RASCO'S HOTEL, assisted by Messrs. BRAUNEIS & EGLAUCH on the Piano Forte, Mr. WOOLCOTT on the Flute, Mr. SWAIN and Mr. WHITTY, all of whom have kindly volunteered their services—when will be performed several popular Overtures, Medleys, Solos, &c.

By the kind permission of Colonel England, the Band of the 71st Regiment will attend, conducted by Mr. MAFFRE.

Doors open at half-past Seven, performance to begin at half-past EIGHT o'clock. Tickets, 5s; Double Tickets, (to admit two Ladies and a Gentleman,) 10s; to be at the principal Music and Book Stores, and at the Door on the evening of the Concert.

May 27, 1843   12

Montreal Transcript
Thursday, June 1, 1843

The Blind Harper's Concert at Rasco's, on Monday evening, was exceedingly well attended, and the performances gave general satisfaction. The tones of Mr. Wall drew forth from his harp were wild and sweet. We were, however, disappointed in the style and execution of the Blind Minstrel, and thought that there was a want of feeling in playing the beautiful air, "Oh, Blame not the Bard."

Mr. Woolcott on the flute, and Messrs. Eglauch and Brauneis on the piano, acquitted themselves well, and Mr. Swain sung several songs in exceedingly good taste. There was one amateur who, if he did not please by his sweet sounds, afforded much amusement of the nasal twang of his tones, and the original motions of his head and body, which put us in mind of the fanciful evolutions of the famous sign of the "Marquis of Granby" on a windy night. He certainly on Monday evening missed his calling. [*The Marquis of Granby was John Manners, son of the 3rd Earl of Rutland, who rose to become a General at a young age; he left the military in 1747 to lead a widely-publicized, debauched life of free-spending, gambling, and sporting.*]

La Minerve
June xx, 1843

MARIAGES.

En cette ville, le 28, par le Révérend M. Whiliber, M. Joseph Maffré Junior, á Delle. Julie Marie Théophile Perrault, ines deux de cette ville.

The Montreal Transcript
Thursday, June 29, 1843
[*This was the first celebration of St. Jean Baptiste to be held at Notre Dame in Montreal.*]

SAINT JEAN BAPTISTE.

On Saturday inst. [*June 24*], a solemn Mass was celebrated in the Catholic Cathedral, in honor of the Patron Saint of the Society of St. Jean Baptiste. The Catholic Bishop of Montreal presided at this august ceremony. The Vicar General, Messire Hudon, celebrated the Mass, and the Reverend Messire Roup gave an excellent and appropriate sermon on the occasion. The *Pain Beni* was unusually splendid, and of eighteen stories high!! All concerned seemed desirous to render this ceremony as imposing as it was magnificent.

The Lady Mayoress accompanied the four bearers of the *Pain Beni*, and offered it at the Altar. [*The third Mayor of Montreal was Joseph Bourret, serving 1843-44 and 1847-48.*]

The collection in the body of the Church was made by Mesdames Lafontaine, Delisle, and Donegani—that in the galleries by Messieurs Cherrier and Leblanc.

The Band of the 71st Regiment was stationed near the Organ, and played several national airs. The Solus was chanted by Messrs. Fortin, pere et fils, of Laprairie, and Mr. F. Cherrier, Organist of the Cathedral. The Choir acquitted themselves admirably in the Chorus.

Some one had spread a report, that in consequence of the terrible disaster at Boucherville, the celebration of this Mass was deferred—notwithstanding which an immense crowd attended divine service.

The members of the Temperance Society, established under the Clergy of the Cathedral, to the number of about one thousand, attended in procession with their beautiful banners, at about half-past eight o'clock. The Mass over, the Temperance Society filed along Notre Dame Street, followed by the band of the 71st Regiment, playing the air of "*Vive la Canadienne.*" After the band was a banner, representing on one side the figures of St. Jean Baptiste—and on the other side a Canadian Habitant—each surrounded with a wreath of maple leaves and buds.

After the banner walked the Honble D. B. Viger, the President of the Association, accompanied by His Honor the Mayor.

After these came a crowd composed of the members of Committee, and other citizens, who marched four deep. The whole, after making a short *detour*, returned to the Cathedral—where God save the Queen having been played, the meeting dispersed.

If the spirit with which this procession would have been got up, had been something damped by the recent terrible catastrophe at Boucherville, there was enough to prepare us for the magnificence and *esprit de corps* likely to be displayed on the next anniversary.

The Montreal Transcript
Tuesday, July 18, 1843

SOIREE MUSICALE,
AT RASCO'S HOTEL.

MRS. BAILEY respectfully informs her friends and the public that she proposes giving a
GRAND CONCERT
OF
VOCAL AND INSTRUMENTAL MUSIC
ON THURSDAY EVENING, JULY 2,
AT RASCO'S HOTEL,
When she will introduce selections from the admired Operas of La Somnambula, Norma, Marino Faliero, L'Ambassadrice, Le Preaux Clercs, and Fra Diavolo; with Scotch and Irish Ballads.

Mr. WARREN, Professor of Music and Organist of Christ's Church, having politely volunteered his services, will preside at the Piano Forte.

By permission of Col. ENGLAND, the Band of the 71st Regiment will assist and perform some favourite pieces.

Concert to commence at half-past EIGHT o'clock.

Tickets HALF-A-DOLLAR each—to be had at the Stores of Messrs. Armour & Ramsay, Messrs. Mead & Co., and at Rasco's Hotel.

July 18, 1843.   34

The Montreal Transcript
Saturday, July 22, 1843

A considerable company was drawn together at Rasco's Room, on Thursday evening, to listen to the charming melody of that delightful vocalist, Mrs. Bailey. Of course every one was delighted. Still we fear that from the lowness of the price, (half-a-dollar,) the amount received at the door, could not have been sufficient, after the expenses, to leave anything for the singer. Mrs. Bailey, however, is about to give another concert, when, we trust, she will have better fortune.

The Montreal Transcript
Saturday, July 29, 1843

DANCING FOR YOUNG LADIES.

MRS. CHARLES HILL,
PROFESSOR & TEACHER OF DANCING, AND THE CALISTHENIC EXERCISES,

At the request of several Families, respectfully announces her intention of opening an Academy for the above elegant accomplishments. Having conducted similar establishments in London, Bath, Cheltenham and Newcastle-upon-Tyne, with eminent success and unqualified satisfaction to her Pupils, their Parents and Friends, Mrs. C. H. can confidently recommend her system for the speedy acquirement of excellence in every branch of BALL ROOM DANCING. The strictest attention paid to the deportment and address, by the practice of easy and graceful CALISTHENIC EXCERCISES, as recommended by the first Medical men for expanding the chest and improving the health and spirits.

Schools and Families attended on moderate terms, regulated according to distance and the number of pupils. Further particulars may be obtained on application, by letter of in person, to Mr. MAFFRE, Professor of Music, Sanguinet Street; Mr. HERBERT's

Music Warehouse, Notre Dame Street; or to Mrs. CHARLES HILL, at Mr. MARTELL's, 31 St. Mary Street, Quebec Suburbs, from 8 to 10, A. M., and from 3 to 5, P. M.

Mrs. C. H. solicits the early attention of those Families who intended to honour her with their patronage.

July 25, 1843.   37

The Montreal Transcript
Saturday, July 29, 1843

HARP, GUITAR AND SINGING.

MISS ROCK begs to intimate her intention of giving instruction in the above elegant accomplishments; and from the success which has attended her system of teaching in Dublin, Edinburgh, Liverpool, and the principal cities of the United States, has no hesitation in insuring those Families who may honor her with their patronage, an easy and speedy knowledge of any or all of the above delightful studies. VOCAL CLASSES organized if desired; SCHOOLS and FAMILIES attended on moderate terms—regulated according to distance and number of pupils. Further particulars may be known at Mr. MARTELL's, 31 St. Mary Street, Quebec Suburbs; Mr. HERBERT's Music Warehouse, Notre Dame Street; and at Mr. MAFFRE's, Professor of Music, Sanguinette St.

July 29, 1843.   39-tf

The Montreal Transcript
Thursday, August 3, 1843

DANCING ACADEMY.

MRS. CHARLES HILL has taken those central and convenient Premises, situated at the Corner of Notre Dame (No. 101) and St. Gabriel Streets, where she will be happy to receive Pupils in

DANCING, AND THE CALISTHENIC EXERCISES,

Schools and Families attended. For terms, apply to Mrs. CHARLES HILL, to Mr. HERBERT, Music Warehouse, Notre Dame street, and to Mr. MAFFRE, Professor of Music, Sanguinet Street.

Montreal, August 2.   41-lm

The Montreal Transcript
Thursday, September 21, 1843
[Maffre is not mentioned in this first announcement for the Choral Society but he was leading it at the Concert weeks later.]

The Montreal Choral Society meet this evening at 8 o'clock, in the British and Canadian School, when all persons desirous of becoming members, may do so. As the society intends to give a public Concert in a few weeks, the practice room will in future be closed to all but honorary members.

The Montreal Transcript
Saturday, September 23, 1843
[*Miss Maffre later employed Mr. Crerar as a confectioner.*]

Mr. Crerar's Dancing Academy.

In Mr. F. MULLIN's Buildings, Steamboat Wharf, (formerly occupied as Mechanic's Institute).

PUBLIC CLASSES are now OPEN on MONDAYS, WEDNESDAYS, and FRIDAYS, from 4 till 6, and from 8 till 10.

Private Families and Schools attended at moderate charges.

Orders left at Mr. F. MULLIN's, and at Mr. D. W. CRERAR's, Notre Dame Street, will be pointedly attended to.

Montreal, September 23, 1843   63-tf

Montreal Gazette
November 13, 1923

SCIENCE OF MUSIC
IMPROVED MORALS

Montreal Choral Society Made Claim to Mayor Eighty Years Ago

Montreal was not lacking in amenities in 1843, and indeed, possessed what appears to have been an admirable organization in the "Montreal Choral Society." Some records of the society remain in the archives of the City, and one in particular exists in the form of a petition forwarded to the Mayor on September 22, 1843.

The writer directs to the attention of His Worship, and the Aldermen and Councillors, "That a Society of the Science and Practice of Music has been formed in this City styled "The Montreal Choral Society."

[*The remainder of this article quotes from the petition and constitution, which are reproduced in full in the next entry.*]

Constitution of the Montreal Choral Society
Probably drafted June 1843
From the Archives of the City of Montreal

CONSTITUTION
OF THE
MONTREAL CHORAL SOCIETY

RULE I.

That this Society be called "The Montreal Choral Society," and shall have for its object: improvement in and the cultivation of a taste for the science of Music and shall confine itself exclusively to the practice and performance of Sacred Music.

II.

That the Society be composed of Practical and Honorary Members.

III.

That the Officers of the Society, viz: a President, Vice President, Secretary and Treasurer, and Six Members, compose a Committee for the transaction of business.

IV.

That said Committee be chosen from the Practical Members, at the Annual Meeting of the Society.

V.

That the Annual Meeting be held on the first Tuesday in June.

VI.

That it shall be the duty of the President to attend and preside at all Meetings of the Committee.

VII.

That the Vice President shall preside in the absence of the President.

VIII.

That it shall be the duty of the Secretary to attend all Meetings of the Society, to record all proceedings, and to issue all notices and advertisements requisite.

IX.

That the Treasurer shall receive and pay all monies, and shall keep a book of accounts for the purpose.

X.

That power to transact all business, connected with the Society, be vested in the Committee.

XI.

That at the request of ten Members, the Committee shall, at any time, call a General Meeting.

XII.

That any person desiring to join this Society, must be proposed at one General Meeting—a majority of voices at the next, constituting full membership—admission of said Member to be subject to the approval of the Committee.

XIII.

That all Persons admitted into this Society, as Practical Members do pay the sum of 2s. 6d. on their entry, and the sum of 2d. per week in addition, to be paid quarterly in advance. [*Since 1 shilling = 12 pence, they paid 30 cents on entry, and 26 cents quarterly.*]

XIV.

That the payment of 5s. on entry, and 3s. 9d. quarterly, (in advance,) shall entitle any one, approved of by the Committee, to the privileges of an Honorary Member. [*They paid 60 cents on entry and 45 cents quarterly.*]

XV.

That Honorary Members have the privilege of attending all Practices and Concerts of the Society.

XVI.

That the Practical Members meet once in each week for Practice.

LOVELL AND GIBBON, PRINTERS

Montreal Choral Society to Mayor Joseph Bourret to use the Rooms over St. Ann's Market; prior to Sept. 22, 1843 From the Archives of the City of Montreal [*Joseph Bourret was the third Mayor of Montreal in 1843-44 and was re-elected for 1847-48.*]

To His Worship the Mayor, Aldermen & Common Councillors of the City of Montreal

This representation is respectfully made.

That a Society for the promotion and cultivation of the Science and Practice of Music has been formed in this City styled "The Montreal Choral Society" a copy of the constitution of which is respectfully presented.

That this Society already numbers upwards of ninety practical, exclusive of Honorary, members.

That it has for its object not only the improvement of its own members in music, but aware of the great influence the cultivation of a taste for that Science must have on improving the moral tone of the Community, they are desirous to contribute to so desirous an end.

That this Society purpose [*propose*] holding periodical Public Concerts the proceeds of which shall, after the liquidation of necessary expences, be appropriated to Public Charity.

That the Room over the St. Ann's Market, being the most central as well as suitable place for a Public Performance the Society respectfully solicit the use of it for their first Concert, which will take place in the beginning of October, they defraying all expence that may be incurred for Extra Insurance, for lights.

And the Society is in City found will ever prosper.

[*C. S. Butler ?*]

Pres Montreal Choral Society

Handwritten note from Mayor Joseph Bourret on Sept. 22, 1843 From the Archives of the City of Montreal

Montreal Choral Society Constitution— Soliciting to occupy the room over St. Ann's Market. Granted 22 Sept 1843

The Montreal Transcript Thursday, September 28, 1843

GRAND CONCERT,
UNDER THE PATRONAGE OF
HIS WORSHIP THE MAYOR

THE MONTREAL CHORAL SOCIETY will hold their FIRST PUBLIC CONCERT in the Large Room over the ST. ANN'S MARKET, on THURSDAY EVENING, the 5th October.

Tickets —price 1s 3d—may be had at the different Bookstores, with a Programme of the Performance.

Concert to commence at EIGHT o'clock precisely.

September 28   65

The Montreal Transcript Thursday, October 5, 1843

The Montreal Choral Society give their first public Concert this evening, in the room over St. Ann's Market. We understand that there are upwards of 100 vocal performers who will take part in the different choruses, and that the orchestra is composed of 25 instruments. This says a great deal for the spirit and good taste of our community, and is a very gratifying circumstance. In addition to the regular members, Miss Rock has kindly volunteered her assistance on the occasion, and is to sing two beautiful selections from Handel's works—"Angels ever bright and fair," and "With verdure clad." On the whole we cannot imagine a more pleasing entertainment, and we trust that the public will show their respect for *native* talent by mustering in strong numbers this evening.

The Montreal Transcript
Thursday, October 5, 1843

GRAND CONCERT,
UNDER THE PATRONAGE OF
HIS WORSHIP THE MAYOR

———

THE MONTREAL CHORAL SOCIETY will hold their FIRST PUBLIC CONCERT in the Large Room over the ST. ANN'S MARKET, on THURSDAY EVENING, the 5th October.

MISS ROCK has kindly volunteered her assistance on the occasion, when she will sing the two Solos, "Angle [*sic*] ever bright and fair," from Handel's Theodor, and "With verdure clad," from Hayden's Creation.

PROGRAMME,
PART I.

1—Grand Overture		
2—Blessed be the Lord God of Israel,	*Chorus,*	*Leach*
3—Stanley,	*Chorus,*	
4—Angels ever bright and fair,	*Solo,*	*Handel*
5—Worthy is the Lamb,	*Chorus,*	*Handel*
6—Avon,	——	*Bannister*
7—Comfort ye my people Every valley, &c	*Solo,*	*Handel*
8—Millenium	*Chorus,*	*Leach*

PART II.

1—Levite's March,	*Instrumental,*	*Wyvill*
2—Missionary,	*Hymn,*	
3—There's nothing true but Heaven,	*Solo,*	
4—26th Psalm	*Anthem,*	——
5—The Heavens are telling,	*Chorus,*	*Hayden*
6—Lovely Place,	*Duet,*	*Handel*
7—With verdure clad,	*Solo,*	*Hayden*
8—Hallelujah,	*Grand Chorus,*	*Handel*
Finale—GOD SAVE THE QUEEN.		

Leader of the Orchestra, • Mr. MAFFRE.

The doors will open at half-past Seven o'clock.—Concert to commence at EIGHT o'clock precisely.

Tickets —price 1s 3d—may be had at the different Bookstores, and the Music Stores with a Programme of the Performance.

September 28   65

The Montreal Transcript
Friday, October 6, 1843

CHORAL SOCIETY.

The great room at the St. Ann's Market was thronged to overflowing on Thursday evening, when the Choral Society gave their first public Concert. There must have been nearly a thousand persons present, and of these, there was not one, we are satisfied, who did not derive the greatest pleasure from the effects of the performance. The choruses, on the whole, were exceedingly well given, and several of the solos would have done no discredit to *artistes* of greater pretensions. Where all exerted themselves to the utmost, it seems invidious to particularlize; but still we cannot avoid noticing the very unaffected and pleasing manner in which the beautiful hymn "There's nothing true but heaven," was sung by one of the female performers. The tones of this lady's voice are exceedingly sweet, and have something bird-like in their quality; added to which, there was a retiring modesty in the singer's manner, which interested the audience, and rendered this solo one of the most effective of the evening. The magnificent anthem, "Comfort ye my people," was also very fairly sung by a gentleman, whose extreme nervousness, however, evidently interfered with his voice, and prevented him from doing so well as he otherwise would have done. The two solos by Miss Rock—"Angels ever bright and fair," and, "With verdure clad," were given with great taste and sweetness. This lady's voice is, however, scarcely strong enough for the room, which is not well adapted for singing.

On the whole, we think this public must have been taken by surprise, and we confess that we were. We had formed no idea that, in so short a space of time, such a Society could have been formed, and it is only another proof of what the combined efforts of a few persons can do.

The Montreal Transcript
Thursday, October 18, 1843

The second division of the 71st Regiment leave this evening for Quebec, *en route* to the West Indies, carrying with them the best wishes and kindest feelings of the inhabitants. There are very few regiments which have left behind them so high a character as the 71st. The excellent conduct of the men, and gentlemanly and courteous demeanour of the officers, rendered them general favorites, and makes their departure a subject of sincere regret. As a military body, they are one of the finest regiments that ever set foot in Canada and the privates are far above the ordinary men, as was shown in their successful attempts to amuse the public during last winter by a series of dramatic performances at the Theatre. Good fortune go with them, say we — a more gallant set of fellows are not to be found even among the thousands of brave men who have the honor of serving Queen Victoria.

[*The following item appeared a few items below.*]

The Montreal Choral Society meet this evening in their practice room at half past seven o'clock, British and Canadian School Room, Lagauchetierre Street.

Petition, November 4, 1843
From the Public Archives of Canada

To His Excellency

Sir Richard Downes Jackson K.G.B.

Commander of the Forces in British North America
The Petition of The Undersigned Musicians residing in the City of Montreal

Most Respectfully Sheweth
That Your Petitioners are now practicing their Profession as Musicians in the City of Montreal, and are wholly dependent on the Profits ensuing therefrom, to enable them to maintain themselves and Families, and to meet the heavy rents and Taxes attendant thereon.

That Your Petitioners Main source of Receipts arise from playing as such musicians at Balls, Quadrille Parties, Public Assemblies as also from attendance at Private residences where their services may be in requisition as musicians aforesaid.

That in consequence of Military Bands being permitted to attend at such Balls Quadrilles parties for in many instances Free of charge & in all cases at very low rates, advantage thereof is meanly taken by the Citizens, who are wholly dependent on such sources for their livelihood and who have been induced to make Montreal their place of Residence, from the very flattering hopes held out to them by a few Friends.

Therefore Your Petitioners Humbly Trust That your Excellency will take the foregoing into your gracious consideration, and mete out such relief to your Petitioners, as to your Excellency's Wisdom may seem most fitting and Your Petitioners will every Pray—

Montreal 4th November 1843

	G Compton	*D. Sallter*
	H. Fastrois	*W. Willison*
	Wm Salter	*J. Warnock*
Juniors	*F. Maffre*	*C. Warnock*
	H. Maffre	*F. Maffre*
	Jos Maffre	

[*Joseph Maffre Sr. probably composed the above petition. It is in the Public Archives of Canada and is document RG8/C76, which means from the British military Record Group 8, C series, volume 76. All documents in volume 76 pertain to the civil government of Lower Canada from 1806-1845.*]

The Montreal Transcript
December 12, 1843

It will be seen by an advertisement, to be found in another column, that the members of the Montreal Harmonic Society intend to give their first Concert, at the large room in the St. Ann's Market, on Wednesday. These musical societies, of which there are now two, the Choral and the Harmonic, are highly creditable to the musical taste of the city, and deserve every encouragement. If the Harmonics only acquit themselves as well as their Choral brethren, they will do wonders.—*See Advertisement.*

[*This group competed with Maffre's. According the review of January 12, the Harmonic Society's Concert was not a success.*]

The Montreal Transcript
Saturday, December 23, 1843

GRAND CONCERT.

THE MONTREAL CHORAL SOCIETY will hold a PUBLIC CONCERT in the ST. GABRIEL STREET CHURCH, on FRIDAY EVENING, the 29th instant, to commence at EIGHT o'clock precisely.

The proceeds of this Concert will be devoted to the Ladies' Benevolent Institution.

Tickets, 1s 3d; may be had at the different Book and Music Stores.

December 21, 1843   101

The Montreal Transcript
Saturday, December 30, 1843

The Concert given by the Choral Society at St. Gabriel's Church last evening was very well attended, and went off much to the satisfaction of every one present.

The Montreal Transcript
January 12, 1844

The concert given by members of the Harmonic Society at the Theatre on Wednesday evening, was not very well attended. There was some good singing but on the whole we are inclined to think that the attempt was premature, and that the Society would do well to wait for a little while, till it has acquired more strength, before it undertakes to give another public entertainment on this scale.

La Minerve [*translation*]
March 7, 1844

Musical Education.

Mr. Maffré, *senior* respectfully informs the men and women of Montreal and surrounding area that he has made his residence in one of the stone houses of MR. SMITH, on Craig Street, facing Champs de Mars and close to the government square, where he proposes to open an ACADEMY OF MUSIC, modeled after the system of Mr. Logier. This system of musical instruction is universally known and meets with the approval of all the sovereigns of Europe. Mr. Maffre can affirm this by his personal observation in the academies of Mr. Logier, there examining its numerous students, that this system is invariably successful. Mr. M. has also had the liberty to play by this system, further he will teach perfect execution on the piano giving knowledge of harmony, thorough-bass, and composition, knowledge that is desirable and essential to render perfect music. Mr. Maffre begs to state also that knowledge of harmony in music is as necessary as the knowledge of grammar in language; and in Mr. Logier's school these essential matters are communicated to the abilities of the very young, in as much as 6-year-old children have begun to learn with success.

Mr. Maffre will structure the classes in his school 2 days a week for instruction in the art of playing the piano; and 2 days to give lectures on harmony, thorough-bass and composition. The ladies and gentlemen who are already advanced in the art of playing may receive lessons in harmony or composition, either in classes or individually. Students may either receive their music lessons in the French, German or English language.

For conditions, etc., contact Mr. Maffre, Craig Street near Champs de Mars.

Montréal 7 March 1844.

The Montreal Transcript
Monday, March 19, 1844

It will be seen on an advertisement that the Choral Society will give another of their musical entertainments on Thursday evening, in the St. Gabriel Church. The previous Concerts given by this Society were exceedingly creditable to the native talent of the City, and we are quite sure that the present one will be no worse.

[*On another page in the same issue.*]

GRAND CONCERT.

THE MONTREAL CHORAL SOCIETY will give a GRAND CONCERT of SACRED MUSIC on THURSDAY EVENING, the 21st instant, in the ST. GABRIEL STREET CHURCH.

Leader of the Orchestra—Mr. MAFFRE.

Tickets—price 1s 2d—may be had at the different Book and Music Stores.

For further particulars see Handbills

Doors open at half past Seven; Concert is to commence at EIGHT o'clock precisely.

GOD SAVE THE QUEEN.

March 19, 1844   130

The Montreal Transcript
Saturday, March 23, 1844

The Choral Society gave their concert at St. Gabriel Church, on Thursday evening. The orchestra was not so well filled as on former occasions, nor was the attendance so numerous; but there was, certainly, no falling off in the execution of the different pieces. On the contrary, the choruses were better managed than we ever heard them, and there was, in all other respects, a marked improvement in the performers, both instrumental and vocal.

We trust that the Society will not be neglected, now that it has advanced so far. There is no saying how far combinations of this kind may carry musical improvement and refine public taste.

La Minerve
Thursday, April 4, 1844

Théàtre Royal.

—o—

ATTRACTION SANS EXAMPLE!

Tragédie, Comédie, Farce, Musique et Danse.

LUNDI, MARDI, JEUDI, ET VENDRE DI SOIRS.

Lundi Soir, le 8 Avril,

La Représentation sera au Bénéfice de

MR. MAFFRÉ,

Chef d'Orchestre et de plusieurs Sociétés Musicales.

Il sera assisté en cette occasion, par MM.

WARREN, WOLCOTT, ANDERSON, FOX,

Et plusieurs autres Musiciens distingués.

Plusieurs Morçeaux de Musiques du premier mérite serent executés par 40 Musiciens.

Après quoi, plusieurs Danses et un Drame populaire seront executés.

The Montreal Transcript
Saturday, April 6, 1844

EASTER HOLIDAYS.
———

THEATRE ROYAL.
———

UNPARALLELED ATTRACTIONS IN
TRAGEDY, COMEDY, FARCE, MUSIC, AND
DANCING,
ON
Monday, Tuesday, Thursday, and Friday Evenings.

ON MONDAY EVENING, APRIL 8,
AN UNPRECEDENTED
MUSICAL AND DRAMATIC
ENTERTAINMENT,
For the Benefit of
MR. MAFFRE,
Leader and Musical Conductor of the Orchestra, Choral Society,
&c.
On which occasion he will be assisted by Mr. WARREN,
Mr. WOLCOTT, Mr. ANDERSON, and the Leading
Professors of the City, Aided by the Messrs. FAX, and
several AMATEUR VOCALISTS.
In the course of the evening, the
OVERTURE TO DER FRIESCHUTZ [*sic*],
and a GRAND BATTLE PIECE,
by KOTZWARRA,
arranged expressly for the occasion by Mr. MAFFRE, will
be executed by a Band comprising FORTY PERFORMERS.
After which, a variety of DANCING, and other
Entertainments.
To conclude with a POPULAR DRAMA.
———

April 2, 1844.   145
[*Maffre was not featured on Tuesday (songs and dances),
Thursday (amateur performance), or Friday (a play).*]

Tipperary Free Press
Wednesday, April 24, 1844

CANADA.
Montreal…St. Patrick's Day [*March 17*]….This Feast
having occured on Sunday this year, the usual extended
procession of the sons of Ireland did not take place; nor
did St. Patrick's Society, as such, join in the
demonstration, which occurred in consequence of some
of its officers and members being of Protestant
demoninations, and having to attend their respective
places of worship. An immense procession, however,
composed of the Irish Teetotal Society, the Hibernian
Benevolent Society, with its president, and a
considerable number of the members of the St. Patrick's
Society, was formed at the Recollet Church as early as
nine o'clock, a.m. [*on Monday, March 18?*], and having
been kindly favoured by the officers of the 89th with the
Band of that regiment, and the St. Patrick's Amateur
Band, under the direction of the well-known musician,
Mr. Maffre, being also in attendance, moved in imposing
order to the French Church, where a grand and solemn
High Mass was celebrated by the Rev. Mr. O'Connell,
assisted by the several priests of the Seminary, and an
eloquent and appropriate sermon was delivered by the
Rev. Mr. Morgan. The united choirs on the College and
Recollet Church assisted in the service of the morning
with grand effect. The blessed bread used upon the
occasion, one of singularly large size, was the offering of
Counsellor Tully. After the sermon, a handsome
collection in aid of St. Patrick's Church was taken up.
We may add that the occasion was, altogether, one of
thrilling importance. It was truly grand and touching
witness such a number, almost to the extent of filling the
immense Cathedral, assembled to celebrate the festival
of their patron saint, according to the blessed spirit of
religion, and exhibiting in their entire demeanour all the
marks of peace, order, and comfort.

The Montreal Transcript
Tuesday, December 3, 1844

The members of the Montreal Choral Society meet on
Wednesday evening the 4th inst., at half-past seven
o'clock for practice, in their Room, Lagauchetiere Street.
As the concert will take place on the 10th instant, every
member is particularly requested to attend punctually at
half-past seven o'clock.

The Montreal Transcript
Tuesday, December 3, 1844

GRAND CONCERT.

A GRAND CONCERT of SACRED CHORAL
MUSIC will be given by the MONTREAL CHORAL
SOCIETY, on TUESDAY EVENING, the 10th instant,
in the WESLEYAN METHODIST CHAPEL, St. James
Street.
For particulars see Programmes.
To commence at EIGHT o'clock precisely.

Tickets, Price 1s 3d; may be had at Messrs MEAD's, and Messrs. J. W. HERBERT & Co.'s Music Stores.

Doors open at Half past 7 o'clock.

Concert to commence at 8 o'clock precisely.

December 3d.   93

The Montreal Transcript
Tuesday, December 10, 1844

The Choral Society will give a Grand Concert of Sacred Music, this evening, at eight o'clock precisely, in the Methodist Church, Great St. James Street. The satisfaction which this Society has, upon all occasions, given to the Public, will, we are sure, ensure them a numerous and respectable audience on this occasion. The price of admittance is only 1s 3d.—*See advertisement.*

Montreal Gazette
Tuesday, December 10, 1844

We feel much pleasure in calling the attention of our musical readers to the Grand Concert to be given this evening, by the Montreal Choral Society, in the Wesleyan Methodist Chapel, Great St. James Street. The encouragement and patronage of sacred music, is highly laudable, both in a scientific and devotional point of view, and we trust that the resources of the Society will be considerably increased by the attendance at the concert of this evening.—*See Advertisement.*

The Montreal Transcript
Thursday, December 12, 1844

We were present on Tuesday night, at the concert of sacred music given by the Choral Society, in the Methodist church, Great St. James street. The pieces selected for the occasion were excellent, and the performance of a superior order. The audience was large and respectable, and evinced their satisfaction as far as the nature of the place would allow. The Choral Society has strong claims on the public, as it has enabled them to pass their leisure hours in a pleasing and rational manner.

Montreal Gazette
Thursday, December 12, 1844

The Grand Concert announced to be given by the Montreal Choral Society took place on Tuesday evening. We are happy to state that the excellent performance both of the vocal and instrumental pieces gave undisguised satisfaction to a numerous and fashionable audience.

The Montreal Gazette
Saturday, December 14, 1844

PROSPECTUS,

WILL be published shortly, THE FIRST MUSICAL WORK EVER PRINTED IN CANADA, to be entitled "NOTES OF THE FOREST, or, Eastern TOWNSHIP MELODIES," being a collection of ORIGINAL AIRS, set as Quadrilles, Waltzes, and Marches, composed by J. CRISPO, and arranged for the Piano Forte by Mr. MAFFRE, Professor of Music. To be dedicated, by permission, to His Excellency, Sir CHARLES THEOPHILUS METCALFE, Bart., G.C.B., Governor General of British North America, &c. &c. &c.

The Work will contain two sets of Quadrilles, six Waltzes, and five Marches;—and will be published at 5s., in neat coloured stiff covers; and about 8s. 6d. or 10 s., half bound, or bound in cloth, with gilt letters on the outside.

The Montreal Transcript
Tuesday, January 7, 1845

PROSPECTUS.

———

WILL be PUBLISHED shortly, the first MUSICAL WORK ever printed in Canada, to be entitled

Notes of the Forest;

on,

EASTERN TOWNSHIP MELODIES;

being a collection of (original) AIRS, set of QUADRILLES, WALTZES AND MARCHES; composed by J. CRISPO, and arranged for the Piano Forte, by Mr. MAFFRE, Professor of Music; to be dedicated (by permission) to—His Excellency Sir C. T. Metcalfe, Bart., G C B., Governor General, of British North America, &c. &c. &c.

———

The WORK will contain two sets of QUADRILLES, six WALTZES and five MARCHES; and will be published at 5s., in neat coloured stiff covers; and about 8s. 6d. or 10 s., if half bound, or bound in cloth, with gilt lettering on the outside.

January 7.   108

[This ad appeared in a few January issues, reappeared in February, and again in March.]

The Montreal Transcript
January 21, 1845

The Montreal Choral Society will meet to practice on Wednesday Evening next, at 8 o'clock. A punctual attendance is earnestly requested.

Montreal Gazette
March 3, 1845

MARRIED.

In this city, on the 27th ultimo, at Trinity Church, by the Rev. Mark Willoughby, William Tate, Esquire, to Miss Maria Maffre, both of this city.

The Montreal Transcript
Thursday, March 13, 1845
[Similar entry in the Montreal Gazette of March 11]

GRAND CONCERT
OF
SACRED MUSIC.

THE Ladies and Gentlemen of this City are respectfully informed, that a CONCERT of VOCAL and INSTRUMENTAL MUSIC will be given at ST. PAUL'S CHURCH, on WEDNESDAY EVENING, the 19th instant, for the benefit of the Choir; when a number of Psalms, Hymns, Anthems, Doxologies, &c,. selected from the best authors, will be sung; also a number of Instrumental Pieces will be played by the Band of the 93d Highlanders.

Leader of the Choir—Mr. S. Fax, assisted by the principal singers of the city.

Mr. Maffre will preside at the Pianoforte and conduct the Instrumental Music.

Single ticket, 2s 6d; family ticket to admit three, 5s; children, 1s 3d. To be had at Messrs. Armour & Ramsay's Bookstore, Mr. Dugald Stewer's Place d'Armes, and from Mr. S. Fax, Alexander Street.

Doors to open at half past seven, and Concert to commence at EIGHT o'clock precisely.

For particulars see Programmes.

March 11.   135

The Montreal Transcript
Tuesday, March 18, 1845

The Concert of SACRED MUSIC, VOCAL and INSTRUMENTAL, at St. Paul's Church, will take place to-morrow evening, at eight o'clock precisely. From the well known abilities of the performers, and the excellence of the Programme, which we subjoin, we have no doubt the Church will be crowded:—

PROGRAMME OF CONCERT.
PART FIRST.

Instrumental Piece, Band,		
Psalm,	Invocation,	R. A. Smith.
Psalm,	Zion Hill, Denmark,	Dr. Madan.
Psalm,	Islay,	
Anthem,	From the 68th Psalm,	R. A. Smith.

PART SECOND.

Instrumental Piece, Band,		
	Arnolds and Doxology,	Dr. Arnolds.
Psalm,	St. George's, Edinburgh,	Rev. Dr. Thomas.
	Watchman, tell us of the night,	L. Mason.
	Old Hundred,	Martin Luther.
	Eastgate and Doxology,	
Anthem, From the 24th Psalm,		R. A. Smith.

PART THIRD.

Instrumental Piece, Band,		
Hymn,	Daughter of Zion,	
	Mount Olivet,	J. Stewart.
	Come ye Disconsolate,	Webbe.
	Creation,	Haydn.
Anthem,	From the 100th Psalm,	R. A. Smith.
Finale,	God Save the Queen.	

In addition to the above attracting selection, the Band of the 93d Highlanders will attend, and execute a number of Instrumental pieces.

—*See Advt.*

Montreal Gazette
July 7, 1845

A Card.

DANCING—LA POLKA.

MISS ST. CLAIR, Principal Dancer of the Park Theatre, New York, begs to announce that she is prepared to teach the above Celebrated Ball-Room Dance to Ladies, in a few lessons. Immediate application must be made, in consequence of Miss St. Clair's short stay in Montreal.

Address, Mr. MAFFRE, Professor of Music, Craig-Street, near St. Denis-street; or, Miss ST. CLAIR, Quebec Hotel, adjoining Rasco's.

July 7.

La Minerve [translation]
Thursday, December 11, 1845

CONCERT,
UNDER THE PATRONAGE
Of His Honor the Mayor.

M. **Maffré** respectfully announces to the public that he will offer a GRAND CONCERT of Vocal and Instrumental Music on TUESDAY, **16**th instant, in the NEW HALL OF ODD FELLOWS, Upper St. James Street. The orchestra will be composed of 50 MUSICIANS.

Principal vocalists:—Miss Levingston [*sic*], Miss Holloway, and Mr. Rogers, Fax, Cameron, Michel, Ronald, Anderson, Hunt, &c. &c.

Leader of the Orchestra—Mr. Maffre,

Tickets of admission **2s 6d**. Doors to open at seven and music to begin at eight.

For details, see the flyers.

La Minerve [translation]
Thursday, December 18, 1845

—We attended Tuesday night's concert by Mr. Maffre. The bright room of Odd Fellows Hall could hardly contain the crowd. We hardly like music concerts melee and yet the singers performed their task well, and everyone seemed satisfied. Among the singers we notice Miss Livingston and Miss Halloway, who certainly have voices that would be noticed in theater. Mr. Maffre played well as usual, with taste and precision. His playing is firm, well accentuated and he showed in his violin solo that he knows the little tricks of the "divine art." Taken as a whole, it was ultimately a pleasant musical feast, and the number of fans seemed large enough to induce us to believe that these concerts should be repeated more often. Those who attend any public performance should know never to whistle at a woman. It is in bad taste and shows a lack of breeding. You must show respect to this beloved part of us on Tuesday! Hissing one of the singers, who returned upon public demand of deafening screams again and again! His embarrassment was painful to see, of this we are sensitive, such that we felt a tear roll down our nose, when the jokes of a neighboring gentleman came to console us. The brave dilettante was standing in the midst of the audience, beating the time of the head and foot, laughing, gesticulating, crying, speaking from time to time to the musicians words of encouragement or blame, saying to one: That's right; to the other: That feat alone was worth the price of admission. He was a great prankster who might not be armed he had the air! It seems to us that we laughed a little and the music and those who listened. It is true that the audience got a lot of laughs from him, and, in this, everyone is compensated.

The Montreal Transcript
All issue are missing from 26 April 1845 to 4 May 1846

The Montreal Transcript
late 1846

Wanted, a good Terrier dog, he must be a first rate ratter.

The Montreal Transcript
Saturday, October 3, 1846

[*Image of three interlocked rings*]

I. O. of O. F.

THE ANNIVERSARY of the MONTREAL DISTRICT of I.O.O.F., M.U., will be Celebrated by a PUBLIC SOIREE in the Hall of the New Market, on TUESDAY, the 6th October.

The room will be fitted up for a Promenade Concert.

Mr. W. J. DAVIS of New York, has kindly consented to perform on the celebrated Boehm Flute.

Monsieur J. B. LABELLE will preside at the Piano Forte.

Miss LIVINGSTON, Mr. ANDERSON and the principal Glee Singers in Montreal will give several Songs, Duetts, Glees, Catches, &c.

Several Gentlemen will address the Assembly on the Principle, Benefits, and Rise and Progress of Odd Fellowship.

The Band belonging to the Order will be in attendance, and will perform several beautiful and appropriate Airs.

Mr. MAFFRE's Splendid Quadrille Band has been secured.

Refreshments during the evening.

Doors open at SEVEN o'clock.

Chair to be taken at 8 o'clock.

Tickets—Single, 5s; do. admitting a Lady and Gentleman, 6s 3d; do, admitting a Gentleman and two Ladies, 8s 9d—to be had at Mead's Music Store, John Hoy, Fancy Store, and R.W.S. MacKay, Monkseller, Notre Dame-street, Caledonian Springs Depot, and Victoria Hotel, Place d'Armes, A.W. Laird, Canada Gazette Office; Ramsay and McArthur, Painters, McGill-street, and J.L. McIntyre, Compson-street, and of any of the Committees or Officers of the Lodges.

Oct. 3   67

The Montreal Transcript
Tuesday, October 6, 1846

The Anniversary Festival of the Independent Order of Odd Fellows of Montreal, will take place this day. The *Gazette* of yesterday has given the following programme of the course the procession will take in the morning, and a list of those persons who will endeavor to render the *Soiree* attractive in the evening. We fully enter late the belief of our contemporary that the *Soiree* will be one of the best conducted affairs ever seen in Montreal:—

The Anniversary Festival of the Independent Order of Odd Fellows, Manchester Unity, will be celebrated this day (Tuesday), and preparations are on foot for its observance with more than usual *éclat*. The brethren of the Order will meet in the Hall, in St. Gabriel Street, at ten o'clock in the morning, whence they will walk in procession to St. Gabriel Street Church, where Divine Service will be performed, and an appropriate address delivered in aid of "the Widows' and Orphans Fund," by the Rev. Mr. Leishman. In the evening a grand Soiree will be held in the spacious hall of the New Market, which will be arranged for a promenade concert, and decorated with much splendour. Stuart Derbishire, Esq., will preside at the Soiree to render which attractive, no pains and expense have been spared. Mr. W. J. Davis, whose talents are highly spoken of by the New York press will perform on the celebrated Boehm flute, Mr. Labelle will preside at the piano forte, and the assistance of the most celebrated vocalists in the city has been secured. The band belonging to the order will perform appropriate pieces at intervals, during the evening; whilst, for the gratification of the votaries of Terpsichore [the Greek Muse of poetry and dance], Mr. Maffre's splendid quadrille band has been engaged. We have no doubt the whole affair will go off with spirit, and that the Soiree will surprise, both in point of numbers and brilliancy anything of the kind we have hitherto seen in Montreal.

The Montreal Transcript
Thursday, October 8, 1846

The Manchester Unity of O. F. celebrated their anniversary Festival on Tuesday evening, in the Hall of the New Market, in a manner that did credit to their taste, spirit, and liberality. The building had been fitted up with great care, and presented the usual embellishments of flags and evergreens, orders, paintings, &c. Although not unfrequently adorned after a similar fashion, it lost nothing by comparison with previous efforts. Some very pretty coloured chandeliers threw a pleasant light over the whole, and made the scene at once lively and showy.

The evening commenced by an introductory speech from the chairman, a fat comfortable looking little man, who rather solemnly exhorted the visitors to make themselves as happy and jolly as possible, a piece of advice which they were evidently perfectly well prepared

to attend to. Afterwards came two speakers, who enlarged on the benefits of the order, proving as plain as a pike-staff that without Odd Fellowship no man can live or die happy, and exhorting the ladies in particular to have nothing to do with any who do not belong to the brotherhood.

Then came singing, now solos, now duets, and now good lively glees, varied by the harmonious roarings of Mr. Maffre's famed band, who surrounded themselves, as often before, with an immortal halo of musical glory. All of a sudden, in the midst of this combination of art and beauty, an adventurous couple, taking advantage of a tripping tune, began to waltz, and soon the infection spread around. In a few minutes the one couple was changed into two, then into three, and before long all the room was jigging. Such are the triumphs of Terpsichore, that the oration of an associated Demosthenes [*Athenian statesman known for his speeches*], the silvery tones of the mysterious chairman's bell, or the fumes of mocha-breathing coffee, would at that moment have been heard and smelt in vain. Henceforth the triumph was Maffre's, and nobly we understand he acquitted himself, playing with his band of heros [*sic*] to "past four o'clock in the morning," when exhausted nature and legs gave in.

Seriously, the affair was exceedingly well managed, and every one seemed to enjoy himself or herself amazingly. The attendance, too, was such as shown the influence Odd Fellowship exercises, not only over the hideous beast man, but over that much more perfect and attractive piece of workmanship, woman. Of the latter, there was by no means a scant master, and either our eyes deceived us, or the lamps and nature aint to be trust, if many of them wer'nt [*sic*] beauty—but there, we wont write the word, but only explain that it is the antithesis of "ugly."

The Montreal Transcript
Thursday, December 24, 1846

GRAND CONCERT.

The Public of Montreal and its vicinity are respectfully

informed that the
FIRST SEASON SUBSCRIPTION
CONCERT,
of

Vocal and Instrumental Music,
UNDER THE IMMEDIATE PATRONAGE OF
His Excellency the Earl Cathcart,
Will take place at
DONEGANA'S HOTEL,

ON
SATURDAY, THE 26TH INSTANT.

The receipts of these Concerts, after expense, will be applied to charity.

Terms to Subscribers, for the three performances, 10s, to be paid on the evening of the First Concert. Family Tickets, to admit three persons, 8s.; to admit four, 10s.; to admit six, 15s to each Concert. Single Tickets, 3s. 9d.

Subscription Lists are open at the Music Stores in Notre Dame Street; Messrs. R. & C. Chalmers, Great St. James Street, and at Donegana's Hotel, at which places Admission Tickets are to be had.

Leader of the Orchestra, Mr. MAFFRE.—Mr. WARREN will preside at the Piano Forte.

December 24.   102

Montreal Transcript
Thursday, December 24, 1846
[*This ad doesn't mention Maffre but the Jan. 9 review does.*]

A CHARITABLE SOIREE
WILL BE HELD AT
DALEY'S HOTEL,
ON TUESDAY, 5TH JANUARY, 1847,
FOR THE BENEFIT OF THE MONTREAL
LYING-IN HOSPITAL,
The Ladies' Directresses of the Institution, will preside.

———

PRICE OF TICKETS.

A Gentleman with two Ladies 10s 6d
A Lady and Gentleman 7s 6d
Single Tickets 5s 0d

To be had at the Book Stores, and at DALEY'S and DONNEGANA'S Hotels.

A MILITARY BAND will be in attendance.

Montreal, December 23.   102

Montreal Transcript
Saturday, December 26, 1846

It will be seen from an advertisement in another column, that the first of a series of subscription Concerts takes place this evening at Donegana's Hotel. The receipts of these Concerts are to be applied, after paying expenses, to charitable purposes, and the price of admission has been rendered so low as to exclude none who really desire to observe the Christmas season by contributing to a benevolent object. The performers, vocal and instrumental, are all residents, and they have obtained the patronage of His Excellency the Governor General in the furtherance of their really deserving scheme. We trust, such being the case, that they will meet with support, and that the hundreds in our good city who are always ready to answer the call of foreign artists, and to hurry where fashion prompts, will not refuse a solitary dollar bill towards the encouragement of a scheme that is at the same time local and charitable.

Montreal Transcript
Saturday, January 2, 1847

The first season subscription Concert of Vocal and Instrumental Music, took place at Donegana's Hotel, on Saturday evening. We are sorry to be compelled to observe, that although the performers, both vocal and instrumental, comprised a great portion of musical talent of Montreal, the concert was but poorly attended. A great number of the ladies and gentlemen who were present, however, were among the *elite* of the city; among who was Major General Gore, Captain Hope, Colonel Wetherall, and several others of the military, and many ladies of fashion. The band, under the leadership of Mr. Maffre, was all that could be desired; and the vocal performers, among who Miss Livingston was the only female, and who therefore bore a very prominent and pleasing part in the concert, acquitted themselves admirably. It is to be desired that the two remaining concerts, both for the musical credit of Montreal, and for the sake of the charity to which the receipts of the concert, after expenses are paid, are to be devoted, will be more numerously attended.

Montreal Transcript
Saturday, January 9, 1847

We omitted to state that the Soiree [*on January 5*], in behalf of the Montreal Lying-In Hospital, went off in gallant style. The dancing was kept up until two o'clock with great spirit. The Quadrille was under the direction of Mr. Joseph Maffre, and it had a most potent charm on the trippers of the light fantastic toe. In fact, the music was excellent. We have not heard the amount of the sum collected, but we learn that the directresses are in every way satisfied.—*Times*

Montreal Transcript
Saturday, January 30, 1847

Grand Concert
of
VOCAL AND INSTRUMENTAL MUSIC.
———

The Public of Montreal are respectfully informed, that the SECOND SEASON CONCERT, under the immediate Patronage of the Earl of Cathcart, will take place on MONDAY EVENING, the FIRST of February, 1847, in the ODD FELLOWS' HALL, Great St. James Street.

After the Concert Mr. T. [sic] Maffre's full Quadrille Band will be in attendance.

Tickets—For a Gentleman and Lady, 7s 6d—Gentleman and two Ladies, 10s—Single Tickets, 5s. To be had at the Music Stores, and at Messrs. Chalmers, Great St. James Street.

Leader of the Band, Mr. Maffre. The proceeds of this Concert, after expenses, to be applied to Charity.
January 26.   116

Montreal Transcript
January 30, 1847

Mr. Maffre's second Concert of Vocal and Instrumental Music takes place on Monday evening. The Concert is under the immediate patronage of the Earl of Cathcart. Mr. Maffre's abilities are too well known, and appreciated, to doubt his having an overflowing house, more especially, as the proceeds, after deducting expenses, are to be applied to charitable purposes.

Montreal Transcript
Tuesday, February 18, 1847

The Annual Soiree of the President and Committee of management of the Mechanics' Institute of Montreal, came off Tuesday evening in splendid style; there could not have been less than 2,500 persons present. In the early part of the evening a short address was read by the President, Mr. Tate.

His Excellency the Earl of Elgin, accompanied by Col. Bruce, and an Aid-de-camp, arrived about half past ten o'clock, and was enthusiastically received by the assembly; [*he gave a short speech, examined the machinery assembled, shouted "Three cheers for the Mechanics' Institute of Montreal", then the Queen, then the Ladies. They responded with "for Lord Elgin" and placed a rosette on his lapel. He said he would mail it to his Lady in his next letter to her.*]

Quadrilles then commenced, and shortly afterwards His Excellency retired amidst the cheers of the assembly.

Dancing was kept up with great spirit until five o'clock on Wednesday morning.

The band of the Rifle Brigade, the Light Infantry band, and Maffre's Quadrille Band were in attendance. The refreshments were excellent and plentiful. All present appeared to enjoy themselves to the utmost—and the Festival turned out to be, as was promised by the committee of management, in all respects the best thing of the kind ever seen in Canada.

Among the many objects of mechanical and scientific interest, were a model of the new bridge across the St. Lawrence, another of the electro magnetic telegraph; numerous railway and locomotive models, an electrifying machine, steam engines and printing presses, a model of the new Theatre Royal, a number of paintings and engravings—some of them of great merit; stuffed birds, models of naval architecture; besides which were a number of others which from the hasty view we took of them we are unable to particularize.

[*The article then praises the people who were in charge of the caps and coats, says that Miss Livingston, Mr. Anderson, and others had sung earlier in the evening, and that speeches had been given by the Hon. Mr. Draper but that the crowd was such that they could not get near enough to hear him.*]

Montreal Transcript
Tuesday, February 23, 1847

GRAND SOIREE
IN AID OF THE FUNDS FOR THE RELIEF
OF THE
SUFFERING POOR
OF
IRELAND AND SCOTLAND
Under the immediate patronage of the
NATIONAL SOCIETIES

THE COMMITTEE OF MANAGEMENT for the late Mechanical Festival, have been induced, by the earnest solicitation of many influential Citizens, as well as by their own sense of duty, to avail themselves of the splendid Decorations, Machinery, Models, Paintings, &c. &c., which now adorn the Magnificent Halls of BONSECOURS MARKET, for the purpose of holding A GRAND SOIREE, on THURSDAY EVENING next, the 25th inst. The proceeds will be devoted to the Relief of their Suffering Fellow-Creatures in Ireland and Scotland.

Chair will be taken at EIGHT o'clock.

Addresses will be delivered by several distinguished Gentlemen.

Miss Livingston and Mr. Anderson, with his Glee Party, as also Mr. Maffre, the Military, and Volunteer Rifle Bands have kindly volunteered their services, for the occasion.

Montreal Transcript
Saturday, February 27, 1847

We should imagine that from 1000 to 1200 persons were assembled on Thursday evening, in the rooms over the Bonsecours Market Hall,—which had been left precisely in the same condition as they were on the night of the Annual Festival. About half past nine o'clock, Mr. Tate addressed the assembly from the platform, in a speech appropriate to the occasion—with the object of introducing the other gentlemen who intended to address the meeting,—when Mr. Tate sat down, "Had rosy morn" was sung by Mr. Anderson and his Glee Party.

The Rev. Mr. Cordae [*gave a speech about the evening's object of charity*]. After some musical entertainments by Miss Livingston and Mr. Anderson, Mr. McGinn rose to address the meeting. He made a long and excellent speech to the same effect as that of the Rev. gentleman who had preceded him…the assembly was addressed in French by M. Rodier, to the same effect…His Worship the Mayor arrived about 10 o'clock, and took the chair [*At half past 11,*] dancing commenced in right earnest, and was continued until an early hour in the morning. The band of Rifle Brigade, the Light Infantry Band, Maffre's Quadrille Band, were in attendance during the evening, and everything passed off with the greatest harmony. The refreshments consisted of every delicacy in the confectionary line that could be imagined, and reflected great credit on the furnisher, Mr. Keiller; they were plentiful almost to profusion, both the coffee and the tea, were as good as they could be, and the whole arrangements were admirably conducted.

Montreal Witness
March 1847

MARRIAGES.

Montreal—25th ult., Mr Thos. Buckley, to Mary Anne, youngest daughter of Mr J. Maffre.

Montreal Transcript
Tuesday, March 9, 1847

ST. DAVID'S BALL.—St. David, who, though the patron of Britons the most ancient, has been quite overlooked by Montrealers in the brotherhood of Saints, was honoured on his anniversary (Monday eve) by a ball and supper given at Mayo & Flagg's Exchange, in a style equal to any, and superior to most things of the kind got up this season. The assemblage of ladies, most young, and all looking so, appeared to have been studiously selected from the most beautiful of the city, and in point of tasteful dress they were all perfection. In the matter for which they were met—dancing—we could only wonder where so many were found so accomplished in the art. Maffre's band appeared really inspired by the graces their music brought into action, and, with little intermission, kept the whole in motion till many hours "ayont the twal'." Nor could anything exceed the excellent…all beneath their roof [*of Mayo & Flagg*] on the even of St. David's Day will long remember it as one of the most brilliant and agreeable in their lives.—*Courier.*

Montreal Transcript
Tuesday, April 13, 1847

The second Elgin Assembly took place on Tuesday evening last, at Hall's Ottawa Hotel, Great St. James Street. The weather proved very unfavorable, it having rained in torrents during the evening, thereby causing the absence of many who intended joining it. This, however, did not prevent some eighty ladies and gentlemen from being present—and dancing with great spirit until five o'clock. The supper table was profusely supplied with every dainty, reflecting great credit—as on a former occasion—to Mr. and Mrs. Hall, for their unwearied exertions to please. Mr. Maffre's quadrille band was in attendance, and played in their customary correct and excellent manner.—*Herald.*

Hampshire Telegraph
August 7, 1847

DIED.

At Montreal, Canada, on July 11th, 1847, John Crispo, aged 30, eldest son of Lieut. J. W. Crispo, R.N. Also, on the same day, Lieut. Wm. Lloyd, R.N.: and, on the following day, the Rev. Mark Willoughby, minister of Trinity Church, Montreal. These three gentlemen died of typhus fever, and fell a sacrifice to their Christian benevolence in visiting the sick and dying Irish immigrants, in the sheds of Montreal.

Montreal Transcript
November 4, 1847

JUST PUBLISHED,
THE
ORIGINAL CANADIAN QUADRILLES,
DEDICATED TO THE
COUNTESS OF ELGIN.

———

THESE QUADRILLES are founded on old Voyageur Airs that have enjoyed an extensive popularity in Manuscript, amongst our resident population, and have been universally admired by all strangers visiting our city. They are beautifully got up, with a characteristic title page.

—ALSO,—

JUST RECEIVED,

A Choice and Extensive selection of EUROPEAN MUSIC, containing all that was new and popular down to the moment of shipment.

J. W. HERBERT & CO.

N.B.—Others in the Trade having conspicuously advertised "American Music at half price," we beg leave to say, that we have never charged more than half price for American Reprints, and were the first to sell Music at moderate price in Canada.

J. W. H. & CO.

GOLDEN LYRE MUSIC WAREHOUSE,
113, Notre Dame Street.
August 21   50

La Minerve
November 8, 1847

Académie de Danae.

MELLE. **Maffré** annonce respectueusement au public de Montréal, qu'elle a ouvert une Académie pour l'instruction des juenes Dame et des jeunes Messieurs dans Pari de la Danse. Elle donnner aursi des leçons dans les familles ou dans les academies de demoiselles á des prix modérés. S'addresser au No. 77, rue Rousseau, près du Quarré Dalhousie— 5 nov.

[By January, her address was listed as No. 11, the same address as Joseph Maffre.]

Montreal Transcript
November 2, 1847
[This ad also ran in January 1848]

EDUCATION.

DANCING ACADEMY.

———

A Card.

MISS MAFFRE respectfully announces to the Montreal Public, that she has opened a DANCING ACADEMY, for the Instruction of Young Ladies and Gentleman.

Seminaries and Private Families punctually attended too. Terms moderate.

For particulars apply at her Residence, 77, Rousseau Street, near Dalhousie Square.

Nov. 2   **80**

La Minerve
January 3, 1848

DECES

Sumedi, le 1r du courant, A l'age de 24 ans., Henry, fils de Mr. J. E. Maffrê, professeur de musique, en cette ville.

[Sunday, the 1st of the current month, at age 24, Henry, son of Mr. J. E. Maffre, Professor of Music, of this village. This is the only time Joseph Maffre is given a middle initial.]

Montreal Witness
January 3, 1848

DEATHS

1st inst…Of consumption, Mr Henry Maffre, second son of Mr. S Maffre, aged 24 years.

New Orleans, 30th Sept. Mr. Thomas Buckley, late of Montreal, aged 36 years.

Montreal Transcript
Tuesday, January 25, 1848

MISS MAFFRE respectfully informs her friends, that her first annual BALL will take place on TUESDAY, the first of Feb. 1848, in the ODD FELLOWS HALL, St. Gabriel street.

Tickets, to admit a Lady and Gentleman, 6s 3d. Single Tickets, 3s 9d. To be had at the Music Stores, Notre Dame Street, and at her residence No. 11 Rousseau Street.

N.B.—Mr. CRERAR, the Confectioner, will be in attendance.

January 25   116

La Minerve
January 27, 1848

Melle. Maffré

INFORME respectueusement ses amis que son premier BAL annuel aura lieu MARDI, le 1r Febrier, dans la Salle des Odd Fellow, rue Saint Gabriel.

Billets admettant un Monsieur et une Dame, 6s 3d, une seul personne 3s 9d. On peut a'en procurer aux magasins de musique, rue Notre-Dame et á se residence, rue Rousseau, No. 11.

Les enfralchiessments serout servis par M. Crerar—27 janv.

Montreal Transcript
Tuesday, January 27, 1848

RATES OF ADVERTISING

	s	d
Six lines and under, first insertion	2	6
Every insertion *after the first*	0	7
Ten lines, and under, first insertion	3	4
Every insertion *after the first*	0	10
Above ten lines, per line,	0	4
Every insertion after the first, per line,	0	1

Montreal Transcript
Thursday, January 27, 1848
[*Maffre performed at this event according to the Feb. 12 review*]

I. O. O. F.
CELEBRATION.

A CELEBRATION of the INDEPENDENT ORDER OF ODD FELLOWS of British North America, will be held at DONEGANA'S HOTEL, on the EVENING of THURSDAY, the 10th Feby, and MEMBERS are requested to appear in Regalia appertaining to their rank.

ADDRESSES, ODES, &c will be given by Brethren of the Order.

Bands of Music will be in attendance during the whole of the Evening.

Tickets of Admission are now in the hands of and can be purchased from, the OFFICERS of the R. W. GRAND, LODGE; the NOBLE GRANDS OF PRINCE of WALES; QUEEN'S; COMMERCIAL; and CANADA LODGES, and at the several Book-Stores in the City.

January 27   117

Montreal Transcript
Saturday, February 12, 1848

After an adjournment to the refreshment room, in which a comfortable supply of the good things there provided having been taken in, the room was cleared for dancing, and soon a hundred feet tripped merrily over the floor, to the exhilarating sounds of Mr. Maffre's Quadrille band, and the still more lilting tones produced by the band of the Montreal Amateurs.

The dancing once commenced, need we say that it was kept up with spirit, till an early hour in the morning; and soon after the last parties quitted the scintillating scene, daylight appeared in the dawn and we are well assured that all parties were highly gratified with the entertainment.

The room was filled with as many persons as could conveniently hold, and we have since learned that about 400 persons were present. The Independent Order of Odd Fellows have reason to congratulate themselves on the success of their First Annual Celebration.

Montreal Gazette
Monday, February 14, 1848

The second annual celebration of the Independent Order of Odd Fellows took place on Thursday evening last, at Donegana's Hotel. [*They explain that they have already reviewed it earlier but wanted to elaborate here. The room is described in general terms and then in particular.*] At one end of the room, on a raised platform, or *dais*, stood the gorgeous tent of the *Encampment*—the walls on each side of which were elegantly festooned with drapery, in colours emblematic of the various degrees of the order. At the opposite end of the room were erected two orchestras, occupied respectively by Maffre's Quadrille band, and the band of the Montreal Light Infantry, both of which acquitted themselves to admiration. [*The review continues and then recounts the speeches.*]

Montreal Transcript
Saturday, February 12, 1848
[*Maffre performed at this event, see next entry.*]

MECHANICS' INSTITUTE
FESTIVAL & EXHIBITION.

THE PRESIDENT and COMMITTEE of MANAGEMENT of the MECHANICS' INSTITUTE of MONTREAL, beg to announce to the public, that the ANNUAL FESTIVAL and EXHIBITION of the INSTITUTE will be held on TUESDAY EVENING the 15th instant, in the MAGNIFICENT HALLS of the BONSECOUR MARKET, which have been kindly placed at their disposal by His Worship the Mayor. From the facilities afforded by this Building, and the extensive arrangements now in progress, and having the experience of past years to guide them, the Committee confidently anticipate that this Festive occasion will be one of surpassing interest and splendour. The Halls will be thoroughly *cleansed* and *heated* in every part.

Tickets may be had at the different Book and Music Stores.

Price of Tickets; Gentlemen's 6s. 3d.; Ladies and Childrens, 3s. 9d.

Members wishing to claim their privilege must apply at the Institute for their Tickets.

February 3   120

Montreal Transcript
Thursday, February 17, 1848

ANNUAL CELEBRATION OF THE MECHANICS' INSTITUTE.

This long talked of, anxiously looked for, and decidedly popular festival, came off on Tuesday evening; and we think the result must have fully equalled, if it did not exceed, the most sanguine expectations of the committee of management. [*Many paragraphs omitted.*]

Alternate songs from the glee singers, and from Mr. and Miss Brown, of Ohio, who kindly favored the Committee with their gratuitous services, and strains from the bands of music stationed in every room—with occasional visits to the abundantly spread refreshment board—then became the order of the evening. About midnight the hall was cleared for dancing, and to the music of Maffre's quadrille band, a hundred couples gaily tripped in giddy mazes through the length of the room in alternate reels and waltzes, till daylight dissolved the magic of the scene, and they retired—if wearied with their exertions—delighted with the entertainment so carefully and unsparingly provided.

[*Many paragraphs omitted.*]

Montreal Gazette
Friday, February 18, 1848

[*Many paragraphs omitted.*]

The President leaving the Chair about eleven, was the signal for striking the fetters from the feet of the company, and two thousand feet were speedily in motion to the strains of Maffre's Band. The fun now "grew fast and furious." Dancing was kept up till a late, we should rather say early, hour, with right good spirit. People seemed half *daft* with the "Polka" and the jolly "Sir Roger." But we must apply the scissors to the thread of our scribbling faculties, by congratulating the President and Committee of Management, on the magnificent manner in which their Festival went off.

Montreal Transcript
March 11, 1848

Miss Maffre

RESPECTFULLY informs the Public, that at the request of her Pupils and Friends, her SECOND and LAST BALL for this Season, will take place on FRIDAY, the 17th instant, at the ODD FELLOWS' HALL, St. Gabriel Street.

TICKETS, to admit a Lady and Gentleman, 7s 6d; Single Tickets, 5s; Tea and Coffee included. To be had at MISS MAFFRE'S Residence, 11 Rousseau Street, and at the ODD FELLOWS' HALL.

Mr. Maffre's full Quadrille Band will attend.

March 11   136

[*This Ball was not reviewed but the large St. Patrick's Day parade on that day was. The parade ended at St. Patrick's church, where Mr. Maffre was the organist. In fact, he was the music master for Montreal's Irish Catholics since 1843.*]

Montreal Transcript
April 22, 1848

UNDER THE PATRONAGE OF HER EXCELLENCY
THE COUNTESS OF ELGIN AND KINCARDINE

THE ANNUAL SOIREE

IN aid of the Funds of the UNIVERSITY LAYING IN HOSPITAL, will be held at DONEGANA'S HOTEL, on the EVENING of THURSDAY, 4th May next.

LADY PATRONESSES.

Hon. Mrs. Gore,	Madame De Bleury,
Mrs. L. T. Drummond,	Mrs. Coffin,
Mrs. Col. Wetherall,	Mrs. Mjr. Campbell

MASTERS OF THE CEREMONY.

Col. Antrobus, Prv. A.D.C.,	Col. De Salaberry,
Gen. Desbarais, Esq.,	Col. Ermatinger,
Mjr. Granville, 23d H.W.F.	Capt. Claremont, D.A. Adjt. Gen.

The Band of the 77th and Maffre's Quadrille Band, will attend.

Cards of Admission to be had after the 10th inst., at Messrs. A. Savage & Co., Lyman, Chalmers, McCoy, &tc, &tc.

April 6   147

The Montreal Transcript
All issues are missing from 22 April 1848 to 31 Dec 1848

La Minerve
May 1, 1848

Sous le Patronage de
MADAME LA COMTESSE D'ELGIN
LA SOIREE ANNUELLE,

En aide de l'Université de l'Hospice de la Maternité aura lieu a L'Hotel Donegana, JEUDI soir, le 4 mai prochain.

DAMES PATRONESSES

Mesdames Gore,	Mesdames DeBleury,
" L.T.Drummond	" Collin
" Wetherall	" Campbell

MAITRES DE CEREMONIES

Col. Antrebus, A.D.C.P.,   Col. DeSalaberry,
George Debarats, Ecr.   Col. Ermatinger
Mj. Grenville, 23rd R.W.F.   Capt.Clermont, D.A.
                                          Adjt. Gen.

La Bande du 77e régt. et de Maffré assisteront en ceite occasion. On pourra se procurer des cartes d'admission après le 10, aux magasins de MM. Savage, Lyman, Chalmers, McCoy, etc.—6 avril.

Montreal Gazette
Friday, February 2, 1849

UNDER THE PATRONAGE
OF HIS EXCELLENCY
THE GOVERNOR GENERAL

———

THE PRESIDENT AND COMMITTEE OF
MANAGEMENT
OF THE
Mechanics' Institute of Montreal
BEG TO ANNOUNCE THAT THEIR
Grand Annual Festival
WILL TAKE PLACE
𝕺𝖓 𝕿𝖚𝖊𝖘𝖉𝖆𝖞 𝕰𝖛𝖊𝖓𝖎𝖓𝖌, 13𝖙𝖍 𝖎𝖓𝖘𝖙𝖆𝖓𝖙,
IN THE
MAGNIFICENT HALLS
OF THE
BONSECOURS MARKET,
Which has been kindly placed at their disposal
by His Worship the Mayor.

———

From the arrangements in progress, it is confidently anticipated that the festive occasion will surpass in interest and splendor all preceding ones.

An EXHIBITION of WORKS OF ART, MODELS, &c. &c. will be open during the Evening.

The public are respectfully invited to send in all descriptions of CANADIAN MANUFACTURES, as the Committee are particularly desirous that the industrial resources of this Province should be prominently brought forward at all their Festivals.

By the kind permission of Colonel HAY, the splendid Band of the 19th Regiment will be in attendance.

The Montreal Light Infantry Band, and MAFFRES Quadrille Band have also been engaged.

ADDRESSES will be delivered by several eminent Gentlemen.

The REFRESHMENT TABLES will be open through the night.

The Chair will be taken at EIGHT o'clock.

Gentlemen's Tickets, 6s 3d; Ladies Tickets, 3s 9d. Can be procured at all principal Book and Music Stores, and at the Hotels.

P.S.—Members who wish to avail themselves of their privilege, must procure Tickets at the Institute.
Montreal, Feb. 2, 1849   15

Montreal Gazette
Friday, February 16, 1849

MECHANICS' FESTIVAL

One of the gayest and most spirit-stirring events that the imagination can picture, was fully realized at the Bonsecours Market Hall, on Tuesday evening on the occasion of the Grand Annual Festival of the Mechanics' Institute. Much was anticipated from the previous displays made by this Institution, and from the promises of the managers that they intended, in the present instance, to exceed all their previous efforts. But we believe few were prepared for the gorgeous display which met the eye upon entering the grand ball, which, splendidly lighted up, and hung with banners and escutcheons, which likewise decorated the halls in profusion, intermingled with evergreens trained in arches, and every variety of fanciful and ingenuous device, gave the place the air of a hall of enchantment such as school boys read with pleasure in the Fairy Tales, or the Arabian Nights. Stationed in a balcony over the entrance, was the splendid brass band of the 19th, and higher up opposite the dais, Maffre's Quadrille band was placed for the entertainment of the dancers at a later period of the evening's amusements.

[The review of the event continues but says no more about Maffre.]—*Transcript.*

La Minerve
Thursday, March 15, 1849

Société Musicale de Montréal.

GRAND CONCERT
DE
Musique Vocale et Instrumentale.

LES soussignés Musiciens de profession, s'étant formés en société Musicale, ent été solicités de donner one SERIE de CONCERTS, et ile informant le public que le premier aura lieu.

MARDI, LE 20 DU COURANT
A L'HOTEL DONEGANA, Prix d'admission un écu.

Les portes s'ouvrirent à huit heures, et le concert commencera à HUIT ET DEMIE.

Pour les autres détails voir les petites affiches.

On petit se procurer des billets aux daféreuts magasins de musique et à l'Hotel Donegana.

MM. WARREN, pres.   MAFFRE, senr.
        FOLLENUS,   VEIT,
        HIRD,   EGLAUCH,

ARTHURSON,   MAFFRE, junr.
SEEBOLD,   GUAITA,
BRAUNEIS,   ZEIGLER, sect.
Montréal, 15 mars 1849.

[Translation: *The undersigned professional musicians, having formed a Musical society, will give a CONCERT SERIES, and they inform the public that the first will take place on Tuesday, the 20th of the current month, at the Hotel Donegana, price of admission is one dollar. The doors open at eight, and the concert will begin at eight thirty. For other details see the playbill. Tickets can be purchased at music stores and at the Hotel Donegana.*]

La Minerve
Monday, March 19, 1849

Concert.—Les amateurs de bonne musique ne doivent pas oublier que c'est domain, mardi, que doit aveir lieu le premier concert donné par la nouvelle compagnie, entre les principaux musiciens' de profession de cette ville. Le programme promet beaucoup, et jamais concert n'aura été donné ici par autant de talents rénnis.

[Translation: *Music lovers should not forget that the first concert by the new company, composed of the chief professional musicians of the city, takes place on Tuesday. The program promises a lot, and never has a concert here been given by so much combined talent.*]

Montreal Transcript
March 24 1849
[*This address is very close to Maffre's of 11 Rousseau.*]

TO LET.
TWO comfortable TWO STORY BRICK HOUSES, situated in Rousseau Street, near the rear of Dalhousie Square, containing each 4 bed Rooms, besides having a Drawing Room and small Parlour, Cellar, Kitchen, Yard, and Stables with Water Pipes and Sink. Rent very low. Apply to the Proprietor, fifth House.
ROBERT UNWIN.
March 24   141

Montreal Transcript
April 22, 1849

UNDER THE PATRONAGE OF HER EX-
CELLENCY THE COUNTESS OF
ELGIN AND KINCARDINE.
———

THE ANNUAL SOIREE

IN aid of the Funds of the UNIVERSITY LYING IN HOSPITAL, will be held at DONEGANA'S HOTEL, on the EVENING of THURSDAY, 4th May next.

LADY PATRONESSES
Hon. Mrs. Gore,   Madame De Bleury,
Mrs. L. T. Drummond,   Mrs. Coffin,
Mrs. Col. Wetherall,   Mrs. Mjr. Campbell

MASTERS OF THE CEREMONY
Col. Antrobus, Prv. A.D.C., Col. De. Salaberry
Geo. Desbarais, Esq.,   Col. Ermatinger,
Mjr. Granville, 23rd H.W.F., Capt. Claremont, D.A.
                                        Adjt. Gen.
———

The Band of the 77th and Maffre's Quadrille Band, will attend.

Cards of Admission to be had after the 10th inst., at Messrs. A. Savage & Co., Lyman, Chalmers, McCoy, &c. &c.
April 6   147

Montreal Transcript
Saturday, June 9, 1849

We beg to direct the attention of our readers to the advertisement of Mr. Maffre's concert, this evening at Donegana's Hotel. Mr. M. is a long resident citizen, and he will, we trust, meet with the support of his friends.

[*In the adjacent column of the paper.*]
CONCERT
OF
Vocal and Instrumental Music.

THE Public are respectfully informed, that MR. MAFFRE, assisted by the Montreal Professional Musical Society, will give a CONCERT of VOCAL AND INSTRUMENTAL MUSIC at DONEGANA'S HOTEL, on TUESDAY, the 19th instant, under the Patronage of Lieut. Col. Sir HEW DALRYMPLE and the Officers of 71st Highland Light Infantry.

Single Tickets, 3s. 6d. each.
Tickets to admit a Lady and Gentleman, 5s.
May be procured at the Music Store, and at Messrs. R. & C. Chalmers' Book Store, Great St. James Street, also at Donegana's.
After the Concert, an Excellent Quadrille Band will be in attendance for the amusement of the Company.
For further particulars, see Programme.
June 9   18

Montreal Transcript
Tuesday, June 12, 1849

Mr. Maffre's Concert, which, we wrongly stated was to take place on Saturday last, instead of Tuesday (to day), is postponed until Friday next.

Montreal Transcript
Thursday, June 14, 1849

Mr. Maffre's Concert comes off to-morrow night. It will be seen by the advertisement that Mr. Maffre has distinguished patronage. We have seen the programme, and certify that it promises well; and no doubt the Quadrille parties that may be formed after the concert will attract numerous visitors.

[*Two columns over.*]
Mr. Maffre's Concert, on Friday evening.

[*On the next page.*]
UNDER THE PATRONAGE OF
LIEUT. COL. SIR HEW DALRYMPLE,
AND THE
Officers of the 71st Highland Light Infantry

———

MR. MAFFRE
Respectfully announces he will give a

GRAND CONCERT,

OF
INSTRUMENTAL AND VOCAL MUSIC
AT
DONEGANA'S HOTEL,
On FRIDAY EVENING, June 15, 1849.

On which occasion, with the kind permission of Lieut. Col. HAY, and of Lieut. Col. Sir HEW DALRYMPLE, he will have the assistance of the splendid Bands of the 19th and 71st Regiments, forming an Orchestra of Fifty Musicians.

———

Tickets, 2s 6d each—may be procured at the Book Store of Messrs. R. & C. Chalmers, and at Donegana's Hotel.

Doors open at EIGHT o'clock. Concert to commence at half-past Eight.

After the Concert, an excellent Quadrille Band will be in attendance, for the amusement of the Company.

June 14   20

The Montreal Gazette
Friday, June 15, 1849, p. 2

Mr. Maffre's Concert comes off to-night, at Donegana's, under the patronage of Sir Hew Dalrymple. The following is the Programme:—

PART I.

1.—Overture, "Zampa" .... Herold
2.—Concerto—Flute—(Lindenberg) ....
3.—Glee..
4.—Oboe—Solo ....Mr. Maffre, jr.

5.—The Drum Polka, in which will be
    introduced 20 Drums ....
This Polka, lately performed by Jullien's celebrated band in London, will be played from the author's Score, including all the original effects.

PART II.

1.—Overture, ... Mr. Maffre.
2.—Solo—On Irish and Scotch
    Melodies—Violin .... Mr. Maffre
3.—Glee..
4.—The Sleigh Polka—Written for
    "The Montreal Sleigh Club," .... Mr. Smyth
5.—God Save the Queen,..
    Tickets only 2s 6d. Doors open at Eight o'clock.

[*Mr. James Smyth (1818-1885) was Bandmaster for the 19th Regiment of Foot beginning in 1841 and for the Royal Artillery from 1854-1881.*]

Montreal Transcript
July 28, 1849

DEATHS

In this city, on the 26th instant, Lucy Thomas Maffre, wife of Mr. Joseph Maffre, senr., professor of music, aged 57 years, a native of Hampshire, England.

Montreal Witness
July 30, 1849

DEATHS

26th inst…Lucy Thomas Maffre, wife of Mr Joseph Maffre, senior, professor of music, a native of Hampshire, England, aged 57 years.

La Minerve
July 30, 1849

DECES.

—En cette ville, le 26 Dime Lucy Thomas, epouse de M. Joseph Maffré, professeur de musique, agée de 59 ans.

[*Translation: In this city, on the 26th instant Lucy Thomas, spouse of Mr. Joseph Maffré, Professor of Music, age 59 years.*]

—Ce matin, après quelques jours de maladie, M. Joseph Maffré, professeur de musique, natif de France, agé ele de 56 ans.

[*Translation: This morning, after a few days illness, Mr. Joseph Maffré, Professor of Music, native of France, age 56 years.*]

Montreal Transcript
August 2, 1849

DEATHS

The late Mr. Joseph Maffre, was formerly Band Master of the 19th Regt., and subsequently of the 71st. He was son of a French loyalist, and, when a child, was, upon the evacuation Toulon by the English in consequence of Napoleon's capture of one its principal outworks, taken by his parents England.

The Montreal Gazette
August 3, 1849

DIED

In this city, on the 29th ult. Mr. Joseph Maffre, formerly Band Master of the 19th Regt., and subsequently of the 71st. He was son of a French loyalist and, when a child, was (upon the evacuation of Toulon by the English in consequence of Napoleon's capture of one of its principal outworks) taken by his parents to England.

On the 26th ultimo, Mrs. Lucy Thomas, wife of Mr. Joseph Maffre, aged 59 years.

Montreal Witness
August 6, 1849

DEATHS

29th ult…Mr Joseph Maffre, formerly band master of the 19th Regiment, and subsequently of the 71st.

Montreal Transcript
August 11, 1849

CHOLERA REGISTER FOR 1849
[*This table was assembled from several news articles.*]

Week	No. Deaths
Prior to July 9	25
July 9 to July 16	97
July 17 to July 23	154
July 24 to July 30	136
July 31 to Aug 6	53
Aug 7 to Aug 10	18
Total Cholera Deaths	483

During the period beginning July 9th, and ending August 8th, at once, the whole number of deaths from all causes, was 986.

To these cases of cholera death there must be added a few more from among the military; […] Probably this may add from ten to fifteen of the above total, as the whole number of cases in the Garrison have, up to this day, been twenty one. One Lieut. Colonel (Holmes), three sergeants, and seventeen privates.

[*Half of all Montreal deaths during this period were due to cholera. Lucy and Joseph died on July 26 and 29 during the second deadliest week.*]

Leicester Chronicle
Saturday, March 2, 1850

DEATHS.

At Montreal, Canada, on the 26th of July, 1849, Mr. Joseph Maffre, formerly in the Duke of Rutland's band, and on the 30th, Mrs. Maffre, both deaths were from cholera. Mr. Maffre was well known in Leicester as a clever musician. He was the son of a French emigrant, formerly in the service of that nation but driven from his country in the Reign of Terror.

[*According to the Montreal papers, Lucy died on the 26th and Joseph on the 30th.*]

"Reminiscences of Canadian Life"
in *The Christian Treasury, by Elizabeth Crispo Cox (Mrs. H. L. Cox), England, 1850, 80 pages. Cox bound her contribution as a book and corrected it with pencil. Cox's copy was donated to the Royal Ontario Museum, University of Toronto Library by her daughter Mrs. Harcourt Roe.*

CHAPTER 1.

It was during the month of July in the year 1835, that my father, who was an officer in the Royal Navy, embarked with his family from Mount's Bay, Cornwall, on board the barque *Geraldine*, bound for Quebec. Many officers that year emigrated to Canada, literally "to turn their swords into plough-shares;" or, in other words, to exchange a sea-life in his Majesty's service for that of a farming one in the new world.

CHAPTER 14. [*Compton township, Quebec, 1837*]

The boys, as well as my father, played extremely well, and it was a great pleasure to us to listen to the numerous operatic and other pieces of music, selected from the *répertoires* of the most celebrated composers. Mozart was an especial favourite. My father was fond of sacred music, and never a day passed without it. My eldest brother composed several pieces of music, entitled "Notes of the Forest, or Eastern Township Melodies," which we highly appreciated.

In course of time we made acquaintance with several families, both at Lennoxville, Compton, and Hatley. We now often attended parties, and small dances, meeting the best society the place afforded. Some of our friends lived quite the English style, being well off, especially those in the neighbourhood of Lennoxville.

CHAPTER 28. [*April 1843*]

My father had by this time given a farming life sufficient trial, and it was evident to him that no suitable living or provision for his family could be made from it. His capital, too, had wofully diminished, and with such a large family only a good income would suffice. To leave them hereafter with little besides the farm would condemn them to a life of toil and penury. He therefore contemplated giving it up as soon as he could arrange to do so, and taking his family to Montreal, where he would endeavour to obtain an appointment for himself, and find suitable employment for his elder sons. The young ones could go to school, and in time get out in life, either in professions, Government appointments, or mercantile houses—all of which about after a twelvemonth came to pass.

"The Charms of Music"
in *The Christian Treasury, by the late John Crispo, England, 1850,* 8 pages, pp. 568-571, 634-638.

[*Endnote, by Mrs. Elizabeth Crispo Cox*]

The late Mr. John Crispo, the author of the above, was the eldest son of Lieutenant J. W. Crispo, R.N. He and a friend had arranged to give each week in turn, at his father's house in Montreal, a series of home lectures for the amusement and instruction of the younger members of their respective families—a plan worthy of imitation.

The address now printed was the last given by Mr. Crispo; for his death occurred soon after [*John Crispo died in Montreal on July 11th, 1847, aged 30*], to the inexpressible grief of his family, who lost a most exemplary son and brother, while many others missed a devoted friend. The circumstances attending his death were of an unusual character, and excited the utmost sympathy and regret in the City of Montreal, generally; and it is believed, that this record will not be considered unacceptable by those who revere the memory of all good men whose lives have been sacrificed in doing work from love to their Heavenly Father and their Saviour, Jesus Christ.

Mr. Crispo, with another gentleman (Lieutenant Lloyd, R.N.), was associated with the Reverend Mark Willoughby, of Trinity Church, in assisting him in his pastoral duties. One ever memorable season a large number of Irish emigrants were landed at Montreal, suffering from malignant typhus fever, and sheds and tents were erected to receive them. Every possible assistance was given; but scores of men, women, and children, died.

It was amongst these terrible scenes that the three friends ministered, and sacrificed their lives; all were stricken down by the fever, and their deaths occurred in the same week.

Upon one occasion Mr. Crispo's mother remarked to him that she feared his health and strength would not hold out if he stayed so many hours each day and evening in the midst of such fearful disease.

His reply was: "Mother, I feel it is to be my duty; and you may be sure I shall not die before it pleases God to take me."

The last day before he was taken ill, he found in one of the tents a dead woman, with her little infant endeavouring to take nourishment from its mother's breast. He took the babe in his arms, and carried it to one of the nurses in a tent some little way off. This was his last work on earth.

When delirium, the usual accompaniment of typhus fever, came on, his wandering thoughts were even then those of Christian love.

One day, when under its influence, he remarked to his sister, who assisted his mother in nursing him:

"Let us go, dear; let us go!"

"Where shall we go?" was the reply.

"Where? Why to our loving Saviour, of course."

Sometimes he sung a hymn, and asked those around to join with him. The last Psalm he repeated before he died was the forty-second, beginning—"Like as the heart desireth tho water-brooks, so longeth my soul after Thee, O God. My soul is athirst for God; yea, even for the living God. When shall I come to appear before the presence of God?"

His love of music was great. He played the violin, and composed several pieces of music, entitled "Notes of the Forest; or, Eastern Township Melodies."

But earthly music has lost its charms to our young friend. For now his voice is mingled with those who, in the palace of the King, are clothed in white, and who sing—"Blessing and honour, and glory, and power, unto Him who sitteth upon the throne, and unto the Lamb for ever and ever."

Chorus
I'm Joseph Maffre
I want to be famous
I have been waiting for two hundred years
I'm Joseph Maffre
Born on the run
Toulon, Corsica, Lymington

I've spent my time
Writing letters, petitions, prospectuses, too
I've spent my time
Leaving a paper trail for you

Chorus

Lucy was cute
She followed me everywhere, what could I do?
Lucy was smart
She had a charcoal-burner's heart

Chorus

Fémy, Viotti, Beethoven
The biggest big shots I could find
Teaching at church, school, and home
I have yet to unwind

Chorus

French, English, Protestant, Catholic
I'll change if you pay me, OK
Ahead of my time
I would be multicultural today

Chorus

Talent, good looks, charm, and energy
Stamina – I had it all
Never too tired
To play nights at a fancy dress ball

Chorus

Damn that Dalrymple!
He cut off my music, influence, and fame
Leaving vain Junior
To carry on the Maffre name

Chorus

REFERENCES

Audio and Video

Biggs, Julian, director. *Lord Elgin: Voice of the People*. Streaming online video from the National Film Board of Canada, originally released 1959.

Gance, Abel, director. *Napoleon*. DVD from South Korea: Premier Entertainment, 2004; movie originally released 1927.

Howe, John, director. *Lord Durham*. Streaming online video from the National Film Board of Canada, originally released 1961.

Prince, Henry, composer. *Mermaid Polka*, 1856. Performed by The Beckwith Ensemble on the *À la Claire Fontaine* compact disk. Burlington, Ontario: Opening Day Recordings, 2000.

Books and Other Texts

Aldrich, Elizabeth. *From the Ballroom to Hell: Grace and Folly in Nineteenth Century Dance*. Evanston, Illinois: Northwestern University Press, 1991.

Alexander, Capt. James Edward. *Transatlantic Sketches, Comprising Visits to the Most Interesting Scenes in North and South America and the West Indies*. Two Volumes. London: Richard Bentley, 1833.

Anonymous. *Regimental Records of the 1st Battalion Highland Light Infantry formerly the 71st Highland Light Infantry, 1777 to 1906*. Dinapore [*now Dinapur*], India: The Watling Printing Works, 1907.

Bailey, Catherine. *The Secret Rooms: A True Story of a Haunted Castle, a Plotting Duchess, & a Family Secret*. New York: Penguin Books, 2012.

Birks, Michael. *Lymington and the French Revolution: The Quiberon Expedition 1795*. Pamphlet. Lymington, Hampshire: St. Barbe Museum, 1995.

Blanchard, David. *Seven Generations: A History of the Kanienkehaka*. Kahnawake Survival School, 1980.

Borthwick, John Douglas. *History and Biographical Gazetteer of Montreal to the Year 1892*. Montreal: John Lovell & Son, 1892.

Bostock, Charles, and Edward Hapgood. *Notes on the Parish Church, Lymington*. Lymington, Hampshire: C. T. King, 1912.

Bosworth, Newton. *Hochelaga Depicta: The Early History and Present Stage of the City and Island of Montreal*, second edition. Montreal: R. W. S. MacKay, 1846.

Brown, A. E., ed. *The Growth of Leicester*. Leicester: University of Leicester Press, 1972.

Bruce, Anthony. *Biography of the British Army, 1660-1914*. London: K. G. Saur, 1985.

Buckley, Roger Norman. *The British Army in the West Indies: Society and the Military in the Revolutionary Age*. Gainesville: University Press of Florida, 1998.

Buckley, R. N. *Slaves in Red Coats: The British West India Regiments, 1795-1815*. New Haven, Connecticut: Yale University Press, 1979.

Buller, Charles. *Sketch of Lord Durham's Mission in Canada*, 1838, reprinted as the appendix to *Letters & Diaries of Lady Durham*, Patricia Godsell, ed. Canada: Oberon Press, 1979.

Bumgardner, Georgia Brady. "Chapter 2. George and William Endicott: Commercial Lithography in New York, 1831-51" in *Prints and Printmakers of New York State, 1825-1940*, David Tatham, ed. Syracuse, New York: University of Syracuse Press, 1986.

Calderisi, Maria. *Music Publishing in the Canadas, 1800-1867*. Ottawa: National Library of Canada, 1981.

Camden History Society. *Streets of St. Pancras: Somers Town and the Railway Lines*. London: Camden History Society, 2002.

Cane, James. *Topographical and pictorial map of the city of Montreal*. Montreal: Robert W. S. Mackay, 1846.

Cannon, James. *Lymington Infirmary: From the Poor Law to the N.H.S.* Highcliffe, Dorset: Eon Graphics, 1992.

Cannon, Richard. *Historical Record of the Nineteenth, or the First Yorkshire North Riding Regiment of Foot (1688-1848)*. London: Parker, Furnivall, and Parker, 1848.

Cannon, Richard. *Historical Record of the Seventy-First Regiment, Highland Light Infantry: Containing an Account of the Formation of the Regiment in 1777, and of its Subsequent Services to 1852*. London: Parker, Furnivall, and Parker, 1852.

Carpenter, Kirsty. *Refugees of the French Revolution: Émigrés in London, 1789-1802*. New York: St. Martin's Press, 1999.

Chancellor, E. Beresford. *Memorials of St James's Street together with the Annals of Almack's*. London: Grant Richards, 1922.

Chartrand, René, and Paul Chappell. *British Forces in the West Indies, 1793-1815*. Men-at-Arms Series, No. 294. London: Osprey Military, 1996.

Chartrand, René, and Patrice Courcelle. *Émigré Foreign Troops in British Service (1), 1793-1802*. Men-at-Arms Series, No. 328. Oxford: Osprey Military, 1999.

Chartrand, René, and Patrice Courcelle. *Émigré Foreign Troops in British Service (2), 1803-1815*. Men-at-Arms Series, No. 335. Oxford: Osprey Military, 2000.

Cheynet, Pierre-Dominique, ed. *Inventaire des Registres des Délibérations et des Minutes des Arrêtés, Lettres et Actes du Directoire, Tome VII* [*Inventory of Entries and Deliberations of the Minutes of Arrests, Letters, and Fines of the Directory, Volume 7*]. 2002, with entries dating from November 1798 to February 1799.

Cockerill, A. W. "The Royal Military Asylum (1803-15)" *Journal of the Society for Army Historical Research, vol. 79*, pages 25-44, 2001.

Coke-Smyth, John. *Sketches in the Canadas*. London: Thomas McLean, [*1840?*].

Coke-Smyth, Jeremy. "Diary of John Coke Smyth: Visit to Canada 1838; On HMS Hastings with Lord Durham", at the Coke Smyth Family History website, online at www.coke-smyth.com/DiaryofJRCS.htm, 2011.

Cox, Mrs. H. L. "Reminiscences of Canadian Life" in *The Christian Treasury*. Edinburgh: John Johnstone, 1850.

Craik, G. L., and MacFarlane, C. *The Pictorial History of England during the Reign of George the Third: Being a History of the People as well as A History of the Kingdom, Volume III*. London: Charles Knight & Co., 1841.

Crook, Malcolm. *Toulon in War and Revolution: From the Ancien Régime to the Restoration, 1750-1820*. Manchester: Manchester University Press, 1991.

Curtis, Bruce "The 'Most Splendid Pageant Ever Seen': Grandeur, the Domestic, and Condescension in Lord Durham's Political Theatre" *The Canadian Historical Review, vol. 89*, pp. 55-88, 2008.

Duchow, Marvin. "Canadian Music Libraries: Some Observations" *Notes, vol. 18*, pp. 33-39, 1960.

Edwards, Francis. *The Jesuits in England*. Tunbridge Wells, Kent: Burns & Oates, 1985.

Ehrlich, Cyril. *First Philharmonic: A History of the Royal Philharmonic Society*. Oxford: Clarendon Press, 1995.

Ehrlich, Cyril. *The Music Profession in Britain since the Eighteenth Century: A Social History*. Oxford: Clarendon Press, 1985.

Farmer, Henry George. *Memoirs of the Royal Artillery Band: Its Origin, History and Progress*. London: Boosey & Co., 1904.

Farmer, Henry George. *Rise and Development of Military Music*. London: William Reeves, 1911.

Ford, Clifford. *Canada's Music: An Historical Survey*. Agincourt, Ontario: GLC Publishers, 1982.

Foster, Josephine. "The Montreal Riot of 1849." *Canadian Historical Review 32*, 61-65, 1951.

Foster, Myles B. *The Philharmonic Society of London, 1813-1912*. London: John Lane, 1912.

Gardiner, William. *Music and Friends; or, Pleasant Recollections of a Dilettante*. 2 vols. London: Longmans, Orme, Brown, and Longman, 1838 & 1853.

Gifford, C. H. *History of the Wars Occasioned by the French Revolution*. 2 vols. London: W. Lewis, 1817.

Godsell, Patricia, ed. *Letters & Diaries of Lady Durham*. Canada: Oberon Press, 1979.

Godsell, Patricia, ed. *The Diary of Jane Ellice*. Canada: Oberon Press, 1975.

Griffiths, Samuel C. *The Military Band: How to Form, Train, and Arrange for Reed and Brass Bands*. London: Rudall, Carte & Co., [*1896*].

Gronow, R[ees] H[owell]. *Reminiscences of Captain Gronow*. Second edition. London: Smith, Elder, & Co., 1872.

Hendrie, Lillian. *Early Days in Montreal and Rambles in the Neighborhood*. Montreal: Mercury, 1932.

Herbert, Trevor, and Helen Barlow. *Music & the British Military in the Long Nineteenth Century*. Oxford: Oxford University Press, 2013.

Hildyard, Henry J. T. *Historical Record of the 71st Highland Light Infantry, from Its Formation in 1777, under the Title of the 73rd, or McLeod's Highlanders, up to the Year 1876*. London: Harrison and Sons, 1876.

Honoré, Louis. *L'émigration dans le Var, 1789-1825*. Draguignan, France: Impr. du Var, 1923.

James, Jude. *Lymington: An Illustrated History*. Wimborne Minster, Dorset: Dovecote Press, 2007.

James, Jude, ed. *Comyn's New Forest: 1817 Directory of Life in the Parishes of Boldre & Brockenhurst*. Lymington, Hampshire: C. J. Newsome & Associates, 1982.

Johnson Reid, Stuart. *Life and Letters of the first Earl of Durham, 1792-1840, Volume 2*, London: Longmans, Green & Co., 1906.

Jones, Robert L. *History of Agriculture in Ontario, 1613-1880*. Toronto: University of Toronto Press, 1946.

Kallman, Helmut. *A History of Music in Canada, 1534-1914*. Toronto: University of Toronto Press, 1960.

Kallman, Helmut, Giles Potvin, and Kenneth Winters, eds. *Encyclopedia of Music in Canada*, Third Printing. Toronto: University of Toronto Press, 1981.

King, Edward. *Old Times Re-visited in the Borough and Parish of Lymington*. Lymington, Hampshire: Simpkins 1900.

King, Edward. *A Walk through Lymington*. New, revised edition. Lymington, Hampshire: Ensign Publications, 1990.

Kyte Senior, Elinor. "The British Garrison in Montreal in the 1840's" *Journal of the Society for Army Historical Research, vol. 50*, pages 111-127, 1974.

Kyte Senior, Elinor. *British Regulars in Montreal: An Imperial Garrison, 1832-1854*. Montreal: McGill-Queen's University Press, 1981.

Kyte Senior, Elinor. *Redcoats and Patriotes: The Rebellions in Lower Canada, 1837-1838*. Ontario: National Museum of Canada, 1985.

Lapalice, Ovide. "Les Organistes et Maitres de Musique a Notre-Dame de Montreal" *Bulletin des Recherches Historiques, vol. 25*, pages 243-249, 1919.

Laws, M. E. S. Lt.-Col. "Foreign Artillery Corps in the British Service. No. 3 – The Royal Foreign Artillery" *Journal of the Royal Artillery, vol. 75*, pages 57-63, 1948.

Laws, M. E. S. Major. "Foreign Artillery Corps in the British Service. 1. The French Emigrant Artillery" *Journal of the Royal Artillery, vol. 65*, pages 356-367, 1938.

Logier, J. B. (1818) *An Authentic Account of the Examination of Pupils, Instructed in the New System of Musical Education before Certain Members of the Philharmonic Society, and Others.* London: J. McCreary, 1818.

Lomas, M. J. "Militia and Volunteer Wind Bands in Southern England in the Late Eighteenth and Early Nineteenth Centuries" *Journal of the Society for Army Historical Research, vol. 67*, pages 154-166, 1989.

MacMillan, Ernest, ed. *Music in Canada.* Toronto: University of Toronto Press, 1955.

Mahan, A. T. *The Influence of Sea Power Upon The French Revolution and Empire 1793-1812.* Boston: Little, Brown & Co., 1894.

Mann, Michael. *A Particular Duty: The Canadian Rebellions 1837-1839.* Salisbury, Wiltshire: Michael Russell, 1986.

McGee, Timothy J. *The Music of Canada.* New York: W. W. Norton, 1985.

McIntyre, Alastair. *Scottish Regiments: Lord MacLeod's Highlanders: 1818-1873.* On the "Electric Scotland" website (www.electricscotland.com/history/scotreg/macleod/1818.htm), last accessed 2015.

Mendoza de Arce, Daniel. *Music in North America and the West Indies from the Discovery to 1850: A Historical Survey.* Lanham, Maryland: Scarecrow Press, 2006.

Morley, Geoffrey. *Smuggling in Hampshire and Dorset, 1700-1850.* Newbury, Berkshire: Countryside Books, 1983.

New, Chester W. *Lord Durham: A Biography of John George Lambton, First Earl of Durham.* Oxford: Clarendon Press, 1929.

Oatts, L. B. *The Highland Light Infantry (The 71st H.L.I. and 74th Highlanders).* London: Leo Cooper, 1969.

Oatts, L. B. Lt.-Col. "Chapter XX: Minor Disturbances" in *Proud Heritage: The Story of the Highland Light Infantry, vol. 1: The 71st H.L.I. 1777-1881.* London: Thomas Nelson & Sons, 1952.

Ormsby, William, ed. *Crisis in the Canadas: 1838-1839: The Grey Journals and Letter.* Toronto: Macmillan, 1964.

Palmer, Roy, ed. *The Rambling Soldier: Life in the Lower Ranks, 1750-1900, through Soldiers' Songs and Writings.* Harmondsworth, Middlesex: Peacock Books, 1977.

Pritchard, Brian W. *The Musical Festival and the Choral Society in England in the Eighteenth and Nineteenth Century: A Social History.* PhD Thesis. Birmingham: University of Birmingham Press, 1968.

Richardson, Major [John]. *Eight Years in Canada; Embracing a Review of the Administrations of Lord Durham and Sydenham, Sir Charles Bagot, and Lord Metcalf.* Montreal: H. H. Cunningham, 1847.

Rohr, Deborah. *The Careers of British Musicians, 1750-1850: A Profession of Artisans.* Cambridge: Cambridge University Press, 2006.

Root, Dean L., editor-in-chief. Grove Music Online (http://www.oxfordmusiconline.com/public/). Oxford: Oxford University Press, last accessed 2015.

Schom, Alan. *Napoleon Bonaparte.* New York: HarperCollins, 1997.

Slemon, Peter. *Montreal's Musical Life Under the Union, with an Emphasis on the Terminal Years, 1841 and 1867.* MA Thesis. Montreal: McGill University Press, 1975.

Stewart, Charles H. *The Service of British Regiments in Canada and North America.* Ottawa: Department of National Defence Library, 1964.

Stevenson, Joan. *Leicester through the Ages*. Leicester: Kairos Press, 1995.

Sullivan, Mrs. Robert. "Extracts from a Diary of the Reverend Henry Scadding, 1837-1838", *The Women's Canadian Historical Society of Toronto*, volume 6, pages 3-32, 1906.

Thompson, Ian. *Corsica*. Harrisburg, Pennsylvania: Stackpole Books, 1971.

Thompson, J. M. *The French Revolution*. New York: Oxford University Press, 1945.

Turner, Barbara Carpenter. *A History of Hampshire*. Second edition. Chichester, West Sussex: Phillimore, 1978.

Turner, Gordon, and Alwyn Turner. *The History of British Military Bands, vol. 1: Cavalry and Corps*. Staplehurst, Kent: Spellmount, 1994.

Turner, Gordon, and Alwyn Turner. *The History of British Military Bands, vol. 2: Guards and Infantry*. Staplehurst, Kent: Spellmount, 1996.

Turner, Gordon, and Alwyn Turner. *The History of British Military Bands, vol. 3: Infantry and Irish*. Staplehurst, Kent: Spellmount, 1997.

Tylden, G. Major. "The West India Regiments, 1795 to 1927, and from 1958" *Journal of the Society for Army Historical Research, vol. 40*, pages 42-49, 1962.

Vitse, Colette. *L'émigré Toulonnais de la Révolution à la Restoration: Essai de Caractérisation*. Master's Thesis. Nice: University of Nice, 1972.

Vitse, G. *La Contre-Révolution à Toulon en 1793*. Master's Thesis. Nice: University of Nice, 1970.

Vitse, G. "La Contre-Révolution Toulon en 1793: Les Agents Royalistes et le Faux Problème de Subsistances." *Prov. Hist. 20*, 1970.

Wade-Matthews, Max. *Musical Leicester*. Leicester: Heart of Albion Press, 1998.

Walrond, Theodore. *Letters and Journals of James, Eighth Earl of Elgin*. London: John Murray, 1872.

Warner, Mary Jane. "Anne Fairbrother Hill: A Chaste and Elegant Dancer" *Theatre Research in Canada, vol. 12*, pp. 169-191, Fall 1991.

Weiner, Margery. *The French Exiles 1789-1815*. New York: William Morrow & Co., 1961.

Winstock, Lewis. *Songs and Music of the Redcoats 1642-1902*. London: Leo Cooper, 1970.

Wollenberg, Susan, and Simon McVeigh, eds. *Concert Life in Eighteenth-Century Britain*, Aldershot, Vermont: Ashgate, 2004.

Young, Brian. *In its Corporate Capacity: The Seminary of Montreal as a Business*. Montreal: McGill Queen's Press, 1986.

Young, Brian. *Respectable Burial: Montreal's Mount Royal Cemetery*. Montreal: McGill Queen's Press, 2003.

NAME INDEX

Name	Description	References
Maffre, Ann	child of Joseph Sr. & Lucy	1, 3, 5, 8, 10
Maffre, Ann Harriet	sibling of Joseph Sr.	1, 2, 3
Maffre, Anna Pillar	child of Joseph Jr. & Jean	10
Maffre, Barthelemy	father of Joseph Sr.	1, 2, 3
Maffre, Cecile	mother of Joseph Sr.	1, 2, 3
Maffre, Charles Antoine	child of Joseph Jr. & Julie	10
Maffre, Charles Henri	child of Joseph Jr. & Julie	10
Maffre, Charlotte	child of Joseph Sr & Lucy; dance instructor; spouse of George McDonnell	1, 5, 8, 10
Maffre, Francis 1 (also Frank)	child of Joseph Sr. & Lucy	3, 4, 5, 10
Maffre, Francis 2	child of Joseph Sr. & Lucy; musician; carpenter	1, 5, 8, 10
Maffre, François (also Francis)	sibling of Joseph Sr.	1, 2, 3, 4
Maffre, Frederick	child of Joseph Sr. & Lucy; musician; carpenter; spouse of Mary Mullen	1, 5, 8, 10
Maffre, Frederick Arthur	child of Joseph Jr. & Julie	10
Maffre, Frederick Jr.	child of Frederick & Mary	8, 10
Maffre, Georgiana Australina	child of Joseph Jr. & Julie	8, 10
Maffre, Henry	child of Joseph Sr. & Lucy; musician	1, 5, 8, 9, 10
Maffre, Jane Pillar	child of Joseph Jr. & Jean	10
Maffre, Joseph III	child of Joseph Jr. & Theresa	10
Maffre, Joseph Ludwig (or Joseph Jr.)	child of Joseph Sr. & Lucy; musician; spouse of Julie Perrault, Jean Carruthers, and Theresa Leseur	1, 4, 5, 6, 8, 9, 10
Maffre, Joseph, Sr.	biographee; spouse of Lucy Thomas	all
Maffre, Julie Virginia	child of Joseph Jr. & Julie	8, 10
Maffre, Leopold Alfred	child of Joseph Jr. & Julie; musician	8, 10
Maffre, Lucie Hermelinde	child of Joseph Jr. & Julie	8, 10
Maffre, Maria	child of Joseph Sr.; spouse of William Tate	1, 2, 5, 7, 8, 10
Maffre, Marie Lucy	child of Joseph Jr. & Theresa	10
Maffre, Mary Anne	child of Joseph Sr. & Lucy; spouse of Thomas Buckley	1, 5, 8, 10
Maffre, Pierre	sibling of Joseph Sr.	1, 2
Maitland, Peregrine	military officer	8
Manners, John Henry	patron; Duke of Rutland	5
Marshall, Mr.	musician (violoncello)	5
Martin, George	photographer	10
Mavius, Charles	music instructor; musician (violin)	5
McDonnell, Emilie Ann (or Amelia)	child of George & Esther	10
McDonnell, George	spouse of Charlotte Maffre & Esther Waldron	8, 10
McKorkell, Charles	musician (harp, piano, organ)	5
McVeigh, Simon	historian	8
Melville, Miss A. H.	vocalist	5
Metcalfe, Charles Theophilus	dedicatee; Governor General; Lord Metcalfe	7, 8
Milon, Sarah	spouse of François Maffre	4
Mitchell, Alfred	military officer	10
Morris, Mr.	vocalist	5
Mozart, Wolfgang Amadeus	composer	4
Mullen, Mary	spouse of Frederick Maffre	8, 10
Muston, Mr.	musician (piano, organ)	5
Muston, Mrs.	vocalist	5
Nagel, Jean	musician (violin)	8
Nash, John	architect	4
Newton, Gabriel "Alderman"	businessman; governance	5
Nicholson, Henry	musician (flute); bandmaster	5
Nickinson, John	actor	8
Nourrit, August	musician	8
O'Connell, Daniel	governance	7
Paoli, Pascal	governance	2
Perrault, Henry	spouse of Marie Raiza; father of Julie Perrault	10
Perrault, Julie Théophile	child of Henry & Marie; spouse of Joseph Maffre Jr.	8, 10
Phipps, Constantine	military officer; Earl of Mulgrave; Lord Lieutenant of Ireland	7
Phipps, John Hornby	military officer	9
Pieltan, Dieudonné-Pascal	musician; composer	5
Pigott, Samuel J.	musician; music business	7
Pillar, E.	marriage witness	8
Pillar, William	spouse of Annie Carruthers	10
Pleydell-Bouverie, Edward	in Durham's suite	7
Ponsonby, William	in Durham's suite	7
Poole, James	military officer	9
Power, William	businessman	10
Preston, Thomas	publisher	5
Prevost, George	military officer	3
Prince, Henry	music business; musician; composer	10
Puisaye, Joseph	military officer	3
Raiza, Marie	spouse of Henry Perrault; mother of Julie Perrault	10
Raper, Timothy	military officer	6
Ricard, Harriet C.	spouse of George Henry Tate	10
Robinson, Mr.	vocalist	5
Rock, Miss	music instructor	8

ABOUT THE AUTHORS

Mark Griep is a chemistry professor at the University of Nebraska-Lincoln, where he studies the function of the enzymes that duplicate DNA in bacteria. His research has been supported by the National Institutes of Health, the National Science Foundation, and the Alfred P. Sloan Foundation. Dr. Griep received a Distinguished Teaching Award from the University of Nebraska-Lincoln and was twice elected to serve as the Chair of the Nebraska Section of the American Chemical Society. He has been studying his family history since age 13 and was delighted to be able to begin investigating Marjorie's family history after they were married.

Marjorie Mikasen is a geometric painter who has exhibited her work nationally and internationally; awards include an Individual Artist Fellowship from the Nebraska Arts Council and the Lincoln Mayor's Arts Award for Artistic Achievement in the Visual Arts. Her work is in public and private collections including the Sheldon Museum of Art. Mikasen was able to whistle from an early age and likes to think her ancestor Joseph Maffre had the same ability.

The authors enjoy collaborating on historical projects involving the arts and sciences.

Made in the USA
Middletown, DE
07 December 2015